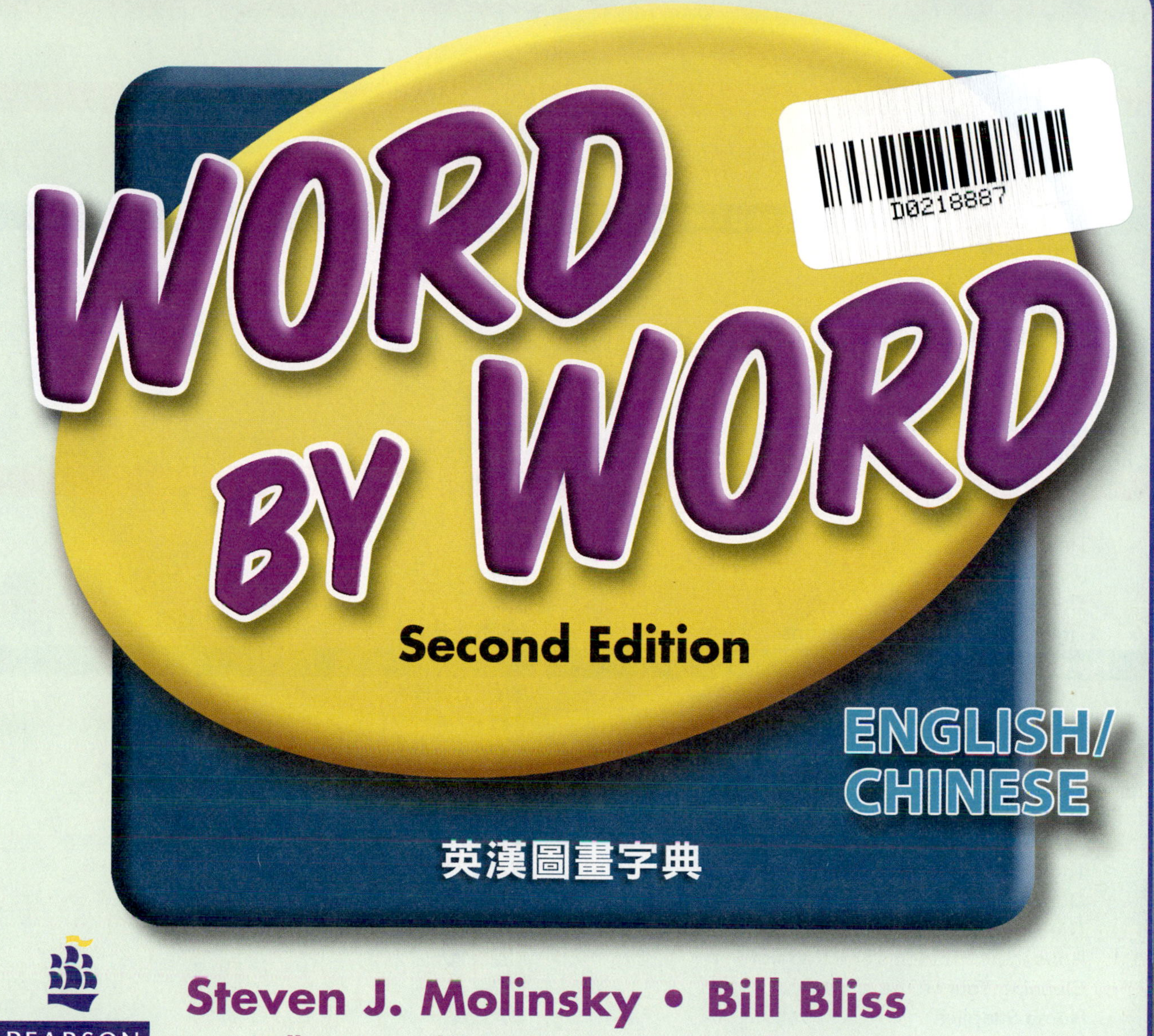

Steven J. Molinsky • Bill Bliss
Hellen Hu and Peter V. S. Smith, Translators

Illustrated by
Richard E. Hill

Word by Word Picture Dictionary,
English/Chinese second edition

Pearson Education, 10 Bank Street, White Plains, NY 10606

Editorial director: Pam Fishman
Vice president, director of design and production: Rhea Banker
Director of electronic production: Aliza Greenblatt
Director of manufacturing: Patrice Fraccio
Senior manufacturing manager: Edith Pullman
Marketing manager: Oliva Fernandez
Associate development editor: Mary Perrotta Rich
Assistant editor: Katherine Keyes
Senior digital layout specialist: Wendy Wolf

Text design: Wendy Wolf
Cover design: Tracey Munz Cataldo
Realia creation: Warren Fischbach, Paula Williams
Illustrations: Richard E. Hill
Contributing artists: Steven Young, Charles Cawley, Willard Gage, Marlon Violette
Reviewers: Susan Y. Rui, ELL Instructional Support Specialist; James Bao, ELL Instructional Support Specialist; Yun Xiao, University of Massachusetts - Amherst; Alicia Chao-Wah Wang, San Francisco City College
Project management by TransPac Education Services, Victoria, BC, Canada with assistance from Robert Zacharias

ISBN-10 0-13-191631-9 ISBN-13 9780131916319
Longman on the Web
Longman.com offers online resources for teachers and students. Access our Companion Websites, our online catalog, and our local offices around the world.

Visit us at www.pearsonlongman.com.

Printed in the United States of America
5 6 7 8 9 10 – V082 – 16 15 14 13

CONTENTS

目錄

Unit / Theme	Communication Skills	Writing & Discussion
1 Personal Information and Family	• Asking for & giving personal information • Identifying information on a form • Spelling name aloud • Identifying family members • Introducing others	• Telling about yourself • Telling about family members • Drawing a family tree
2 Common Everyday Activities and Language	• Identifying classroom objects & locations • Identifying classroom actions • Giving & following simple classroom commands • Identifying everyday & leisure activities • Inquiring by phone about a person's activities • Asking about a person's plan for future activities • Social communication: Greeting people, Leave taking, Introducing yourself & others, Getting someone's attention, Expressing gratitude, Saying you don't understand, Calling someone on the telephone • Describing the weather • Interpreting temperatures on a thermometer (Fahrenheit & Centigrade) • Describing the weather forecast for tomorrow	• Describing a classroom • Making a list of daily activities • Describing daily routine • Making a list of planned activities • Describing favorite leisure activities • Describing the weather
3 Numbers/ Time/ Money/ Calendar	• Using cardinal & ordinal numbers • Giving information about age, number of family members, residence • Telling time • Indicating time of events • Asking for information about arrival & departure times • Identifying coins & currency – names & values • Making & asking for change • Identifying days of the week • Identifying months of the year • Asking about the year, month, day, date • Asking about the date of a birthday, anniversary, appointment • Giving date of birth	• Describing numbers of students in a class • Identifying a country's population • Describing daily schedule with times • Telling about time management • Telling about the use of time in different cultures or countries • Describing the cost of purchases • Describing coins & currency of other countries • Describing weekday & weekend activities • Telling about favorite day of the week & month of the year
4 Home	• Identifying types of housing & communities • Requesting a taxi • Calling 911 for an ambulance • Identifying rooms of a home • Identifying furniture • Complimenting • Asking for information in a store • Locating items in a store • Asking about items on sale • Asking the location of items at home • Telling about past weekend activities • Identifying locations in an apartment building • Identifying ways to look for housing: classified ads, listings, vacancy signs • Renting an apartment • Describing household problems • Securing home repair services • Making a suggestion • Identifying household cleaning items, home supplies, & tools • Asking to borrow an item • Describing current home activities & plans for future activities	• Describing types of housing where people live • Describing rooms & furniture in a residence • Telling about baby products & early child-rearing practices in different countries • Telling about personal experiences with repairing things • Describing an apartment building • Describing household cleaning chores
5 Community	• Identifying places in the community • Exchanging greetings • Asking & giving the location of places in the community • Identifying government buildings, services, & other places in a city/town center • Identifying modes of transportation in a city/town center	• Describing places in a neighborhood • Making a list of places, people, & actions observed at an intersection

Unit / Theme	Communication Skills	Writing & Discussion
6 Describing	• Describing people by age • Describing people by physical characteristics • Describing a suspect or missing person to a police officer • Describing people & things using adjectives • Describing physical states & emotions • Expressing concern about another person's physical state or emotion	• Describing physical characteristics of yourself & family members • Describing physical characteristics of a favorite actor or actress or other famous person • Describing things at home & in the community • Telling about personal experiences with different emotions
7 Food	• Identifying food items (fruits, vegetables, meat, poultry, seafood, dairy products, juices, beverages, deli, frozen foods, snack foods, groceries) • Identifying non-food items purchased in a supermarket (e.g., household supplies, baby products, pet food) • Determining food needs to make a shopping list • Asking the location of items in a supermarket • Identifying supermarket sections • Requesting items at a service counter in a supermarket • Identifying supermarket checkout area personnel & items • Identifying food containers & quantities • Identifying units of measure • Asking for & giving recipe instructions • Complimenting someone on a recipe • Offering to help with food preparation • Identifying food preparation actions • Identifying kitchen utensils & cookware • Asking to borrow an item • Comprehending product advertising • Ordering fast food items, coffee shop items, & sandwiches • Indicating a shortage of supplies to a co-worker or supervisor • Taking customers' orders at a food service counter • Identifying restaurant objects, personnel, & actions • Making & following requests at work • Identifying & correctly positioning silverware & plates in a table setting • Inquiring in person about restaurant job openings • Ordering from a restaurant menu • Taking customers' orders as a waiter or waitress in a restaurant	• Describing favorite & least favorite foods • Describing foods in different countries • Making a shopping list • Describing places to shop for food • Telling about differences between supermarkets & food stores in different countries • Making a list of items in kitchen cabinets & the refrigerator • Describing recycling practices • Describing a favorite recipe using units of measure • Telling about use of kitchen utensils & cookware • Telling about experience with different types of restaurants • Describing restaurants and menus in different countries • Describing favorite foods ordered in restaurants
8 Colors and Clothing	• Identifying colors • Complimenting someone on clothing • Identifying clothing items, including outerwear, sleepwear, underwear, exercise clothing, footwear, jewelry, & accessories • Talking about appropriate clothing for different weather conditions • Expressing clothing needs to a store salesperson • Locating clothing items • Inquiring about ownership of found clothing items • Indicating loss of a clothing item • Asking about sale prices in a clothing store • Reporting theft of a clothing item to the police • Stating preferences during clothing shopping • Expressing problems with clothing & the need for alterations • Identifying laundry objects & activities • Locating laundry products in a store	• Describing the flags of different countries • Telling about emotions associated with different colors • Telling about clothing & colors you like to wear • Describing clothing worn at different occasions (e.g., going to schools, parties, weddings) • Telling about clothing worn in different weather conditions • Telling about clothing worn during exercise activities • Telling about footwear worn during different activities • Describing the color, material, size, & pattern of favorite clothing items • Comparing clothing fashions now & a long time ago • Telling about who does laundry at home

Unit / Theme	Communication Skills	Writing & Discussion
9 Shopping	• Identifying departments & services in a department store • Asking the location of items in a department store • Asking to buy, return, exchange, try on, & pay for department store items • Asking about regular & sales prices, discounts, & sales tax • Interpreting a sales receipt • Offering assistance to customers as a salesperson • Expressing needs to a salesperson in a store • Identifying electronics products, including video & audio equipment, telephones, cameras, & computers • Identifying components of a computer & common computer software • Complimenting someone about an item & inquiring where it was purchased • Asking a salesperson for advice about different brands of a product • Identifying common toys & other items in a toy store • Asking for advice about an appropriate gift for a child	• Describing a department store • Telling about stores that have sales • Telling about an item purchased on sale • Comparing different types & brands of video & audio equipment • Describing telephones & cameras • Describing personal use of a computer • Sharing opinions about how computers have changed the world • Telling about popular toys in different countries • Telling about favorite childhood toys
10 Community Services	• Requesting bank services & transactions (e.g., deposit, withdrawal, cashing a check, obtaining traveler's checks, opening an account, applying for a loan, exchanging currency) • Identifying bank personnel • Identifying bank forms • Asking about acceptable forms of payment (cash, check, credit card, money order, traveler's check) • Identifying household bills (rent, utilities, etc.) • Identifying family finance documents & actions • Following instructions to use an ATM machine • Requesting post office services & transactions • Identifying types of mail & mail services • Identifying different ways to buy stamps • Requesting non-mail services available at the post office (money order, selective service registration, passport application) • Identifying & locating library sections, services, & personnel • Asking how to find a book in the library • Identifying community institutions, services, and personnel (police, fire, city government, public works, recreation, sanitation, religious institutions) • Identifying types of emergency vehicles • Reporting a crime • Identifying community mishaps (gas leak, water main break, etc.) • Expressing concern about community problems	• Describing use of bank services • Telling about household bills & amounts paid • Telling about the person responsible for household finances • Describing use of ATM machines • Describing use of postal services • Comparing postal systems in different countries • Telling about experience using a library • Telling about the location of community institutions • Describing experiences using community institutions • Telling about crime in the community • Describing experience with a crime or emergency
11 Health	• Identifying parts of the body & key internal organs • Describing ailments, symptoms, & injuries • Asking about the health of another person • Identifying items in a first-aid kit • Describing medical emergencies • Identifying emergency medical procedures (CPR, rescue breathing, Heimlich maneuver) • Calling 911 to report a medical emergency • Identifying major illnesses • Talking with a friend or co-worker about illness in one's family • Following instructions during a medical examination • Identifying medical personnel, equipment, & supplies in medical & dental offices • Understanding medical & dental personnel's description of procedures during treatment • Understanding a doctor's medical advice and instructions • Identifying over-the-counter medications • Understanding dosage instructions on medicine labels • Identifying medical specialists • Indicating the date & time of a medical appointment • Identifying hospital departments & personnel • Identifying equipment in a hospital room • Identifying actions & items related to personal hygiene • Locating personal care products in a store • Identifying actions & items related to baby care	• Describing self • Telling about a personal experience with an illness or injury • Describing remedies or treatments for common problems (cold, stomachache, insect bite, hiccups) • Describing experience with a medical emergency • Describing a medical examination • Describing experience with a medical or dental procedure • Telling about medical advice received • Telling about over-the-counter medications used • Comparing use of medications in different countries • Describing experience with a medical specialist • Describing a hospital stay • Making a list of personal care items needed for a trip • Comparing baby products in different countries

Unit / Theme	Communication Skills	Writing & Discussion

12 **School, Subjects, and Activities**	• Identifying types of educational institutions
	• Giving information about previous education during a job interview
	• Identifying school locations & personnel
	• Identifying school subjects
	• Identifying extracurricular activities
	• Sharing after-school plans
	• MATH:
	  • Asking & answering basic questions during a math class
	  • Using fractions to indicate sale prices
	  • Using percents to indicate test scores & probability in weather forecasts
	  • Identifying high school math subjects
	  • Using measurement terms to indicate height, width, depth, length, distance
	  • Interpreting metric measurements
	  • Identifying types of lines, geometric shapes, & solid figures
	• ENGLISH LANGUAGE ARTS:
	  • Identifying types of sentences
	  • Identifying parts of speech
	  • Identifying punctuation marks
	  • Providing feedback during peer-editing
	  • Identifying steps of the writing process
	  • Identifying types of literature
	  • Identifying forms of writing
	• GEOGRAPHY:
	  • Identifying geographical features & bodies of water
	  • Identifying natural environments (desert, jungle, rainforest, etc.)
	• SCIENCE:
	  • Identifying science classroom/laboratory equipment
	  • Asking about equipment needed to do a science procedure
	  • Identifying steps of the scientific method
	  • Identifying key terms to describe the universe, solar system, & space exploration
		• Telling about different types of schools in the community
		• Telling about schools attended, where, when, & subjects studied
		• Describing a school
		• Comparing schools in different countries
		• Telling about favorite school subject
		• Telling about extracurricular activities
		• Comparing extracurricular activities in different countries
		• Describing math education
		• Telling about something bought on sale
		• Researching & sharing information about population statistics using percents
		• Describing favorite books & authors
		• Describing newspapers & magazines read
		• Telling about use of different types of written communication
		• Describing the geography of your country
		• Describing geographical features experienced
		• Describing experience with scientific equipment
		• Describing science education
		• Brainstorming a science experiment & describing each step of the scientific method
		• Drawing & naming a constellation
		• Expressing an opinion about the importance of space exploration

13 **Work**	• Identifying occupations • Stating work experience (including length of time in an occupation) during a job interview • Talking about occupation during social conversation • Expressing job aspirations • Identifying job skills & work activities • Indicating job skills during an interview (including length of time) • Identifying types of job advertisements (help wanted signs, job notices, classified ads) • Interpreting abbreviations in job advertisements • Identifying each step in a job-search process • Identifying workplace locations, furniture, equipment, & personnel • Identifying common office tasks • Asking the location of a co-worker • Engaging in small-talk with co-workers • Identifying common office supplies • Making requests at work • Repeating to confirm understanding of a request or instruction • Identifying factory locations, equipment, & personnel • Asking the location of workplace departments & personnel to orient oneself as a new employee • Asking about the location & activities of a co-worker • Identifying construction site machinery, equipment, and building materials • Asking a co-worker for a workplace item • Warning a co-worker of a safety hazard • Asking whether there is a sufficient supply of workplace materials • Identifying job safety equipment • Interpreting warning signs at work • Reminding someone to use safety equipment • Asking the location of emergency equipment at work	• Career exploration: sharing ideas about occupations that are interesting, difficult • Describing occupation & occupations of family members • Describing job skills • Describing a familiar job (skill requirements, qualifications, hours, salary) • Telling about how people found their jobs • Telling about experience with a job search or job interview • Describing a familiar workplace • Telling about office & school supplies used • Describing a nearby factory & working conditions there • Comparing products produced by factories in different countries • Describing building materials used in ones dwelling • Describing a nearby construction site • Telling about experience with safety equipment • Describing the use of safety equipment in the community

Unit / Theme	Communication Skills	Writing & Discussion
14 Transportation and Travel	• Identifying modes of local & inter-city public transportation • Expressing intended mode of travel • Asking about a location to obtain transportation (bus stop, bus station, train station, subway station) • Locating ticket counters, information booths, fare card machines, & information signage in transportation stations • Identifying types of vehicles • Indicating to a car salesperson need for a type of vehicle • Describing a car accident • Identifying parts of a car & maintenance items • Indicating a problem with a car • Requesting service or assistance at a service station • Identifying types of highway lanes & markings, road structures (tunnels, bridges, etc.), traffic signage, & local intersection road markings • Reporting the location of an accident • Giving & following driving directions (using prepositions of motion) • Interpreting traffic signs • Warning a driver about an upcoming sign • Interpreting compass directions • Asking for driving directions • Following instructions during a driver's test • Repeating to confirm instructions • Identifying airport locations & personnel (check-in, security, gate, baggage claim, Customs & Immigration) • Asking for location of places & personnel at an airport • Indicating loss of travel documents or other items • Identifying airplane sections, seating areas, emergency equipment, & flight personnel • Identifying steps in the process of airplane travel (actions in the security area, at the gate, boarding, & being seated) • Following instructions of airport security personnel, gate attendants, & flight crew • Identifying sections of a hotel & personnel • Asking for location of places & personnel in a hotel	• Describing mode of travel to different places in the community • Describing local public transportation • Comparing transportation in different countries • Telling about common types of vehicles in different countries • Expressing opinion about favorite type of vehicle & manufacturer • Expressing opinion about most important features to look for when making a car purchase • Describing experience with car repairs • Describing a local highway • Describing a local intersection • Telling about dangerous traffic areas where many accidents occur • Describing your route from home to school • Describing how to get to different places from home and school • Describing local traffic signs • Comparing traffic signs in different countries • Describing a familiar airport • Telling about an experience with Customs & Immigration • Describing an air travel experience • Using imagination: being an airport security officer giving passengers instructions; being a flight attendant giving passengers instructions before take-off • Describing a familiar hotel • Expressing opinion about hotel jobs that are most interesting, most difficult
15 Recreation and Entertainment	• Identifying common hobbies, crafts, & games & related materials/equipment • Describing favorite leisure activities • Purchasing craft supplies, equipment, & other products in a store • Asking for & offering a suggestion for a leisure activity • Identifying places to go for outdoor recreation, entertainment, culture, etc. • Describing past weekend activities • Describing activities planned for a future day off or weekend • Identifying features & equipment in a park & playground • Asking the location of a park feature or equipment • Warning a child to be careful on playground equipment • Identifying features of a beach, common beach items, & personnel • Identifying indoor & outdoor recreation activities & sports, & related equipment & supplies • Asking if someone remembered an item when preparing for an activity • Identifying team sports & terms for players, playing fields, & equipment • Commenting on a player's performance during a game • Indicating that you can't find an item • Asking the location of sports equipment in a store • Reminding someone of items needed for a sports activity • Identifying types of winter/water sports, recreation, & equipment • Engaging in small talk about favorite sports & recreation activities • Using the telephone to inquire whether a store sells a product • Making & responding to an invitation • Following a teacher or coach's instructions during sports practice, P.E. class, & an exercise class • Identifying types of entertainment & cultural events, & the performers • Commenting on a performance • Identifying genres of music, plays, movies, & TV programs • Expressing likes about types of entertainment • Identifying musical instruments • Complimenting someone on musical ability	• Describing a favorite hobby, craft, or game • Comparing popular games in different countries, and how to play them • Describing favorite places to go & activities there • Describing a local park & playground • Describing a favorite beach & items used there • Describing an outdoor recreation experience • Describing favorite individual sports & recreation activities • Describing favorite team sports & famous players • Comparing popular sports in different countries • Describing experience with winter or water sports & recreation • Expressing opinions about Winter Olympics sports (most exciting, most dangerous) • Describing exercise habits & routines • Using imagination: being an exercise instructor leading a class • Telling about favorite types of entertainment • Comparing types of entertainment popular in different countries • Telling about favorite performers • Telling about favorite types of music, movies, & TV programs • Describing experience with a musical instrument • Comparing typical musical instruments in different countries

Unit / Theme	Communication Skills	Writing & Discussion
16 Nature	• Identifying places & people on a farm • Identifying farm animals & crops • Identifying animals & pets • Identifying birds & insects • Identifying fish, sea animals, amphibians, & reptiles • Asking about the presence of wildlife in an area • Identifying trees, plants, & flowers • Identifying key parts of a tree and flower • Asking for information about trees & flowers • Warning someone about poisonous vegetation in an area • Identifying sources of energy • Describing the kind of energy used to heat homes & for cooking • Expressing an opinion about good future sources of energy • Identifying behaviors that promote conservation (recycling, conserving energy, conserving water, carpooling) • Expressing concern about environmental problems • Identifying different kinds of natural disasters	• Comparing farms in different countries • Telling about local animals, animals in a zoo, & common local birds & insects • Comparing common pets in different countries • Using imagination: what animal you would like to be, & why • Telling a popular folk tale or children's story about animals, birds, or insects • Describing fish, sea animals, & reptiles in different countries • Identifying endangered species • Expressing opinions about wildlife – most interesting, beautiful, dangerous • Describing local trees & flowers, & favorites • Comparing different cultures' use of flowers at weddings, funerals, holidays, & hospitals • Expressing an opinion about an environmental problem • Telling about how people prepare for natural disasters
17 U.S. Civics	• Producing correct form of identification when requested (driver's license, social security card, student I.D. card, employee I.D. badge, permanent resident card, passport, visa, work permit, birth certificate, proof of residence) • Identifying the three branches of U.S. government (legislative, executive, judicial) & their functions • Identifying senators, representatives, the president, vice-president, cabinet, Supreme Court justices, & the chief justice, & the branches of government in which they work • Identifying the key buildings in each branch of government (Capitol Building, White House, Supreme Court Building) • Identifying the Constitution as "the supreme law of the land" • Identifying the Bill of Rights • Naming freedoms guaranteed by the 1st Amendment • Identifying key amendments to the Constitution • Identifying key events in United States history • Answering history questions about events and the dates they occurred • Identifying key holidays & dates they occur • Identifying legal system & court procedures (arrest, booking, obtaining legal representation, appearing in court, standing trial, acquittal, conviction, sentencing, prison, release) • Identifying people in the criminal justice system • Engaging in small talk about a TV crime show's characters & plot • Identifying rights & responsibilities of U.S. citizens • Identifying steps in applying for citizenship	• Telling about forms of identification & when needed • Describing how people in a community "exercise their 1st Amendment rights" • Brainstorming ideas for a new amendment to the Constitution • Expressing an opinion about the most important event in United States history • Telling about important events in the history of different countries • Describing U.S. holidays you celebrate • Describing holidays celebrated in different countries • Describing the legal system in different countries • Telling about an episode of a TV crime show • Expressing an opinion about the most important rights & responsibilities of people in their communities • Expressing an opinion about the rights of citizens vs. non-citizens

Welcome to the second edition of the WORD BY WORD Picture Dictionary! This text presents more than 4,000 vocabulary words through vibrant illustrations and simple accessible lesson pages that are designed for clarity and ease-of-use with learners at all levels. Our goal is to prepare students for success using English in everyday life, in the community, in school, and at work.

WORD BY WORD organizes the vocabulary into 17 thematic units, providing a careful research-based sequence of lessons that integrates students' development of grammar and vocabulary skills through topics that begin with the immediate world of the student and progress to the world at large. Early lessons on the family, the home, and daily activities lead to lessons on the community, school, workplace, shopping, recreation, and other topics. The text offers extensive coverage of important lifeskill competencies and the vocabulary of school subjects and extracurricular activities, and it is designed to meet the objectives of current national, state, and local standards-based curricula you can find in the Scope & Sequence on the previous pages.

Since each lesson in *Word by Word* is self-contained, it can be used either sequentially or in any desired order. For users' convenience, the lessons are listed in two ways: sequentially in the Table of Contents, and alphabetically in the Thematic Index. These resources, combined with the Glossary in the appendix, allow students and teachers to quickly and easily locate all words and topics in the Picture Dictionary.

The *Word by Word* Picture Dictionary is the centerpiece of the complete *Word by Word* Vocabulary Development Program, which offers a wide selection of print and media support materials for instruction at all levels.

A unique choice of workbooks at Beginning and Intermediate levels offers flexible options to meet students' needs. Vocabulary Workbooks feature motivating vocabulary, grammar, and listening practice, and standards-based Lifeskills Workbooks provide competency-based activities and reading tied to national, state, and local curriculum frameworks. A Literacy Workbook is also available.

The Teacher's Guide and Lesson Planner with CD-ROM includes lesson-planning suggestions, community tasks, Internet weblinks, and reproducible masters to save teachers hours of lesson preparation time. An Activity Handbook with step-by-step teaching strategies for key vocabulary development activities is included in the Teacher's Guide.

The Audio Program includes all words and conversations for interactive practice and —as bonus material—an expanded selection of WordSongs for entertaining musical practice with the vocabulary.

Additional ancillary materials include Color Transparencies, Vocabulary Game Cards, and a Testing Program. Bilingual Editions are also available.

Teaching Strategies

Word by Word presents vocabulary words in context. Model conversations depict situations in which people use the words in meaningful communication. These models become the basis for students to engage in dynamic, interactive practice. In addition, writing and discussion questions in each lesson encourage students to relate the vocabulary and themes to their own lives as they share experiences, thoughts, opinions, and information about themselves, their cultures, and their countries. In this way, students get to know each other "word by word."

In using *Word by Word*, we encourage you to develop approaches and strategies that are compatible with your own teaching style and the needs and abilities of your students. You may find it helpful to incorporate some of the following techniques for presenting and practicing the vocabulary in each lesson.

1. **Preview the Vocabulary:** Activate students' prior knowledge of the vocabulary by brainstorming with students the words in the lesson they already know and writing them on the board, or by having students look at the transparency or the illustration in *Word by Word* and identify the words they are familiar with.

2. **Present the Vocabulary:** Using the transparency or the illustration in the Picture Dictionary, point to the picture of each word, say the word, and have the class repeat it chorally and individually. (You can also play the word list on the Audio Program.) Check students' understanding and pronunciation of the vocabulary.

3. **Vocabulary Practice:** Have students practice the vocabulary as a class, in pairs, or in small groups. Say or write a word, and have students point to the item or tell the number. Or, point to an item or give the number, and have students say the word.

4. **Model Conversation Practice:** Some lessons have model conversations that use the first word in the vocabulary list. Other models are in the form of skeletal dialogs, in which vocabulary words can be inserted. (In many skeletal dialogs, bracketed numbers indicate which words can be used for practicing the conversation. If no bracketed numbers appear, all the words in the lesson can be used.)

   The following steps are recommended for Model Conversation Practice:

   a. Preview: Have students look at the model illustration and discuss who they think the speakers are and where the conversation takes place.
   b. The teacher presents the model or plays the audio one or more times and checks students' understanding of the situation and the vocabulary.
   c. Students repeat each line of the conversation chorally and individually.
   d. Students practice the model in pairs.
   e. A pair of students presents a conversation based on the model, but using a different word from the vocabulary list.
   f. In pairs, students practice several conversations based on the model, using different words on the page.
   g. Pairs present their conversations to the class.

5. **Additional Conversation Practice:** Many lessons provide two additional skeletal dialogs for further conversation practice with the vocabulary. (These can be found in the yellow-shaded area at the bottom of the page.) Have students practice and present these conversations using any words they wish. Before they practice the additional conversations, you may want to have students listen to the sample additional conversations on the Audio Program.

6. **Spelling Practice:** Have students practice spelling the words as a class, in pairs, or in small groups. Say a word, and have students spell it aloud or write it. Or, using the transparency, point to an item and have students write the word.

7. **Themes for Discussion, Composition, Journals, and Portfolios:** Each lesson of *Word by Word* provides one or more questions for discussion and composition. (These can be found in a blue-shaded area at the bottom of the page.) Have students respond to the questions as a class, in pairs, or in small groups. Or, have students write their responses at home, share their written work with other students, and discuss as a class, in pairs, or in small groups.

   Students may enjoy keeping a journal of their written work. If time permits, you may want to write a response in each student's journal, sharing your own opinions and experiences as well as reacting to what the student has written. If you are keeping portfolios of students' work, these compositions serve as excellent examples of students' progress in learning English.

8. **Communication Activities:** The *Word by Word* Teacher's Guide and Lesson Planner with CD-ROM provides a wealth of games, tasks, brainstorming, discussion, movement, drawing, miming, role-playing, and other activities designed to take advantage of students' different learning styles and particular abilities and strengths. For each lesson, choose one or more of these activities to reinforce students' vocabulary learning in a way that is stimulating, creative, and enjoyable.

WORD BY WORD aims to offer students a communicative, meaningful, and lively way of practicing English vocabulary. In conveying to you the substance of our program, we hope that we have also conveyed the spirit: that learning vocabulary can be genuinely interactive . . . relevant to our students' lives . . . responsive to students' differing strengths and learning styles . . . and fun!

Steven J. Molinsky
Bill Bliss

PERSONAL INFORMATION

個人資料

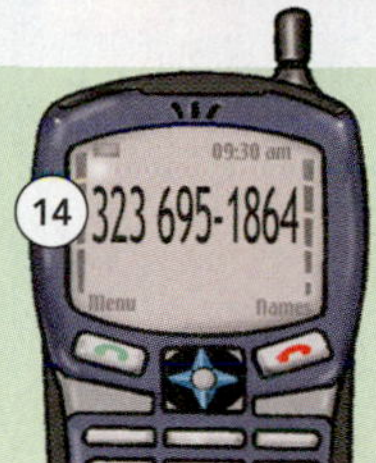

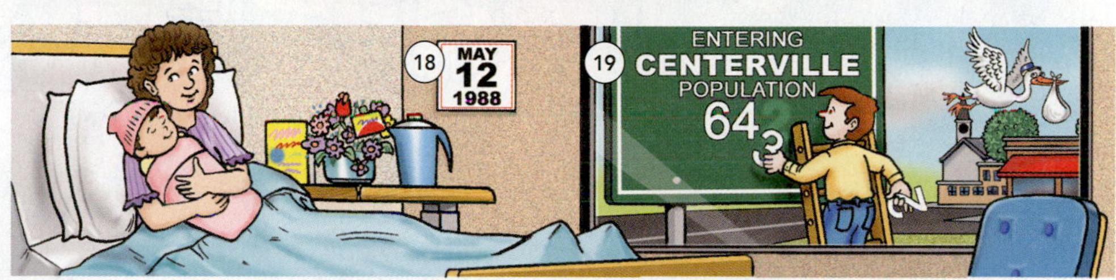

Registration Form

Name: Gloria (First) P. (Middle Initial) Sánchez (Last)

Address: 95 (Number) Garden Street (Street) 3G (Apartment Number)
Los Angeles (City) CA (State) 90036 (Zip Code)

Telephone: 323-524-3278 Cell Phone: 323-695-1864

E-Mail Address: gloria97@ail.com SSN: 227-93-6185 Sex M__ F X

Date of Birth: 5/12/88 Place of Birth: Centerville, Texas

姓名	**1**	name	郵政編碼	**11**	zip code
名字(不含姓)	**2**	first name	電話區號	**12**	area code
中間名的首字母	**3**	middle initial	電話號碼	**13**	telephone number/ phone number
姓	**4**	last name/family name/ surname	手機號碼	**14**	cell phone number
地址	**5**	address	電子郵件地址	**15**	e-mail address
門牌號碼	**6**	street number	社會安全號碼	**16**	social security number
街道	**7**	street	性別	**17**	sex
公寓號碼	**8**	apartment number	出生日期	**18**	date of birth
城市	**9**	city	出生地	**19**	place of birth
州	**10**	state			

A. What's your **name**?
B. Gloria P. Sánchez.

A. What's your ________?
B. ....
A. Did you say ....?
B. Yes. That's right.

A. What's your last name?
B. ....
A. How do you spell that?
B. ....

Tell about yourself:
My name is ....
My address is ....
My telephone number is ....

Now interview a friend.

FAMILY MEMBERS I

家庭成員 1

先生 **1** husband
太太 **2** wife

父母 parents
爸爸 **3** father
媽媽 **4** mother

孩子們 children
女兒 **5** daughter
兒子 **6** son
嬰兒 **7** baby

兄弟姊妹 siblings
姊姊/妹妹 **8** sister
哥哥/弟弟 **9** brother

(外)祖父母 grandparents
(外)祖母 **10** grandmother
(外)祖父 **11** grandfather

(外)孫兒孫女們 grandchildren
(外)孫女 **12** granddaughter
(外)孫子 **13** grandson

A. Who is he?
B. He's my **husband**.
A. What's his name?
B. His name is *Jack*.

A. Who is she?
B. She's my **wife**.
A. What's her name?
B. Her name is *Nancy*.

A. I'd like to introduce my ______.
B. Nice to meet you.
C. Nice to meet you, too.

A. What's your ______'s name?
B. His/Her name is ....

Who are the people in your family?
What are their names?

Tell about photos of family members.

家庭成員 2

伯父/叔父/ 舅父/姑丈/姨丈等	**1**	uncle
姑母/姨母/嬸母/伯母/舅母等	**2**	aunt
姪女/外甥女	**3**	niece
姪兒/外甥	**4**	nephew
(堂)表兄弟姊妹	**5**	cousin
婆婆/岳母	**6**	mother-in-law
公公/岳父	**7**	father-in-law
女婿	**8**	son-in-law
媳婦	**9**	daughter-in-law
內兄/內弟/大伯/小叔/姊夫/妹夫/連襟(配偶之姊妹的丈夫)	**10**	brother-in-law
大姑/小姑/小姨/大姨/嫂嫂/弟媳/妯娌/丈夫的嫂子/弟媳	**11**	sister-in-law

1. Jack is Alan's ____.
2. Nancy is Alan's ____.
3. Jennifer is Frank and Linda's ____.
4. Timmy is Frank and Linda's ____.
5. Alan is Jennifer and Timmy's ____.
6. Helen is Jack's ____.
7. Walter is Jack's ____.
8. Jack is Helen and Walter's ____.
9. Linda is Helen and Walter's ____.
10. Frank is Jack's ____.
11. Linda is Jack's ____.

A. Who is he/she?
B. He's/She's my ________.
A. What's his/her name?
B. His/Her name is ________.

A. Let me introduce my ________.
B. I'm glad to meet you.
C. Nice meeting you, too.

Tell about your relatives:
What are their names?
Where do they live?

Draw your family tree and tell about it.

THE CLASSROOM

教室

老師 **1** teacher	投影機 **8** overhead projector	地球儀 **16** globe
助教 **2** teacher's aide	銀幕 **9** screen	書櫃/書架 **17** bookcase/bookshelf
學生 **3** student	黑板/白板 **10** chalkboard/board	老師書桌 **18** teacher's desk
書桌 **4** desk	時鐘 **11** clock	廢紙簍 **19** wastebasket
座位/椅子 **5** seat/chair	地圖 **12** map	
桌子 **6** table	佈告欄 **13** bulletin board	
電腦 **7** computer	擴音系統/擴音器 **14** P.A. system/loudspeaker	
	白板/黑板 **15** whiteboard/board	

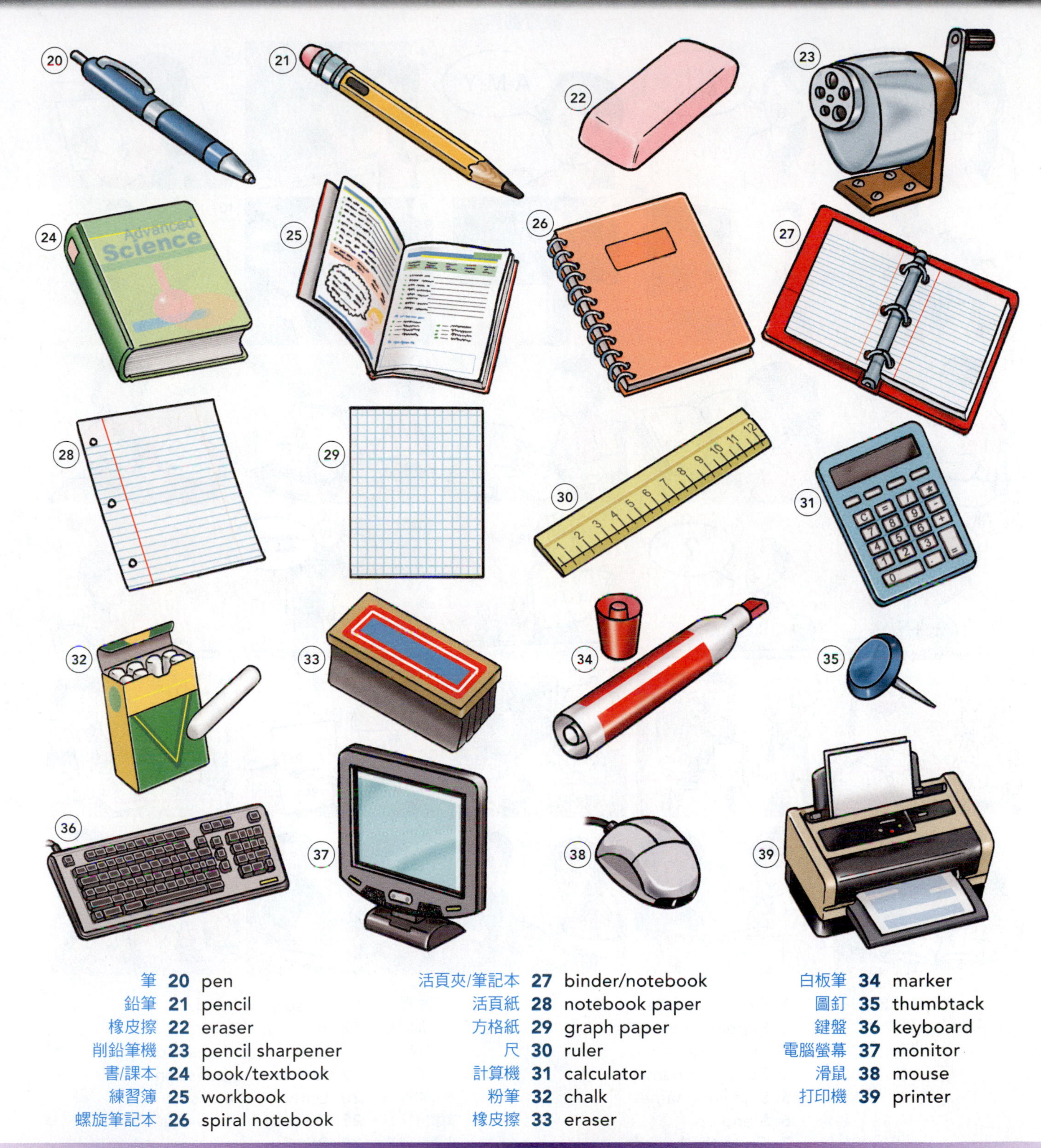

筆 **20** pen	活頁夾/筆記本 **27** binder/notebook	白板筆 **34** marker
鉛筆 **21** pencil	活頁紙 **28** notebook paper	圖釘 **35** thumbtack
橡皮擦 **22** eraser	方格紙 **29** graph paper	鍵盤 **36** keyboard
削鉛筆機 **23** pencil sharpener	尺 **30** ruler	電腦螢幕 **37** monitor
書/課本 **24** book/textbook	計算機 **31** calculator	滑鼠 **38** mouse
練習簿 **25** workbook	粉筆 **32** chalk	打印機 **39** printer
螺旋筆記本 **26** spiral notebook	橡皮擦 **33** eraser	

A. Where's the **teacher**?
B. The **teacher** is *next to* the **board**.

A. Where's the **globe**?
B. The **globe** is *on* the **bookcase**.

A. Is there a/an _____ in your classroom?*
B. Yes. There's a/an _____ next to/on the _____.

A. Is there a/an _____ in your classroom?*
B. No, there isn't.

Describe your classroom. (There's a/an ....)

* *With 28, 29, 32, use:* Is there _____ in your classroom?

教室動作

說出你的名字。 **1** Say your name.
重複你的名字。 **2** Repeat your name.
拼出你的名字。 **3** Spell your name.
寫出你的名字。 **4** Print your name.
請你簽名。 **5** Sign your name.
站起來。 **6** Stand up.
走到黑板/白板前。 **7** Go to the board.
寫在黑板/白板上。 **8** Write on the board.
擦黑板/白板。 **9** Erase the board.
坐下。 **10** Sit down./Take your seat.
打開書本。 **11** Open your book.
唸第10頁。 **12** Read page ten.
學習第10頁。 **13** Study page ten.
闔起書本。 **14** Close your book.
把書收起來。 **15** Put away your book.

請舉手。 **16** Raise your hand.
問問題。 **17** Ask a question.
聽問題。 **18** Listen to the question.
回答問題。 **19** Answer the question.
聽答案。 **20** Listen to the answer.
做家庭作業。 **21** Do your homework.
帶家庭作業。 **22** Bring in your homework.
對答案。 **23** Go over the answers.
訂正錯誤。 **24** Correct your mistakes.
交家庭作業。 **25** Hand in your homework.
共用一本書。 **26** Share a book.
討論問題。 **27** Discuss the question.
互相幫助。 **28** Help each other.
分工合作。 **29** Work together.
和同學分享。 **30** Share with the class.

查字典。 **31** Look in the dictionary.
查一個單字。 **32** Look up a word.
發出單字的音。 **33** Pronounce the word.
唸出釋義。 **34** Read the definition.
抄寫單字。 **35** Copy the word.
自己做功課。/ 做自己的功課。 **36** Work alone./ Do your own work.
和搭擋合作。 **37** Work with a partner.
分成小組。 **38** Break up into small groups.
小組活動。 **39** Work in a group.
全班活動。 **40** Work as a class.
拉下窗簾。 **41** Lower the shades.
關燈。 **42** Turn off the lights.
看銀幕。 **43** Look at the screen.
做筆記。 **44** Take notes.
開燈。 **45** Turn on the lights.

拿出一張紙。 **46** Take out a piece of paper.
發考卷。 **47** Pass out the tests.
回答問題。 **48** Answer the questions.
檢查答案。 **49** Check your answers.
收考卷。 **50** Collect the tests.
選出正確答案。 **51** Choose the correct answer.
圈選正確答案。 **52** Circle the correct answer.
填寫空格。 **53** Fill in the blank.
在答案卷(紙/卡)上作答。/ 將答案塗黑。 **54** Mark the answer sheet./ Bubble the answer.
單字配對。 **55** Match the words.
在單字下畫線。 **56** Underline the word.
在單字上打叉。 **57** Cross out the word.
字母重組，完成單字。 **58** Unscramble the word.
重組單字完成正確的句子。 **59** Put the words in order.
寫在另一張紙上。 **60** Write on a separate sheet of paper.

PREPOSITIONS

介系詞

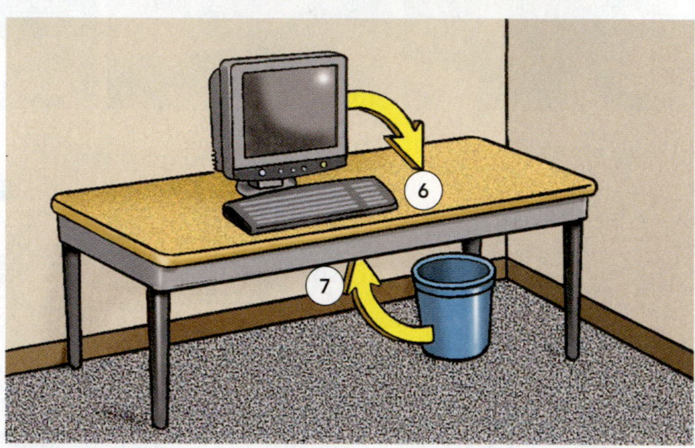

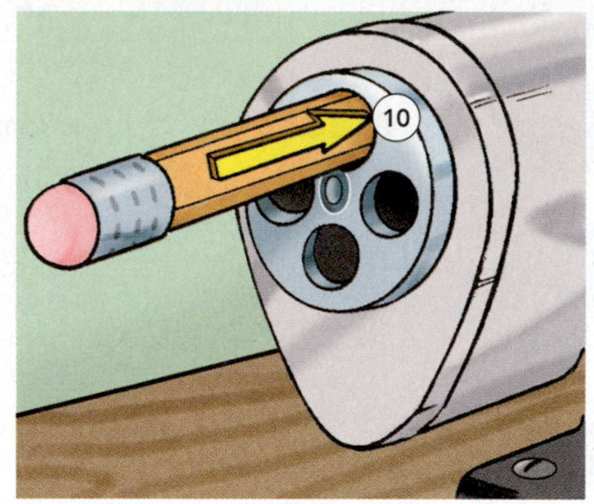

在…之上 **1** above
在…之下 **2** below
在…之前 **3** in front of
在…之後 **4** behind

在…旁邊 **5** next to
在…上面 **6** on
在…下面 **7** under
在…左邊 **8** to the left of

在…右邊 **9** to the right of
在…裡面 **10** in
在…和…之間 **11** between

[1–10]
A. Where's the *clock*?
B. The *clock* is **above** the *bulletin board*.

[11]
A. Where's the *dictionary*?
B. The *dictionary* is **between** the *globe* and the *pencil sharpener*.

Tell about the classroom on page 4. Use the prepositions in this lesson.

Tell about your classroom.

EVERYDAY ACTIVITIES I

日常活動 1

起床	**1**	get up
洗淋浴	**2**	take a shower
刷我的牙齒	**3**	brush *my** teeth
刮鬍子	**4**	shave
穿衣服	**5**	get dressed
洗我的臉	**6**	wash *my** face
化妝	**7**	put on makeup
梳我的頭髮	**8**	brush *my** hair
梳理我的頭髮	**9**	comb *my** hair
整理床鋪	**10**	make the bed
脫下衣服	**11**	get undressed
洗澡	**12**	take a bath
去睡覺	**13**	go to bed
睡覺	**14**	sleep
做早餐	**15**	make breakfast
做午餐	**16**	make lunch
做晚餐	**17**	cook/make dinner
吃早餐	**18**	eat/have breakfast
吃午餐	**19**	eat/have lunch
吃晚餐	**20**	eat/have dinner

* my, his, her, our, your, their

A. What do you do every day?
B. I **get up**, I **take a shower**, and I **brush my teeth**.

A. What does he do every day?
B. He _______s, he _______s, and he _______s.

A. What does she do every day?
B. She _______s, she _______s, and she_______s.

What do you do every day? Make a list.

Interview some friends and tell about their everyday activities.

日常活動 2

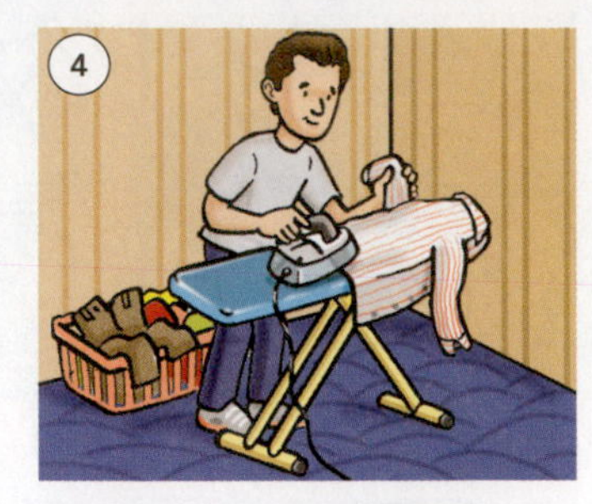

打掃公寓/打掃房子 **1** clean the apartment/clean the house
洗餐具 **2** wash the dishes
洗衣服 **3** do the laundry
燙衣服 **4** iron
餵嬰兒 **5** feed the baby
餵貓 **6** feed the cat
溜狗 **7** walk the dog
學習 **8** study
上班 **9** go to work
上學 **10** go to school
開車上班 **11** drive to work
搭乘巴士上學 **12** take the bus to school
工作 **13** work
下班 **14** leave work
去商店 **15** go to the store
回家/回到家 **16** come home/get home

A. Hello. What are you doing?
B. I'm **clean**ing the **apartment**.

A. Hello, ... This is ....
What are you doing?
B. I'm ________ing. How about you?
A. I'm ________ing.

A. Are you going to ________ soon?
B. Yes. I'm going to ________ in a little while.

What are you going to do tomorrow? Make a list of everything you are going to do.

LEISURE ACTIVITIES

休閒活動

看電視 **1** watch TV
聽收音機 **2** listen to the radio
聽音樂 **3** listen to music
看書 **4** read a book
看報紙 **5** read the newspaper
玩耍 **6** play
打紙牌 **7** play cards
打籃球 **8** play basketball
彈吉他 **9** play the guitar
練習彈鋼琴 **10** practice the piano
運動 **11** exercise
游泳 **12** swim
種花 **13** plant flowers
用電腦 **14** use the computer
寫信 **15** write a letter
放鬆/休息一下 **16** relax

A. Hi. What are you doing?
B. I'm **watch**ing **TV**.

A. Hi, ... Are you ________ing?
B. No, I'm not. I'm ________ing.

A. What's your (husband/wife/son/daughter/. . .) doing?
B. He's/She's ________ing.

What leisure activities do you like to do?

What do your family members and friends like to do?

日常會話

Greeting People 問候他人

Leave Taking 道別

哈囉。/嗨。 **1** Hello. / Hi.
早安。 **2** Good morning.
午安。 **3** Good afternoon.
晚安(傍晚見面時用語)。 **4** Good evening.
你好嗎？ **5** How are you? / How are you doing?
很好。/很好，謝謝。 **6** Fine. / Fine, thanks. / Okay.

有什麼新鮮事？ **7** What's new? / What's new with you?
沒什麼。 **8** Not much. / Not too much.
再見。 **9** Good-bye. / Bye.
晚安(晚上道別時用語)。 **10** Good night.
待會見。 **11** See you later. / See you soon.

Introducing Yourself and Others 介紹自己及他人

Getting Someone's Attention
引起他人注意

Expressing Gratitude
表示感謝

Saying You Don't Understand
表示不明白

Calling Someone on the Telephone
打電話給某人

你好，我的名字叫…。/ 嗨，我是…。 **12** Hello. My name is ..../ Hi. I'm ....

很高興認識你。 **13** Nice to meet you.

我也很高興認識你。 **14** Nice to meet you, too.

讓我向你介紹…。/ 這位是…。 **15** I'd like to introduce ..../ This is ....

對不起。 **16** Excuse me.

我可以問一個問題嗎？ **17** May I ask a question?

謝謝你。/謝謝。 **18** Thank you./Thanks.

不用客氣。 **19** You're welcome.

我不懂。/ 對不起，我不懂。 **20** I don't understand./ Sorry. I don't understand.

你可以再說一遍嗎？ **21** Can you please repeat that?/ Can you please say that again?

你好，我是…。 我可以和…說話嗎？ **22** Hello. This is .... May I please speak to ....?

可以，等一下。 **23** Yes. Hold on a moment.

對不起…現在不在這裡。 **24** I'm sorry. .... isn't here right now.

Practice conversations with other students. Use all the expressions on pages 12 and 13.

天氣

天氣		**Weather**
晴天	**1**	sunny
多雲	**2**	cloudy
晴朗	**3**	clear
有薄霧	**4**	hazy
多霧	**5**	foggy
煙霧瀰漫	**6**	smoggy
大風	**7**	windy
潮濕/悶熱	**8**	humid / muggy
下雨	**9**	raining
下毛毛雨	**10**	drizzling
下雪	**11**	snowing
下冰雹	**12**	hailing
下凍雨	**13**	sleeting
閃電	**14**	lightning
大雷雨	**15**	thunderstorm
暴風雪	**16**	snowstorm
塵暴	**17**	dust storm
熱浪	**18**	heat wave

氣溫		**Temperature**
溫度計	**19**	thermometer
華氏	**20**	Fahrenheit
攝氏	**21**	Centigrade / Celsius
熱	**22**	hot
暖和	**23**	warm
涼	**24**	cool
寒冷	**25**	cold
極冷	**26**	freezing

[1–13]
A. What's the weather like?
B. It's ________.

[14–18]
A. What's the weather forecast?
B. There's going to be __[14]__ / a __[15–18]__.

[20–26]
A. How's the weather?
B. It's __[22–26]__.
A. What's the temperature?
B. It's . . . degrees __[20–21]__.

What's the weather like today? What's the temperature?

What's the weather forecast for tomorrow?

数字

Cardinal Numbers 基數

0	zero	11	eleven	21	twenty-one	101	one hundred (and) one
1	one	12	twelve	22	twenty-two	102	one hundred (and) two
2	two	13	thirteen	30	thirty	1,000	one thousand
3	three	14	fourteen	40	forty	10,000	ten thousand
4	four	15	fifteen	50	fifty	100,000	one hundred thousand
5	five	16	sixteen	60	sixty	1,000,000	one million
6	six	17	seventeen	70	seventy	1,000,000,000	one billion
7	seven	18	eighteen	80	eighty		
8	eight	19	nineteen	90	ninety		
9	nine	20	twenty	100	one hundred		
10	ten						

A. How old are you?
B. I'm _______ years old.

A. How many people are there in your family?
B. _______.

Ordinal Numbers 序數

1st	first	11th	eleventh	21st	twenty-first	101st	one hundred (and) first
2nd	second	12th	twelfth	22nd	twenty-second	102nd	one hundred (and) second
3rd	third	13th	thirteenth	30th	thirtieth	1,000th	one thousandth
4th	fourth	14th	fourteenth	40th	fortieth	10,000th	ten thousandth
5th	fifth	15th	fifteenth	50th	fiftieth	100,000th	one hundred thousandth
6th	sixth	16th	sixteenth	60th	sixtieth	1,000,000th	one millionth
7th	seventh	17th	seventeenth	70th	seventieth	1,000,000,000th	one billionth
8th	eighth	18th	eighteenth	80th	eightieth		
9th	ninth	19th	nineteenth	90th	ninetieth		
10th	tenth	20th	twentieth	100th	one hundredth		

A. What floor do you live on?
B. I live on the _______ floor.

A. Is this your first trip to our country?
B. No. It's my _______ trip.

How many students are there in your class?

How many people are there in your country?

What were the names of your teachers in elementary school? (My *first*-grade teacher was Ms./Mrs./Mr. . . .)

TIME

時間

two o'clock

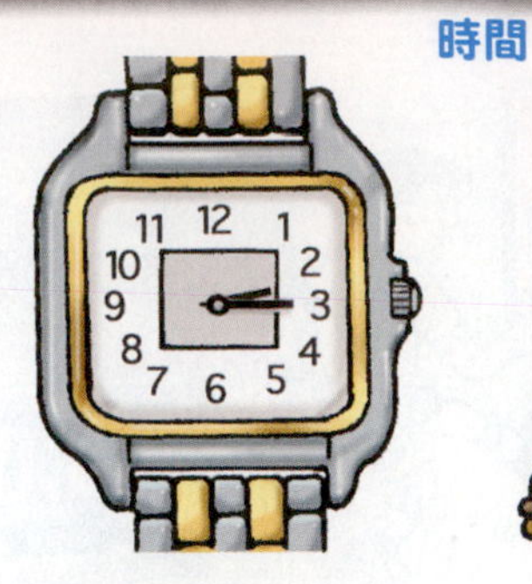
two fifteen/
a quarter after *two*

two thirty/
half past *two*

two forty-five
a quarter to *three*

two oh five

two twenty/
twenty after *two*

two forty/
twenty to *three*

two fifty-five
five to *three*

A. What time is it?
B. It's ______.

A. What time does the movie begin?
B. At ______.

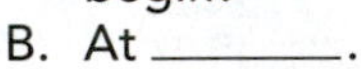

two A.M.

two P.M.

noon/
twelve noon

midnight/
twelve midnight

A. When does the train leave?
B. At ______.

A. What time will we arrive?
B. At ______.

Tell about your daily schedule:
What do you do? When?
(I get up at ______. I ....)

Do you usually have enough time to do things, or do you "run out of time"? Tell about it.

Tell about the use of time in different cultures or countries you know:
Do people arrive on time for work? appointments? parties?
Do trains and buses operate exactly on schedule?
Do movies and sports events begin on time?
Do workplaces use time clocks or timesheets to record employees' work hours?

錢幣

Coins 錢幣

1  2  3  4  5  6 

	Name	Value	Written as:	
1	penny	one cent	1¢	$ .01
2	nickel	five cents	5¢	$ .05
3	dime	ten cents	10¢	$ .10
4	quarter	twenty-five cents	25¢	$ .25
5	half dollar	fifty cents	50¢	$ .50
6	silver dollar	one dollar		$1.00

A. How much is a **penny** worth?
B. A **penny** is worth **one cent**.

A. *Soda* costs *ninety-five cents*. Do you have enough change?
B. Yes. I have a/two/three ____(s) and . . . .

Currency 貨幣

	Name	We sometimes say:	Value	Written as:
7	(one-) dollar bill	a one	one dollar	$ 1.00
8	five-dollar bill	a five	five dollars	$ 5.00
9	ten-dollar bill	a ten	ten dollars	$ 10.00
10	twenty-dollar bill	a twenty	twenty dollars	$ 20.00
11	fifty-dollar bill	a fifty	fifty dollars	$ 50.00
12	(one-) hundred dollar bill	a hundred	one hundred dollars	$100.00

A. I'm going to the supermarket. Do you have any cash?
B. I have a **twenty-dollar bill**.
A. **Twenty dollars** is enough. Thanks.

A. Can you change a **five-dollar bill/a five**?
B. Yes. I have ***five one-dollar bills/ five ones***.

Written as:	We say:
$1.30	a dollar and thirty cents a dollar thirty
$2.50	two dollars and fifty cents two fifty
$56.49	fifty-six dollars and forty-nine cents fifty-six forty-nine

Tell about some things you usually buy. What do they cost?

Name and describe the coins and currency in your country. What are they worth in U.S. dollars?

日曆

年	**1**	year
月	**2**	month
星期	**3**	week
日	**4**	day
週末	**5**	weekend

一週的日子 Days of the Week

星期日	**6**	Sunday
星期一	**7**	Monday
星期二	**8**	Tuesday
星期三	**9**	Wednesday
星期四	**10**	Thursday
星期五	**11**	Friday
星期六	**12**	Saturday

月份 Months of the Year

一月	**13**	January
二月	**14**	February
三月	**15**	March
四月	**16**	April
五月	**17**	May
六月	**18**	June
七月	**19**	July
八月	**20**	August
九月	**21**	September
十月	**22**	October
十一月	**23**	November
十二月	**24**	December

2012年1月3日	**25**	January 3, 2012 January third, two thousand twelve
生日	**26**	birthday
週年紀念	**27**	anniversary
約定時間	**28**	appointment

A. What year is it?
B. It's ________.

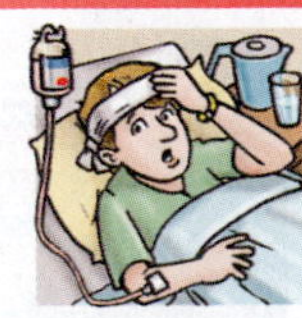

[13–24]
A. What month is it?
B. It's ________.

[6–12]
A. What day is it?
B. It's ________.

A. What's today's date?
B. It's ________.

[26–28]
A. When is your ________?
B. It's on ________.

Which days of the week do you go to work/school?
(I go to work/school on ________.)

What do you do on the weekend?

What is your date of birth?
(I was born on ...*month day, year*....)

What's your favorite day of the week? Why?

What's your favorite month of the year? Why?

時間表達及季節

- 昨天 **1** yesterday
- 今天 **2** today
- 明天 **3** tomorrow
- 早上 **4** morning
- 下午 **5** afternoon
- 傍晚 **6** evening
- 夜晚 **7** night
- 昨天早上 **8** yesterday morning
- 昨天下午 **9** yesterday afternoon
- 昨天傍晚 **10** yesterday evening
- 昨晚 **11** last night
- 今天早上 **12** this morning
- 今天下午 **13** this afternoon
- 今天傍晚 **14** this evening
- 今晚 **15** tonight
- 明天早上 **16** tomorrow morning
- 明天下午 **17** tomorrow afternoon
- 明天傍晚 **18** tomorrow evening
- 明晚 **19** tomorrow night
- 上週 **20** last week
- 本週 **21** this week
- 下週 **22** next week
- 每週一次 **23** once a week
- 每週兩次 **24** twice a week
- 每週三次 **25** three times a week
- 每天 **26** every day

季節 Seasons

- 春天 **27** spring
- 夏天 **28** summer
- 秋天 **29** fall/autumn
- 冬天 **30** winter

What did you do yesterday morning/afternoon/evening? What did you do last night?

What are you going to do tomorrow morning/afternoon/evening/night?

What did you do last week?

What are your plans for next week?

How many times a week do you have English class?/go to the supermarket?/exercise?

What's your favorite season? Why?

房屋及社區種類

公寓大樓 **1** apartment building
房子 **2** house
雙聯式房屋/兩家合居，但各自分開的房屋 **3** duplex/two-family house
二層或三層樓多棟聯建住宅 **4** townhouse/townhome
各戶有獨立產權的公寓(大樓) **5** condominium/condo
宿舍 **6** dormitory/dorm
移動式房屋 **7** mobile home
養老院 **8** nursing home
庇護所 **9** shelter
農場 **10** farm
牧場 **11** ranch
船房 **12** houseboat
城市 **13** the city
郊區 **14** the suburbs
鄉村 **15** the country
小鎮/村莊 **16** a town/village

A. Where do you live?
B. I live
- in a/an [1–9].
- on a [10–12].
- in [13–16].

[1–12]
A. Town Taxi Company.
B. Hello. Please send a taxi to ......*(address)*......
A. Is that a house or an apartment building?
B. It's a/an ________.
A. All right. We'll be there right away.

[1–12]
A. This is the Emergency Operator.
B. Please send an ambulance to ......*(address)*......
A. Is that a private home?
B. It's a/an ________.
A. What's your name and telephone number?
B. ....

Tell about people you know and where they live.

Discuss:
Who lives in dormitories?
Who lives in nursing homes?
Who lives in shelters?
Why?

THE LIVING ROOM

客廳

書櫃	1	bookcase
照片	2	picture/photograph
畫	3	painting
壁爐臺	4	mantel
壁爐	5	fireplace
壁爐屏幕	6	fireplace screen
數碼光碟播放機	7	DVD player
電視	8	television/TV
卡式錄放影機	9	VCR/video cassette recorder
牆壁	10	wall
天花板	11	ceiling
簾/幔	12	drapes
窗戶	13	window
雙人小沙發	14	loveseat
牆櫃	15	wall unit
喇叭	16	speaker
立體音響系統	17	stereo system
雜誌架	18	magazine holder
抱枕	19	(throw) pillow
沙發	20	sofa/couch
植物	21	plant
茶几	22	coffee table
小地毯	23	rug
燈	24	lamp
燈罩	25	lampshade
小茶几	26	end table
地板	27	floor
落地燈	28	floor lamp
單人沙發椅	29	armchair

A. Where are you?
B. I'm in the living room.
A. What are you doing?
B. I'm dusting* the **bookcase**.

* dusting/cleaning

A. You have a very nice living room!
B. Thank you.
A. Your ________ is/are beautiful!
B. Thank you for saying so.

A. Uh-oh! I just spilled coffee on your ________!
B. That's okay. Don't worry about it.

Tell about your living room.
(In my living room there's ....)

THE DINING ROOM

飯廳

餐桌 **1** (dining room) table	瓷器 **12** china	桌巾/桌布 **23** tablecloth
餐椅 **2** (dining room) chair	沙拉碗 **13** salad bowl	餐巾 **24** napkin
餐具櫃 **3** buffet	盛菜碗 **14** serving bowl	叉子 **25** fork
托盤 **4** tray	盛菜盤 **15** serving dish	盤子 **26** plate
茶壺 **5** teapot	花瓶 **16** vase	餐刀 **27** knife
咖啡壺 **6** coffee pot	蠟燭 **17** candle	湯匙 **28** spoon
糖罐子 **7** sugar bowl	燭臺 **18** candlestick	碗 **29** bowl
鮮奶壺 **8** creamer	大淺盤 **19** platter	馬克杯 **30** mug
水壺 **9** pitcher	奶油盤 **20** butter dish	玻璃杯 **31** glass
吊燈 **10** chandelier	鹽瓶 **21** salt shaker	茶杯 **32** cup
瓷器櫃 **11** china cabinet	胡椒瓶 **22** pepper shaker	淺盤 **33** saucer

A. This **dining room table** is very nice.
B. Thank you. It was a gift from my *grandmother*.*

*grandmother/grandfather/aunt/uncle/. . .

[In a store]

A. May I help you?
B. Yes, please. Do you have ________s?*
A. Yes. ________s* are right over there.
B. Thank you.

**With 12, use the singular.*

[At home]

A. Look at this old ________ I just bought!
B. Where did you buy it?
A. At a yard sale. How do you like it?
B. It's VERY unusual!

Tell about your dining room.
(In my dining room there's ....)

臥室

床	**1**	bed
床頭板	**2**	headboard
枕頭	**3**	pillow
枕頭套	**4**	pillowcase
床包	**5**	fitted sheet
平床單	**6**	(flat) sheet
毯子	**7**	blanket
電毯	**8**	electric blanket
床裙	**9**	dust ruffle
床罩	**10**	bedspread
蓋被/拼湊圖案的被褥	**11**	comforter/quilt
地毯	**12**	carpet
五斗櫃/衣櫃	**13**	chest (of drawers)
百葉窗	**14**	blinds
窗簾	**15**	curtains
燈	**16**	lamp
鬧鐘	**17**	alarm clock
鬧鐘收音機	**18**	clock radio
床頭櫃/床頭桌	**19**	night table/nightstand
鏡子	**20**	mirror
首飾盒	**21**	jewelry box
五斗櫃/梳妝臺	**22**	dresser/bureau
床墊	**23**	mattress
彈簧座	**24**	box spring
床架	**25**	bed frame

A. Ooh! Look at that big bug!
B. Where?
A. It's on the **bed**!
B. I'LL get it.

[In a store]
A. Excuse me. I'm looking for a/an ________.*
B. We have some very nice ________s, and they're all on sale this week!
A. Oh, good!

* *With 14 & 15, use:* Excuse me. I'm looking for _____.

[In a bedroom]
A. Oh, no! I just lost my contact lens!
B. Where?
A. I think it's on the ________.
B. I'll help you look.

Tell about your bedroom.
(In my bedroom there's ....)

THE KITCHEN

廚房

- 電冰箱 **1** refrigerator
- 冷凍庫 **2** freezer
- 垃圾桶 **3** garbage pail
- 電動攪拌器 **4** (electric) mixer
- 廚櫃 **5** cabinet
- 紙巾架 **6** paper towel holder
- 罐子 **7** canister
- 廚房工作檯面 **8** (kitchen) counter
- 洗碗機專用洗潔劑 **9** dishwasher detergent
- 洗碗精 **10** dishwashing liquid
- 水龍頭 **11** faucet
- 廚房水槽 **12** (kitchen) sink
- 洗碗機 **13** dishwasher
- 垃圾清除器 **14** (garbage) disposal
- 擦碗巾 **15** dish towel
- 碗碟架/碗碟瀝水架 **16** dish rack/dish drainer
- 調味品架 **17** spice rack
- 電動開罐器 **18** (electric) can opener
- 果汁機 **19** blender
- 小烤箱 **20** toaster oven
- 微波爐 **21** microwave (oven)
- 隔熱墊 **22** potholder
- 燒水壺 **23** tea kettle
- 爐台 **24** stove/range
- 爐頭 **25** burner
- 烤箱 **26** oven
- 烤麵包機 **27** toaster
- 咖啡機 **28** coffeemaker
- 垃圾壓縮機 **29** trash compactor
- 切菜板/砧板 **30** cutting board
- 食譜 **31** cookbook
- 食物處理機 **32** food processor
- 廚房椅子 **33** kitchen chair
- 廚房桌子 **34** kitchen table
- 餐墊 **35** placemat

A. I think we need a new **refrigerator**.
B. I think you're right.

[In a store]

A. Excuse me. Are your ________s still on sale?
B. Yes, they are. They're twenty percent off.

[In a kitchen]

A. When did you get this/these new ________(s)?
B. I got it/them last week.

Tell about your kitchen.
(In my kitchen there's ....)

THE BABY'S ROOM

嬰兒室

泰迪熊	1	teddy bear
嬰兒監聽器/對講機	2	baby monitor/intercom
五斗櫃/衣櫃	3	chest (of drawers)
嬰兒床	4	crib
床圍	5	crib bumper/bumper pad
吊飾	6	mobile
換尿布台	7	changing table
連身衣	8	stretch suit
換尿布護墊	9	changing pad
尿布垃圾桶	10	diaper pail
小夜燈	11	night light
玩具箱	12	toy chest
填充動物玩具	13	stuffed animal
洋娃娃	14	doll
嬰兒盪鞦韆	15	swing
嬰兒圍欄	16	playpen
手搖鈴	17	rattle
學步車	18	walker
搖籃	19	cradle
摺疊式嬰兒車	20	stroller
嬰兒車	21	baby carriage
兒童安全座椅	22	car seat/safety seat
嬰兒提籃	23	baby carrier
食物保溫盒	24	food warmer
幼兒加高座椅	25	booster seat
嬰兒座椅	26	baby seat
高腳椅	27	high chair
攜式嬰兒床	28	portable crib
嬰兒便盆	29	potty
胸前背袋	30	baby frontpack
嬰兒背架	31	baby backpack

A. Thank you for the **teddy bear**. It's a very nice gift.
B. You're welcome. Tell me, when are you due?
A. In a few more weeks.

A. That's a very nice ______.
Where did you get it?
B. It was a gift from ....

A. Do you have everything you need before the baby comes?
B. Almost everything. We're still looking for a/an ______ and a/an ______.

Tell about your country:
What things do people buy for a new baby?
Does a new baby sleep in a separate room, as in the United States?

浴室

廢紙簍 **1** wastebasket	吹風機 **14** hair dryer	空氣清香劑 **25** air freshener
梳妝台/洗手台 **2** vanity	架子 **15** shelf	馬桶 **26** toilet
肥皂 **3** soap	髒衣籃 **16** hamper	馬桶座 **27** toilet seat
肥皂盒 **4** soap dish	風扇 **17** fan	淋浴 **28** shower
皂液器 **5** soap dispenser	浴巾 **18** bath towel	蓮蓬頭 **29** shower head
洗臉槽 **6** (bathroom) sink	手巾 **19** hand towel	浴簾 **30** shower curtain
水龍頭 **7** faucet	洗臉毛巾 **20** washcloth/facecloth	浴缸 **31** bathtub/tub
藥櫃 **8** medicine cabinet	毛巾架 **21** towel rack	橡膠墊 **32** rubber mat
鏡子 **9** mirror	橡膠吸盤 **22** plunger	排水孔 **33** drain
茶杯 **10** cup	馬桶刷 **23** toilet brush	海綿 **34** sponge
牙刷 **11** toothbrush	衛生紙 **24** toilet paper	浴墊 **35** bath mat
牙刷架 **12** toothbrush holder		體重計 **36** scale
電動牙刷 **13** electric toothbrush		

A. Where's the **hair dryer**?
B. It's *on* the **vanity**.

A. Where's the **soap**?
B. It's *in* the **soap dish**.

A. Where's the **plunger**?
B. It's *next to* the **toilet brush**.

A. [Knock. Knock.] Did I leave my glasses in there?
B. Yes. They're on/in/next to the _______.

A. *Bobby*? You didn't clean up the bathroom! There's toothpaste on the _______, and there's powder all over the _______!
B. Sorry. I'll clean it up right away.

Tell about your bathroom.
(In my bathroom there's ....)

家的外圍

前院 Front Yard

路燈 **1** lamppost
信箱 **2** mailbox
前門小路 **3** front walk
前門階梯 **4** front steps
前門門廊 **5** (front) porch
防風門/外重門 **6** storm door
前門 **7** front door
門鈴 **8** doorbell
前門燈 **9** (front) light
窗戶 **10** window
紗窗 **11** (window) screen
窗板 **12** shutter
屋頂 **13** roof
車庫 **14** garage
車庫門 **15** garage door
車道 **16** driveway

後院 Backyard

躺椅 **17** lawn chair
割草機 **18** lawnmower
工具房 **19** tool shed
紗門 **20** screen door
後門 **21** back door
門把 **22** door knob
屋外的平台 **23** deck
烤肉架/戶外烤架 **24** barbecue/(outdoor) grill
露台 **25** patio
排水溝/簷溝 **26** gutter
排水管 **27** drainpipe
衛星接收器/小耳朵 **28** satellite dish
電視天線 **29** TV antenna
煙囪 **30** chimney
側門 **31** side door
籬笆 **32** fence

A. When are you going to repair the **lamppost**?
B. I'm going to repair it next Saturday.

[On the telephone]
A. Harry's Home Repairs.
B. Hello. Do you fix ________s?
A. No, we don't.
B. Oh, okay. Thank you.

[At work on Monday morning]
A. What did you do this weekend?
B. Nothing much. I repaired my ________ and my ________.

Do you like to repair things?
What things can you repair yourself?
What things can't you repair? Who repairs them?

THE APARTMENT BUILDING
公寓大樓

找公寓 Looking for an Apartment

租房廣告/分類廣告 **1** apartment ads/ classified ads
公寓出租廣告 **2** apartment listings
空屋出租廣告 **3** vacancy sign

簽租約 Signing a Lease

房客 **4** tenant
房東 **5** landlord
租約 **6** lease
押金 **7** security deposit

搬入 Moving In

搬家卡車/搬家貨車 **8** moving truck/ moving van
鄰居 **9** neighbor
大樓管理員 **10** building manager
看門人 **11** doorman
鑰匙 **12** key
鎖 **13** lock
一樓 **14** first floor
二樓 **15** second floor
三樓 **16** third floor
四樓 **17** fourth floor
屋頂 **18** roof

(室外)逃生梯 **19** fire escape
室內停車場 **20** parking garage
陽台 **21** balcony
庭院 **22** courtyard
停車場 **23** parking lot
停車位 **24** parking space
游泳池 **25** swimming pool
水力按摩池 **26** whirlpool
垃圾桶 **27** trash bin
冷氣 **28** air conditioner

一樓大廳 Lobby

對講機 **29** intercom/speaker
門鈴 **30** buzzer
信箱 **31** mailbox
電梯 **32** elevator
樓梯 **33** stairway

門口 Doorway

窺視孔/門孔 **34** peephole
門鏈 **35** (door) chain
多段鎖 **36** dead-bolt lock
煙熱警告器 **37** smoke detector

走廊 Hallway

緊急出口/(室內)逃生梯 **38** fire exit/emergency stairway
火警警報 **39** fire alarm
噴水滅火系統 **40** sprinkler system
管房人 **41** superintendent
垃圾滑槽 **42** garbage chute/trash chute

地下室 Basement

儲藏室 **43** storage room
儲藏櫃 **44** storage locker
自助洗衣房 **45** laundry room
安檢門 **46** security gate

[19–46]
A. Is there a **fire escape**?
B. Yes, there is. Do you want to see the apartment?
A. Yes, I do.

[19–46]
[Renting an apartment]
A. Let me show you around.
B. Okay.
A. This is the ________, and here's the ________.
B. I see.

[19–46]
[On the telephone]
A. Mom and Dad? I found an apartment.
B. Good. Tell us about it.
A. It has a/an ________ and a/an ________.
B. That's nice. Does it have a/an ________?
A. Yes, it does.

Do you or someone you know live in an apartment building? Tell about it.

HOUSEHOLD PROBLEMS AND REPAIRS

房屋問題及修理

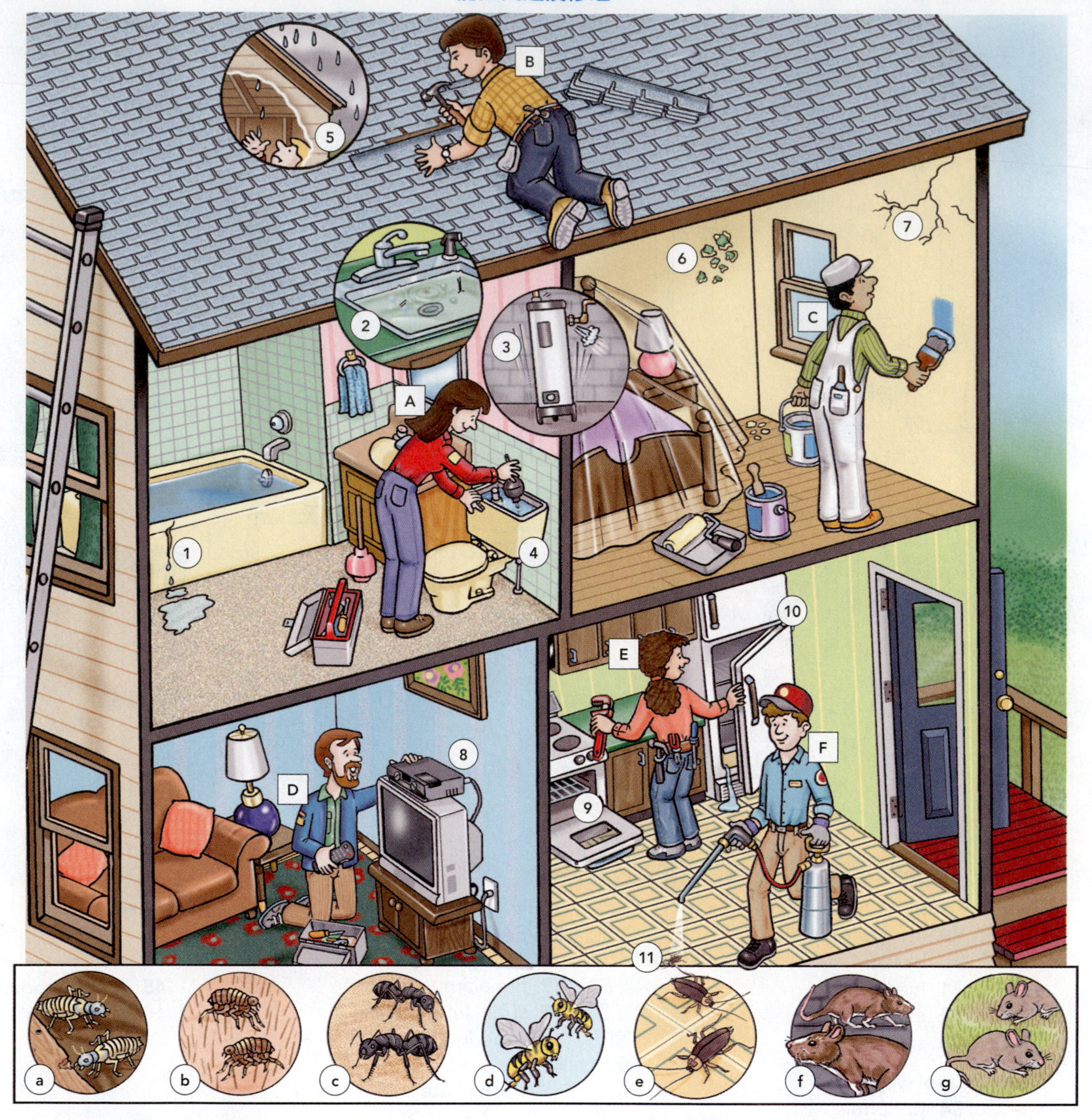

水管工人 **A plumber**

浴缸漏水。 **1** The bathtub is leaking.

洗臉槽堵塞了。 **2** The sink is clogged.

熱水氣故障。 **3** The hot water heater isn't working.

馬桶壞了。 **4** The toilet is broken.

屋頂工人 **B roofer**

屋頂漏水。 **5** The roof is leaking.

油漆工人 **C (house) painter**

油漆剝落。 **6** The paint is peeling.

牆壁有裂縫。 **7** The wall is cracked.

有線電視公司 **D cable TV company**

有線電視故障。 **8** The cable TV isn't working.

家電修理人員 **E appliance repairperson**

爐具故障。 **9** The stove isn't working.

電冰箱壞了。 **10** The refrigerator is broken.

滅蟲害人員 **F exterminator/ pest control specialist**

廚房裡有…。 **11** There are ____ in the kitchen.

白蟻 **a** termites

跳蚤 **b** fleas

螞蟻 **c** ants

蜜蜂 **d** bees

蟑螂 **e** cockroaches

老鼠 **f** rats

小老鼠 **g** mice

鎖匠	**G**	**locksmith**
鎖壞了。	**12**	The lock is broken.
電工	**H**	**electrician**
前門燈不亮。	**13**	The front light doesn't go on.
門鈴不響。	**14**	The doorbell doesn't ring.
客廳停電。	**15**	The power is out in the living room.
煙囱清潔工	**I**	**chimneysweep**
煙囱髒了。	**16**	The chimney is dirty.
修理工/雜活工	**J**	**home repairperson/"handyman"**
浴室的瓷磚鬆動了。	**17**	The tiles in the bathroom are loose.
木工/木匠	**K**	**carpenter**
台階壞了。	**18**	The steps are broken.
門打不開。	**19**	The door doesn't open.
暖氣及空調服務	**L**	**heating and air conditioning service**
供暖系統壞了。	**20**	The heating system is broken.
冷氣故障。	**21**	The air conditioning isn't working.

A. What's the matter?
B. [1–21].
A. I think we should call a/an [A–L].

[1–21]
A. I'm having a problem in my apartment/house.
B. What's the problem?
A. ______.

[A–L]
A. Can you recommend a good ______?
B. Yes. You should call ....

What do you do when there are problems in your home? Do you fix things yourself, or do you call someone?

CLEANING YOUR HOME

打掃房子

掃地 **A** sweep the floor
吸塵器 **B** vacuum
拖地板 **C** mop the floor
洗窗戶 **D** wash the windows
除灰塵 **E** dust
地板打蠟 **F** wax the floor
擦亮家具 **G** polish the furniture
清理浴室 **H** clean the bathroom
丟垃圾 **I** take out the garbage

掃把 **1** broom
簸箕 **2** dustpan
小掃帚 **3** whisk broom
掃毯器 **4** carpet sweeper
吸塵器 **5** vacuum (cleaner)
吸塵器附件 **6** vacuum cleaner attachments
吸塵器袋 **7** vacuum cleaner bag
手提吸塵器 **8** hand vacuum
抹塵拖把/乾拖把 **9** (dust) mop/(dry) mop
海綿拖把 **10** (sponge) mop
濕拖把 **11** (wet) mop
紙巾 **12** paper towels
玻璃清潔劑 **13** window cleaner
氨水 **14** ammonia
擦塵布 **15** dust cloth
羽毛撣子 **16** feather duster
地板打蠟劑 **17** floor wax
木製家具亮光蠟 **18** furniture polish
清潔劑 **19** cleanser
刷子 **20** scrub brush
海綿 **21** sponge
桶子 **22** bucket/pail
垃圾桶 **23** trash can/garbage can
回收桶 **24** recycling bin

[A–I]
A. What are you doing?
B. I'm **sweep**ing **the floor**.

[1–24]
A. I can't find the **broom**.
B. Look over there!

[1–12, 15, 16, 20–24]
A. Excuse me. Do you sell ________(s)?
B. Yes. They're at the back of the store.
A. Thanks.

[13, 14, 17–19]
A. Excuse me. Do you sell ________?
B. Yes. It's at the back of the store.
A. Thanks.

What household cleaning chores do people do in your home? What things do they use?

家用器具

碼尺	**1**	yardstick
蒼蠅拍	**2**	fly swatter
橡膠吸盤	**3**	plunger
手電筒	**4**	flashlight
延長線	**5**	extension cord
測量捲尺	**6**	tape measure
踏板梯子	**7**	step ladder
捕鼠器	**8**	mousetrap
遮蓋膠帶	**9**	masking tape
電工膠帶	**10**	electrical tape
管道膠帶	**11**	duct tape
電池	**12**	batteries
電燈泡	**13**	lightbulbs/bulbs
保險絲	**14**	fuses
機油	**15**	oil
膠水	**16**	glue
工作手套	**17**	work gloves
殺蟲劑	**18**	bug spray/insect spray
殺蟑螂劑	**19**	roach killer
砂紙	**20**	sandpaper
油漆	**21**	paint
油漆稀釋劑	**22**	paint thinner
油漆刷子	**23**	paintbrush/brush
油漆盤	**24**	paint pan
滾筒油漆刷	**25**	paint roller
噴漆槍	**26**	spray gun

A. I can't find the **yardstick**!
B. Look in the utility cabinet.
A. I did.
B. Oh! Wait a minute! I lent the **yardstick** to the neighbors.

[1–8, 23–26]
A. I'm going to the hardware store. Can you think of anything we need?
B. Yes. We need a/an ________.
A. Oh, that's right.

[9–22]
A. I'm going to the hardware store. Can you think of anything we need?
B. Yes. We need ________.
A. Oh, that's right.

What home supplies do you have? How and when do you use each one?

TOOLS AND HARDWARE

工具及五金器具

- 槌子 **1** hammer
- 大頭槌 **2** mallet
- 斧頭 **3** ax
- 鋸子/手鋸 **4** saw/handsaw
- 鋼鋸 **5** hacksaw
- 水平儀 **6** level
- 螺絲起子 **7** screwdriver
- 十字型螺絲起子 **8** Phillips screwdriver
- 扳手 **9** wrench
- 可調扳手/管板鉗 **10** monkey wrench/pipe wrench
- 鑿子 **11** chisel
- 刮刀 **12** scraper
- 剝線鉗 **13** wire stripper
- 手鑽 **14** hand drill
- 台虎鉗 **15** vise
- 鉗子 **16** pliers
- 工具箱 **17** toolbox
- 刨子 **18** plane
- 電鑽 **19** electric drill
- 鑽頭 **20** (drill) bit
- 電圓鋸/電鋸 **21** circular saw/power saw
- 電磨沙機 **22** power sander
- 手動木工鑽 **23** router
- 電線 **24** wire
- 釘子 **25** nail
- 墊圈 **26** washer
- 螺絲母 **27** nut
- 木用螺絲釘 **28** wood screw
- 機械螺絲 **29** machine screw
- 螺栓 **30** bolt

A. Can I borrow your **hammer**?
B. Sure.
A. Thanks.

* *With 25–30, use:* Could I borrow some ________s?

[1–15, 17–24]
A. Where's the ________?
B. It's on/next to/near/over/under the ________.

[16, 25–30]
A. Where are the ________s?
B. They're on/next to/near/over/under the ________.

Do you like to work with tools? What tools do you have in your home?

園藝工具及活動

割草	**A**	mow the lawn
種菜	**B**	plant vegetables
種花	**C**	plant flowers
澆花	**D**	water the flowers
耙葉子	**E**	rake leaves
修剪樹籬	**F**	trim the hedge
修剪灌木叢	**G**	prune the bushes
除雜草	**H**	weed

割草機	**1**	lawnmower
汽油桶	**2**	gas can
修邊機	**3**	line trimmer
鏟子	**4**	shovel
菜種子	**5**	vegetable seeds
鋤頭	**6**	hoe
泥刀/小鏟子	**7**	trowel
獨輪小推車	**8**	wheelbarrow
肥料	**9**	fertilizer
橡膠水管/花園水管	**10**	(garden) hose

噴頭	**11**	nozzle
灑水器	**12**	sprinkler
澆水桶	**13**	watering can
草耙	**14**	rake
吹葉機	**15**	leaf blower
庭院垃圾袋	**16**	yard waste bag
樹籬剪	**17**	(hedge) clippers
樹籬修剪器	**18**	hedge trimmer
修枝剪	**19**	pruning shears
除草器	**20**	weeder

[A–H]
A. Hi! Are you busy?
B. Yes. I'm **mowing the lawn**.

[1–20]
A. What are you looking for?
B. The **lawnmower**.

[A–H]
A. What are you going to do tomorrow?
B. I'm going to ________.

[1–20]
A. Can I borrow your ________?
B. Sure.

Do you ever work with any of these tools? Which ones? What do you do with them?

城鎮場所 1

麵包店/糕餅店 **1** bakery	賣車行 **7** car dealership	服飾店 **12** clothing store
銀行 **2** bank	卡片商店 **8** card store	咖啡店 **13** coffee shop
理髮店 **3** barber shop	托兒所 **9** child-care center / day-care center	電腦商店 **14** computer store
書店 **4** book store	洗衣店/乾洗店 **10** cleaners / dry cleaners	便利店 **15** convenience store
巴士車站 **5** bus station	診所 **11** clinic	影印店 **16** copy center
糖果店 **6** candy store		

熟食店 **17** delicatessen/deli
百貨公司 **18** department store
折扣店 **19** discount store
甜甜圈店 **20** donut shop
藥房 **21** drug store/pharmacy
電子商店 **22** electronics store
眼科中心/眼科中心 **23** eye-care center/optician
速食店 **24** fast-food restaurant
花店/花店 **25** flower shop/florist
家具店 **26** furniture store
加油站 **27** gas station/ service station
雜貨店 **28** grocery store

A. Where are you going?
B. I'm going to the **bakery**.

A. Hi! How are you today?
B. Fine. Where are you going?
A. To the ________. How about you?
B. I'm going to the ________.

A. Oh, no! I can't find my wallet/purse!
B. Did you leave it at the ________?
A. Maybe I did.

Which of these places are in your neighborhood?
(In my neighborhood there's a/an ....)

城鎮場所 2

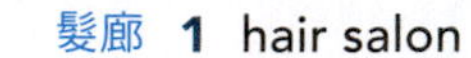

髮廊 **1** hair salon
五金行 **2** hardware store
健身俱樂部 **3** health club
醫院 **4** hospital
旅館 **5** hotel
冰淇淋店 **6** ice cream shop
珠寶店 **7** jewelry store
自助洗衣店 **8** laundromat
圖書館 **9** library
孕婦裝店 **10** maternity shop
汽車旅館 **11** motel
電影院 **12** movie theater
音樂商店 **13** music store
美甲沙龍 **14** nail salon
公園 **15** park
寵物店 **16** pet shop/ pet store

照片沖洗店 **17** photo shop
披薩店 **18** pizza shop
郵局 **19** post office
餐廳 **20** restaurant

學校 **21** school
鞋店 **22** shoe store
購物中心 **23** (shopping) mall
超級市場 **24** supermarket

玩具店 **25** toy store
火車站 **26** train station
旅行社 **27** travel agency
影視租售店 **28** video store

A. Where's the **hair salon**?
B. It's right over there.

A. Is there a/an ________ nearby?
B. Yes. There's a/an ________ around the corner.
A. Thanks.

A. Excuse me. Where's the ________?
B. It's down the street, next to the ________.
A. Thank you.

Which of these places are in your neighborhood?
(In my neighborhood there's a/an ....)

城市

法院大樓	1	courthouse
計程車	2	taxi/cab/taxicab
計程車招呼站	3	taxi stand
計程車司機	4	taxi driver/ cab driver
消防栓	5	fire hydrant
垃圾桶	6	trash container
市政廳	7	city hall
火警箱	8	fire alarm box
郵筒	9	mailbox
下水道	10	sewer
警察局	11	police station
監獄	12	jail
人行道	13	sidewalk
街道	14	street
街燈	15	street light
停車場	16	parking lot
開停車罰單女警	17	meter maid
停車收費器	18	parking meter
垃圾車	19	garbage truck
地鐵/捷運	20	subway
地鐵站/捷運站	21	subway station

報刊販賣攤	**22**	newsstand
交通號誌燈	**23**	traffic light / traffic signal
十字路口	**24**	intersection
警察	**25**	police officer
行人穿越道/斑馬線	**26**	crosswalk
行人	**27**	pedestrian
冰淇淋販賣車	**28**	ice cream truck
路緣/路邊	**29**	curb
停車庫	**30**	parking garage
消防隊	**31**	fire station
公車站	**32**	bus stop
公車	**33**	bus
公車司機	**34**	bus driver
辦公大樓	**35**	office building
公用電話	**36**	public telephone
路牌	**37**	street sign
下水道出入孔	**38**	manhole
摩托車	**39**	motorcycle
街頭攤販	**40**	street vendor
免下車服務窗口	**41**	drive-through window

A. Where's the _______?
B. On/In/Next to/Between/Across from/
In front of/Behind/Under/Over the _______.

[An Election Speech]

If I am elected mayor, I'll take care of all the problems in our city. We need to do something about our _______s. We also need to do something about our _______s. And look at our _______s! We REALLY need to do something about THEM! We need a new mayor who can solve these problems. If I am elected mayor, we'll be proud of our _______s, _______s, and _______s again! Vote for me!

Go to an intersection in your city or town. What do you see? Make a list. Then tell about it.

人物及身體的特徵

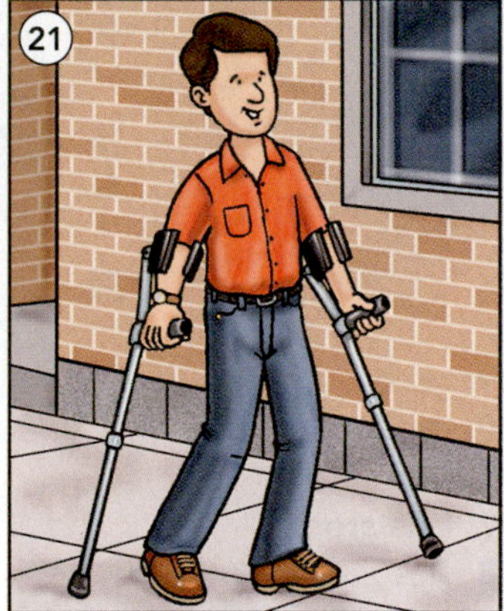

孩子(單數) - 孩子(複數) **1 child-children**
嬰兒 **2** baby/infant
幼童 **3** toddler
男孩 **4** boy
女孩 **5** girl
青少年 **6** teenager

成人 **7 adult**
男人(單數) - 男人(複數) **8** man–men
女人(單數) - 女人(複數) **9** woman–women
年長者 **10** senior citizen/ elderly person

年紀 age
年輕 **11** young
中年 **12** middle-aged
年老/年長 **13** old/elderly

身高 height
高 **14** tall
中等高度 **15** average height
矮 **16** short

體重 weight
重 **17** heavy
中等體重 **18** average weight
苗條 **19** thin/slim
懷孕 **20** pregnant

身體殘疾 **21** physically challenged
視障 **22** vision impaired
聽障 **23** hearing impaired

描述頭髮 Describing Hair

長 **24** long
肩長 **25** shoulder length
短 **26** short

直 **27** straight
波浪 **28** wavy
捲 **29** curly
黑色 **30** black

褐色 **31** brown
金色 **32** blond
紅色 **33** red
灰色 **34** gray

禿 **35** bald

鬍鬚 **36** beard
小鬍子 **37** mustache

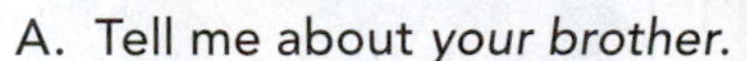

A. Tell me about *your brother.*
B. *He's a tall heavy boy* with *short curly brown* hair.

A. What does *your new boss* look like?
B. *She's average height*, and *she* has *long straight black* hair.

A. Can you describe *the person?*
B. *He's a tall thin middle-aged man.*
A. Anything else?
B. Yes. *He's bald*, and *he* has *a mustache.*

A. Can you describe *your grandmother?*
B. *She's a short thin elderly person* with *long wavy gray* hair.
A. Anything else?
B. Yes. *She's hearing impaired.*

Tell about yourself.

Tell about people in your family.

Tell about your favorite actor or actress or other famous person.

描述人物和物品

新 - 舊 **1–2** new – old
年輕 - 年老 **3–4** young – old
高 - 矮 **5–6** tall – short
長 - 短 **7–8** long – short
大 - 小 **9–10** large/big – small/little
快 - 慢 **11–12** fast – slow
重/胖 - 苗條/瘦 **13–14** heavy/fat – thin/skinny
重 - 輕 **15–16** heavy – light
直 - 彎曲的 **17–18** straight – crooked
直的 - 捲的 **19–20** straight – curly
寬 - 窄 **21–22** wide – narrow
厚 - 薄 **23–24** thick – thin
暗 - 亮 **25–26** dark – light
高 - 低 **27–28** high – low
鬆 - 緊 **29–30** loose – tight
好 - 壞 **31–32** good – bad
熱 - 冷 **33–34** hot – cold
整齊 - 亂七八糟 **35–36** neat – messy
乾淨 - 髒 **37–38** clean – dirty
軟 - 硬 **39–40** soft – hard
簡單 - 困難/難 **41–42** easy – difficult/hard
光滑 - 粗糙 **43–44** smooth – rough
吵/大聲 - 安靜 **45–46** noisy/loud – quiet
已婚 - 單身 **47–48** married – single

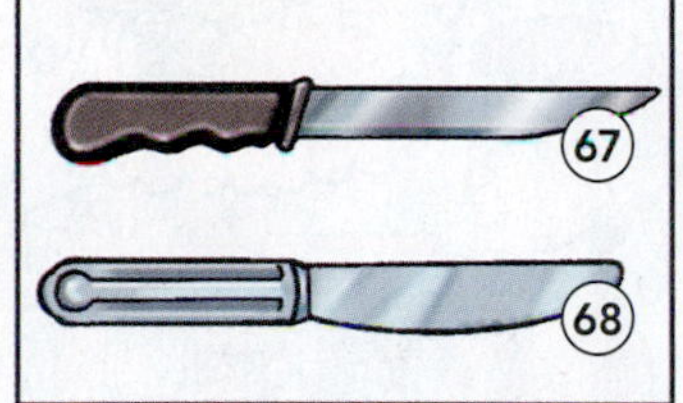

富有/富裕 - 貧窮 **49–50** rich/wealthy – poor
漂亮/美麗 - 醜 **51–52** pretty/beautiful – ugly
英俊 - 醜 **53–54** handsome – ugly
濕 - 乾 **55–56** wet – dry
打開 - 關著 **57–58** open – closed
滿的 - 空的 **59–60** full – empty

昂貴 - 便宜/不貴 **61–62** expensive – cheap/inexpensive
華麗 - 樸素 **63–64** fancy – plain
亮麗 - 無光澤 **65–66** shiny – dull
尖銳 - 鈍的 **67–68** sharp – dull
舒服 - 不舒服 **69–70** comfortable – uncomfortable
誠實 - 不誠實 **71–72** honest – dishonest

[1–2]
A. Is your car **new**?
B. No. It's **old**.

1–2 Is your car _____?
3–4 Is he _____?
5–6 Is your sister _____?
7–8 Is his hair _____?
9–10 Is their dog _____?
11–12 Is the train _____?
13–14 Is your friend _____?
15–16 Is the box _____?
17–18 Is the road _____?
19–20 Is her hair _____?
21–22 Is the tie _____?
23–24 Is the line _____?

25–26 Is the room _____?
27–28 Is the bridge _____?
29–30 Are the pants _____?
31–32 Are your neighbor's children _____?
33–34 Is the water _____?
35–36 Is your desk _____?
37–38 Are the windows _____?
39–40 Is the mattress _____?
41–42 Is the homework _____?
43–44 Is your skin _____?
45–46 Is your neighbor _____?
47–48 Is your sister _____?

49–50 Is your uncle _____?
51–52 Is the witch _____?
53–54 Is the pirate _____?
55–56 Are the clothes _____?
57–58 Is the door _____?
59–60 Is the pitcher _____?
61–62 Is that restaurant _____?
63–64 Is the dress _____?
65–66 Is your kitchen floor _____?
67–68 Is the knife _____?
69–70 Is the chair _____?
71–72 Is he _____?

A. Tell me about your ....
B. He's/She's/It's/They're _____.

A. Do you have a/an _____ ....?
B. No. I have a/an _____ ....

Describe yourself.
Describe a person you know.
Describe some things in your home.
Describe some things in your community.

描述身體狀況及情緒

疲累 **1** tired
想睡 **2** sleepy
精疲力竭 **3** exhausted
生病 **4** sick/ill
熱 **5** hot
冷 **6** cold

餓 **7** hungry
渴 **8** thirsty
飽 **9** full
高興 **10** happy
難過/不高興 **11** sad/unhappy

痛苦 **12** miserable
興奮 **13** excited
失望 **14** disappointed
心煩 **15** upset
氣惱 **16** annoyed

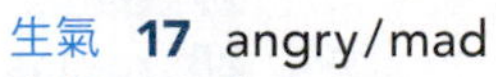

生氣 **17** angry/mad
大怒 **18** furious
憎惡 **19** disgusted
煩/為…傷腦筋 **20** frustrated
驚喜 **21** surprised
震驚 **22** shocked

孤獨 **23** lonely
想家 **24** homesick
緊張 **25** nervous
擔心 **26** worried
害怕 **27** scared/afraid
無聊 **28** bored

以…為榮 **29** proud
窘困 **30** embarrassed
忌妒 **31** jealous
困惑 **32** confused

A. You look ______.
B. I am. I'm VERY ______.

A. Are you ______?
B. No. Why do you ask? Do I LOOK ______?
A. Yes. You do.

What makes you happy? sad? mad?

What do you do when you feel nervous? annoyed?

Do you ever feel embarrassed? When?

FRUITS

水果

蘋果 **1** apple	無花果 **12** fig	柳橙 **22** orange
桃子 **2** peach	椰子 **13** coconut	橘子 **23** tangerine
梨子 **3** pear	酪梨/牛油果 **14** avocado	葡萄 **24** grapes
香蕉 **4** banana	羅馬甜瓜 **15** cantaloupe	櫻桃 **25** cherries
大蕉 **5** plantain	哈密瓜 **16** honeydew (melon)	梅乾 **26** prunes
李子 **6** plum	西瓜 **17** watermelon	棗子 **27** dates
杏 **7** apricot	鳳梨 **18** pineapple	葡萄乾 **28** raisins
油桃 **8** nectarine	葡萄柚 **19** grapefruit	堅果 **29** nuts
奇異果 **9** kiwi	檸檬 **20** lemon	覆盆子 **30** raspberries
木瓜 **10** papaya	青檸 **21** lime	藍莓 **31** blueberries
芒果 **11** mango		草莓 **32** strawberries

[1–23]
A. This **apple** is delicious! Where did you get it?
B. At *Sam's Supermarket*.

[24–32]
A. These **grapes** are delicious! Where did you get them?
B. At *Franny's Fruit Stand*.

A. I'm hungry. Do we have any fruit?
B. Yes. We have ________s* and ________s.*

** With 15–19, use:*
We have ______ and ______.

A. Do we have any more ________s?†
B. No. I'll get some more when I go to the supermarket.

† With 15–19, use:
Do we have any more ______?

What are your favorite fruits? Which fruits don't you like?

Which of these fruits grow where you live?

Name and describe other fruits you know.

VEGETABLES
蔬菜

芹菜	1	celery
玉米	2	corn
綠花椰菜	3	broccoli
白花椰菜	4	cauliflower
菠菜	5	spinach
洋芫荽	6	parsley
蘆筍	7	asparagus
茄子	8	eggplant
生菜	9	lettuce
高麗菜	10	cabbage
(小)白菜/青江菜	11	bok choy
義大利瓜	12	zucchini
小青南瓜	13	acorn squash
白胡桃南瓜	14	butternut squash
大蒜	15	garlic
豌豆	16	pea
四季豆	17	string bean/ green bean
皇帝豆	18	lima bean
黑豆	19	black bean
芸豆/菜豆	20	kidney bean
球芽甘藍	21	brussels sprout
黃瓜	22	cucumber
蕃茄	23	tomato
紅蘿蔔	24	carrot
小蘿蔔	25	radish
蘑菇	26	mushroom
朝鮮薊	27	artichoke
馬鈴薯/洋芋	28	potato
番薯	29	sweet potato
紅薯	30	yam
青椒/甜椒	31	green pepper/ sweet pepper
紅椒	32	red pepper
墨西哥辣椒	33	jalapeño (pepper)
辣椒	34	chili pepper
甜菜	35	beet
洋蔥	36	onion
青蔥	37	scallion/ green onion
蕪菁	38	turnip

A. What do we need from the supermarket?
B. We need **celery*** and **peas**.†

* 1–15 † 16–38

A. How do you like the ___[1–15]___/___[16–38]___s?
B. It's/They're delicious.

A. *Bobby*? Finish your vegetables!
B. But you KNOW I hate ___[1–15]___/___[16–38]___s!
A. I know. But it's/they're good for you!

Which vegetables do you like?
Which vegetables don't you like?

Which of these vegetables grow where you live?

Name and describe other vegetables you know.

MEAT, POULTRY, AND SEAFOOD

肉類，家禽肉類，海鮮類

肉 Meat

- 牛排 **1** steak
- 絞牛肉 **2** ground beef
- 小塊(紅燒用)瘦牛肉 **3** stewing beef
- 烤牛肉 **4** roast beef
- 排骨 **5** ribs
- 小羊腿 **6** leg of lamb
- 小羊排 **7** lamb chops
- 可食用的動物肚子 **8** tripe
- 肝臟 **9** liver
- 豬肉 **10** pork
- 豬排 **11** pork chops
- 香腸 **12** sausages
- 火腿 **13** ham
- 培根 **14** bacon

家禽肉 Poultry

- 雞 **15** chicken
- 雞胸 **16** chicken breasts
- 雞腿/雞小腿 **17** chicken legs/drumsticks
- 雞翅 **18** chicken wings
- 雞大腿 **19** chicken thighs
- 火雞 **20** turkey
- 鴨 **21** duck

海鮮 Seafood

魚 FISH

- 鮭魚 **22** salmon
- 比目魚(大) **23** halibut
- 鱈魚 **24** haddock
- 鰈魚/比目魚 **25** flounder
- 鱒魚 **26** trout
- 鯰魚 **27** catfish
- 鰨魚片 **28** filet of sole

貝類海產 SHELLFISH

- 蝦 **29** shrimp
- 扇貝 **30** scallops
- 螃蟹 **31** crabs
- 蛤蜊 **32** clams
- 貽貝/淡菜 **33** mussels
- 牡蠣/蠔 **34** oysters
- 龍蝦 **35** lobster

A. I'm going to the supermarket. What do we need?
B. Please get some **steak**.
A. **Steak**? All right.

A. Excuse me. Where can I find ________?
B. Look in the ________ Section.
A. Thank you.

A. This/These ________ looks/look very fresh!
B. Let's get some for dinner.

Do you eat meat, poultry, or seafood?
Which of these foods do you like?

Which of these foods are popular in your country?

奶製品，果汁，飲料

奶製品 Dairy Products

- 牛奶 1 milk
- 低脂牛奶 2 low-fat milk
- 脫脂牛奶 3 skim milk
- 巧克力牛奶 4 chocolate milk
- 柳橙汁 5 orange juice*
- 乳酪 6 cheese
- 奶油 7 butter
- 人造奶油 8 margarine
- 酸奶油 9 sour cream
- 奶油乳酪 10 cream cheese
- 卡迪吉乳酪/鬆軟的白乾酪 11 cottage cheese
- 優酪乳/酸乳 12 yogurt
- 豆腐* 13 tofu*
- 雞蛋 14 eggs

水果 Juices

- 蘋果汁 15 apple juice
- 鳳梨汁 16 pineapple juice
- 葡萄柚汁 17 grapefruit juice
- 蕃茄汁 18 tomato juice
- 葡萄汁 19 grape juice
- 綜合果汁 20 fruit punch
- 盒裝果汁 21 juice paks
- 即溶飲料粉 22 powdered drink mix

飲料 Beverages

- 汽水 23 soda
- 無糖汽水 24 diet soda
- 瓶裝水 25 bottled water

咖啡和茶 Coffee and Tea

- 咖啡 26 coffee
- 低咖啡因咖啡 27 decaffeinated coffee/decaf
- 即溶咖啡 28 instant coffee
- 茶 29 tea
- 花草茶 30 herbal tea
- 可可/熱巧克力粉 31 cocoa/hot chocolate mix

* 柳橙汁和豆腐不屬奶製品，但通常被放置在這個區域。

A. I'm going to the supermarket to get some **milk**. Do we need anything else?
B. Yes. Please get some **apple juice**.

A. Excuse me. Where can I find ________?
B. Look in the ________ Section.
A. Thanks.

A. Look! ________ is/are on sale this week!
B. Let's get some!

Which of these foods do you like?
Which of these foods are good for you?
Which brands of these foods do you buy?

熟食 Deli

烤牛肉 **1** roast beef
粗香腸 **2** bologna
義大利蒜味香腸 **3** salami
火腿 **4** ham
火雞 **5** turkey
鹽醃牛肉 **6** corned beef
醃燻牛肉 **7** pastrami
瑞士乾酪 **8** Swiss cheese
波伏洛乾酪 **9** provolone
美國乾酪 **10** American cheese
瑪芝瑞拉乳酪 **11** mozzarella
切達乾酪 **12** cheddar cheese
馬鈴薯沙拉 **13** potato salad
高麗菜沙拉 **14** cole slaw
通心粉沙拉 **15** macaroni salad
義大利麵沙拉 **16** pasta salad
海鮮沙拉 **17** seafood salad

冷凍食品 Frozen Foods

冰淇淋 **18** ice cream
冷凍蔬菜 **19** frozen vegetables
冷凍晚餐 **20** frozen dinners
冷凍濃縮檸檬汁 **21** frozen lemonade
冷凍濃縮柳橙汁 **22** frozen orange juice

休閒食品 Snack Foods

洋芋片 **23** potato chips
玉米片 **24** tortilla chips
椒鹽脆餅 **25** pretzels
堅果 **26** nuts
爆玉米花 **27** popcorn

A. Should we get some **roast beef**?
B. Good idea. And let's get some **potato salad**.

[1–17]
A. May I help you?
B. Yes, please. I'd like some ________.

[1–27]
A. Excuse me. Where is/are ________?
B. It's/They're in the ________ Section.

What kinds of snack foods are popular in your country?

Are frozen foods common in your country? What kinds of foods are in the Frozen Foods Section?

雜貨

包裝食品 Packaged Goods

- 穀類早餐 1 cereal
- 餅乾 2 cookies
- 薄片餅乾 3 crackers
- 義大利通心麵 4 macaroni
- 麵 5 noodles
- 義大利麵 6 spaghetti
- 米 7 rice

罐頭食品 Canned Goods

- 湯 8 soup
- 鮪魚 9 tuna (fish)
- 罐頭蔬菜 10 (canned) vegetables
- 水果罐頭 11 (canned) fruit

果醬 Jams and Jellies

- 果醬 12 jam
- 果醬 13 jelly
- 花生醬 14 peanut butter

佐料/調味料 Condiments

- 蕃茄醬 15 ketchup
- 芥末醬 16 mustard
- 碎黃瓜醬 17 relish
- 酸黃瓜 18 pickles
- 橄欖 19 olives
- 鹽 20 salt
- 胡椒 21 pepper
- 香料 22 spices
- 醬油 23 soy sauce
- 美奶滋 24 mayonnaise
- 炒菜油 25 (cooking) oil
- 橄欖油 26 olive oil
- 墨西哥辣醬 27 salsa
- 醋 28 vinegar
- 沙拉醬 29 salad dressing

烘焙食品 Baked Goods

- 麵包 30 bread
- 小麵包 31 rolls
- 英式鬆餅 32 English muffins
- 口袋餅 33 pita bread
- 蛋糕 34 cake

烘焙用料 Baking Products

- 麵粉 35 flour
- 糖 36 sugar
- 蛋糕粉 37 cake mix

A. I got **cereal** and **soup**. What else is on the shopping list?
B. **Ketchup** and **bread**.

A. Excuse me. I'm looking for ______.
B. It's/They're next to the ______.

A. Pardon me. I'm looking for ______.
B. It's/They're between the ______ and the ______.

Which of these foods do you like?

Which brands of these foods do you buy?

家庭用品，嬰兒用品，寵物食品

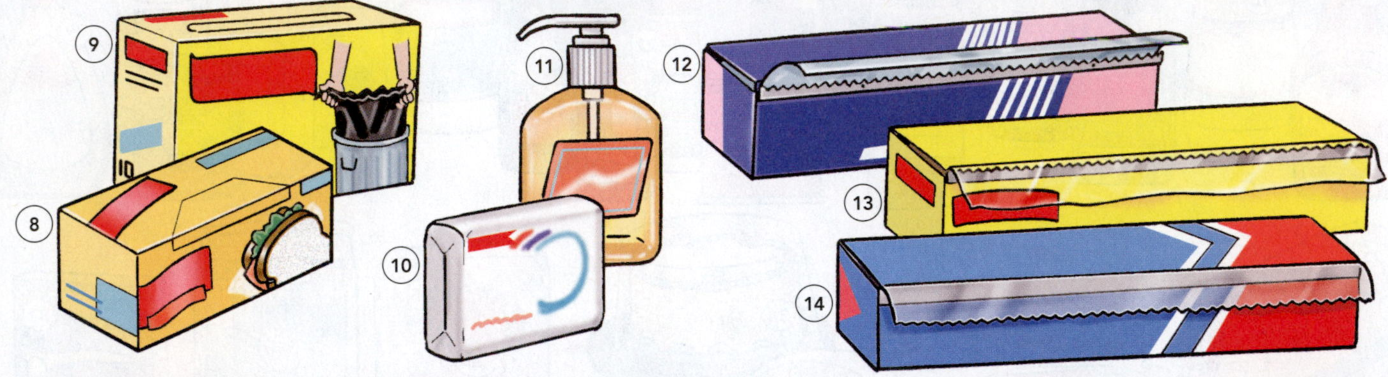

紙製品 Paper Products

- 餐巾紙 **1** napkins
- 紙杯 **2** paper cups
- 衛生紙 **3** tissues
- 吸管 **4** straws
- 紙盤 **5** paper plates
- 紙巾 **6** paper towels
- 衛生紙 **7** toilet paper

家庭用品 Household Items

- 三明治袋 **8** sandwich bags
- 垃圾袋 **9** trash bags
- 香皂 **10** soap
- 液體肥皂 **11** liquid soap
- 鋁箔紙 **12** aluminum foil
- 保鮮膜 **13** plastic wrap
- 蠟紙 **14** waxed paper

嬰兒用品 Baby Products

- 嬰兒麥片 **15** baby cereal
- 嬰兒食品 **16** baby food
- 嬰兒奶粉 **17** formula
- 濕巾 **18** wipes
- 即棄紙尿片 **19** (disposable) diapers

寵物食品 Pet Food

- 貓食 **20** cat food
- 狗食 **21** dog food

A. Excuse me. Where can I find **napkins**?
B. **Napkins**? Look in Aisle 4.

[7, 10–17, 20, 21]
A. We forgot to get ________!
B. I'll get it. Where is it?
A. It's in Aisle ________.

[1–6, 8, 9, 18, 19]
A. We forgot to get ________!
B. I'll get them. Where are they?
A. They're in Aisle ________.

What do you need from the supermarket? Make a complete shopping list!

超級市場

- 走道 **1** aisle
- 購物者/顧客 **2** shopper/customer
- 購物籃 **3** shopping basket
- 結帳隊伍 **4** checkout line
- 結帳櫃檯 **5** checkout counter
- 輸送帶 **6** conveyor belt
- 收銀機 **7** cash register
- 購物推車 **8** shopping cart
- 口香糖 **9** (chewing) gum
- 糖果 **10** candy
- 減價優待券 **11** coupons
- 收銀員 **12** cashier
- 紙袋 **13** paper bag
- 裝袋員 **14** bagger/packer
- 快速結帳隊伍 **15** express checkout (line)
- 小報 **16** tabloid (newspaper)
- 雜誌 **17** magazine
- 掃描機 **18** scanner
- 塑膠袋 **19** plastic bag
- 蔬果區 **20** produce
- 經理 **21** manager
- 店員 **22** clerk
- 秤 **23** scale
- 鐵罐回收機 **24** can-return machine
- 瓶子回收機 **25** bottle-return machine

[1–8, 11–19, 21–25]
A. This is a gigantic supermarket!
B. It is! Look at all the **aisle**s!

[9, 10, 20]
A. This is a gigantic supermarket!
B. It is. Look at all the **produce**!

Where do you usually shop for food? Do you go to a supermarket, or do you go to a small grocery store? Describe the place where you shop.

Describe the differences between U.S. supermarkets and food stores in your country.

CONTAINERS AND QUANTITIES

容器及數量

袋子 **1** bag	(一)顆 **9** head	(一)條 **16** stick
瓶子 **2** bottle	瓶罐 **10** jar	軟管/(一)條 **17** tube
盒子 **3** box	(一)條 - 條(複數) **11** loaf–loaves	(一)品脫 **18** pint
串/束 **4** bunch	(一)包 **12** pack	(一)夸脫 **19** quart
鐵罐 **5** can	包裝/(一)包 **13** package	半加侖 **20** half-gallon
紙盒 **6** carton	(一)捲 **14** roll	(一)加侖 **21** gallon
容器 **7** container	半打 **15** six-pack	(一)公升 **22** liter
(一)打 **8** dozen*		(一)磅 **23** pound

* 應說 "a dozen eggs," 而不是 "a dozen of eggs"

A. Please get a **bag** of *flour* when you go to the supermarket.
B. A **bag** of *flour*? Okay.

A. Please get two **bottles** of *ketchup* when you go to the supermarket.
B. Two **bottles** of *ketchup*? Okay.

[At home]

A. What did you get at the supermarket?
B. I got ______, ______, and ______.

[In a supermarket]

A. Is this the express checkout line?
B. Yes, it is. Do you have more than eight items?
A. No. I only have ______, ______, and ______.

Open your kitchen cabinets and refrigerator. Make a list of all the things you find.

What do you do with empty bottles, jars, and cans? Do you recycle them, reuse them, or throw them away?

計量單位

茶匙 teaspoon
tsp.

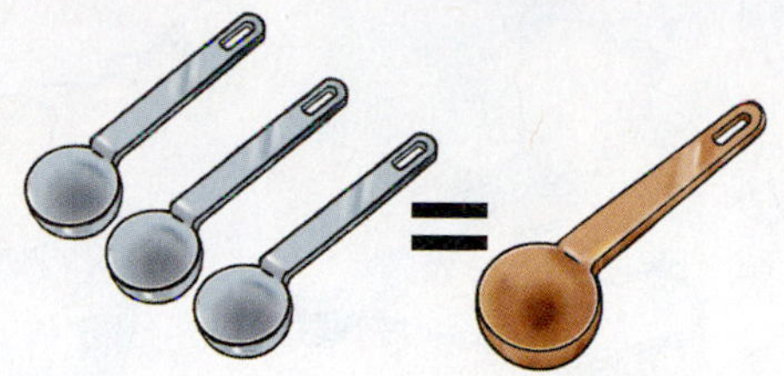

湯匙 tablespoon
Tbsp.

一(液體)盎司 1 (fluid) ounce
1 fl. oz.

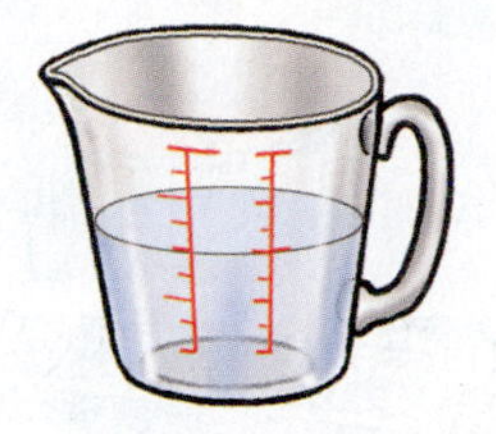

量杯 cup
c.
8 fl. ozs.

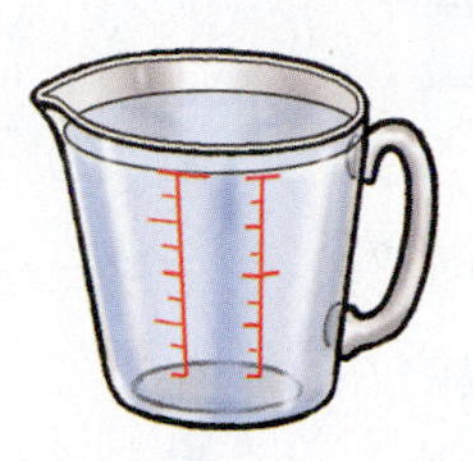

(一)品脫 pint
pt.
16 fl. ozs.

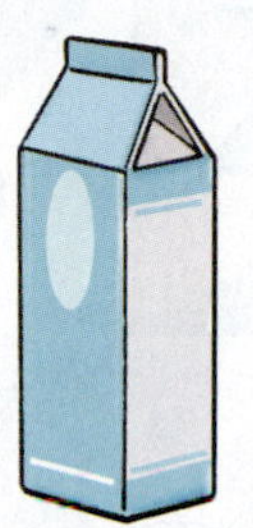

(一)夸脫 quart
qt.
32 fl. ozs.

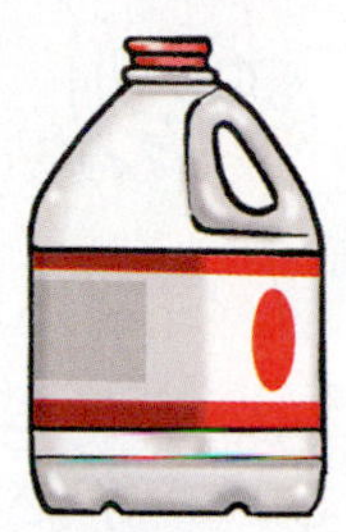

(一)加侖 gallon
gal.
128 fl. ozs.

A. How much water should I put in?
B. The recipe says to add one _______ of water.

A. This fruit punch is delicious! What's in it?
B. Two _______s of apple juice, three _______s of orange juice, and a _______ of grape juice.

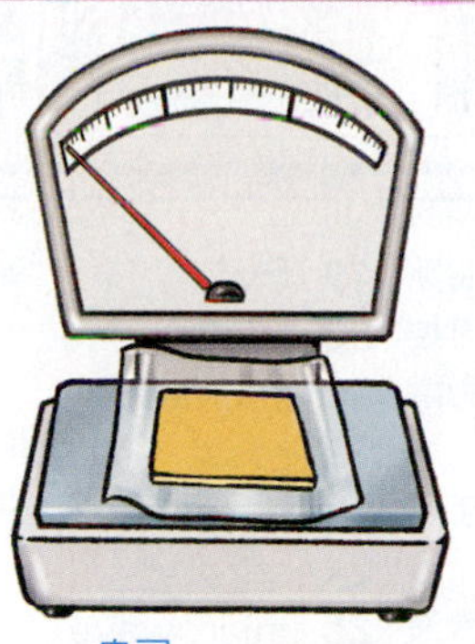

一盎司 an ounce
oz.

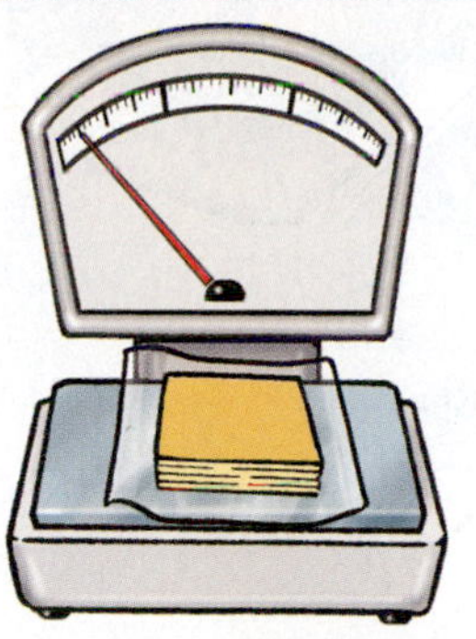

1/4磅 a quarter of a pound
1/4 lb.
4 ozs.

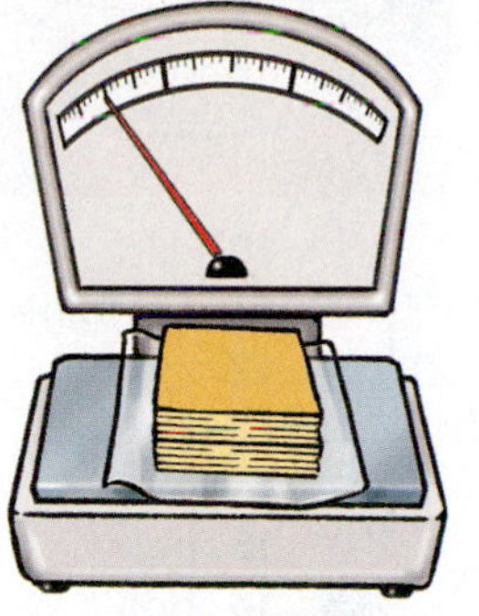

1/2磅 half a pound
1/2 lb.
8 ozs.

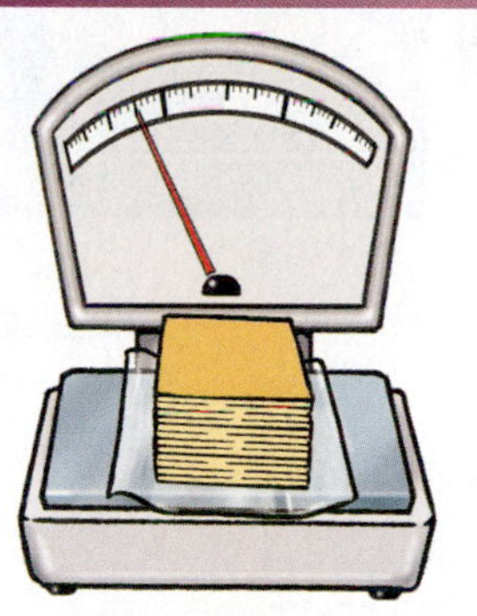

3/4磅 three-quarters of a pound
3/4 lb.
12 ozs.

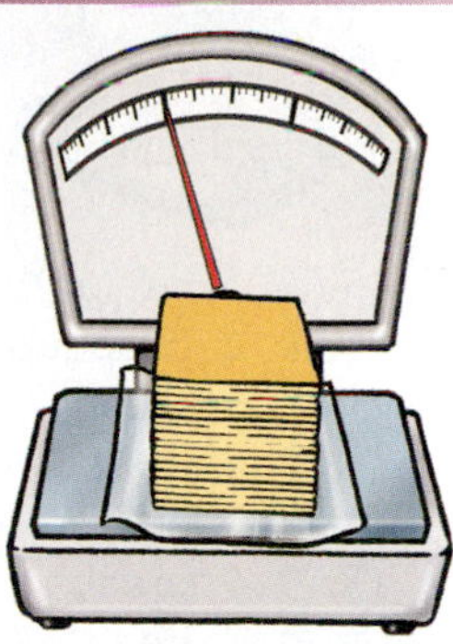

一磅 a pound
lb.
16 ozs.

A. How much roast beef would you like?
B. I'd like _______, please.
A. Anything else?
B. Yes. Please give me _______ of Swiss cheese.

A. This chili tastes very good! What did you put in it?
B. _______ of ground beef, _______ of beans, _______ of tomatoes, and _______ of chili powder.

食物製備及食譜

切 **1** cut (up)
切塊 **2** chop (up)
切片 **3** slice
刨 **4** grate
剝 **5** peel
打(破) **6** break
打(蛋等) **7** beat
攪拌 **8** stir
倒 **9** pour
加 **10** add
將 ____ 和 ____ 加在一起 **11** combine ____ and ____
將 ____ 和 ____ 混合在一起 **12** mix ____ and ____
將 ____ 放入 ____ **13** put ____ in ____
烹調/煮 **14** cook
烘烤 **15** bake
水煮 **16** boil
燒烤 **17** broil
蒸 **18** steam
油炸/油煎 **19** fry
煎炒 **20** saute
煨/燉 **21** simmer
烤 **22** roast
用烤架烤 **23** barbecue/grill
炒 **24** stir-fry
微波 **25** microwave

A. Can I help you?
B. Yes. Please **cut up** the vegetables.

[1–25]
A. What are you doing?
B. I'm ________ing the ....

[14–25]
A. How long should I ________ the ....?
B. ________ the .... for .... minutes/seconds.

What's your favorite recipe? Give instructions and use the units of measure on page 57. For example:

Mix a cup of flour and two tablespoons of sugar.
Add half a pound of butter.
Bake at 350° (degrees) for twenty minutes.

廚房器皿及用具

冰淇淋勺	**1**	ice cream scoop
開罐器	**2**	can opener
開瓶器	**3**	bottle opener
蔬菜削皮器	**4**	(vegetable) peeler
打蛋器	**5**	(egg) beater
蓋子	**6**	lid/cover/top
鍋子	**7**	pot
平底煎鍋	**8**	frying pan/skillet
雙層鍋	**9**	double boiler
炒菜鍋	**10**	wok
長柄杓	**11**	ladle
過濾器	**12**	strainer
煎鏟	**13**	spatula
蒸架	**14**	steamer
刀子	**15**	knife
大蒜鉗	**16**	garlic press
刨子	**17**	grater
陶瓷烤盤	**18**	casserole dish
燒烤盤	**19**	roasting pan
燒烤架	**20**	roasting rack
切肉刀	**21**	carving knife
煮鍋	**22**	saucepan
瀝水盆	**23**	colander
廚房計時器	**24**	kitchen timer
桿麵棍	**25**	rolling pin
派盤	**26**	pie plate
水果刀	**27**	paring knife
餅乾烤盤	**28**	cookie sheet
餅乾模型	**29**	cookie cutter
攪拌碗	**30**	(mixing) bowl
攪拌器	**31**	whisk
量杯	**32**	measuring cup
量匙	**33**	measuring spoon
蛋糕烤盤	**34**	cake pan
木杓	**35**	wooden spoon

A. Could I possibly borrow your **ice cream scoop**?
B. Sure. I'll be happy to lend you my **ice cream scoop**.
A. Thanks.

A. What are you looking for?
B. I can't find the ________.
A. Look in that drawer/in that cabinet/ on the counter/next to the ________/ ....

[A Commercial]
Come to *Kitchen World*! We have everything you need for your kitchen, from ________s and ________s, to ________s and ________s. Are you looking for a new ________? Is it time to throw out your old ________? Come to *Kitchen World* today! We have everything you need!

What kitchen utensils and cookware do you have in your kitchen?

Which things do you use very often?

Which things do you rarely use?

速食

漢堡	1	hamburger
起士漢堡	2	cheeseburger
熱狗	3	hot dog
魚排三明治	4	fish sandwich
雞排三明治	5	chicken sandwich
炸雞	6	fried chicken
炸薯條	7	french fries
墨西哥玉米片	8	nachos
墨西哥玉米餅	9	taco
墨西哥捲餅	10	burrito
一片披薩餅	11	slice of pizza
一碗墨西哥辣豆醬	12	bowl of chili
沙拉	13	salad
冰淇淋	14	ice cream
冷凍酸奶/冷凍優格	15	frozen yogurt
奶昔	16	milkshake
汽水	17	soda
蓋子	18	lids
紙杯	19	paper cups
吸管	20	straws
餐巾紙	21	napkins
塑膠餐具	22	plastic utensils
蕃茄醬	23	ketchup
芥末醬	24	mustard
美奶滋	25	mayonnaise
碎黃瓜醬	26	relish
沙拉醬	27	salad dressing

A. May I help you?
B. Yes. I'd like a/an [1–5, 9–17] / an order of [6–8].

A. Excuse me. We're almost out of [18–27].
B. I'll get some more from the supply room. Thanks for telling me.

Do you go to fast-food restaurants? Which ones? How often? What do you order?

Are there fast-food restaurants in your country? Are they popular? What foods do they have?

咖啡店及三明治

甜甜圈 **1** donut
鬆糕 **2** muffin
貝果圈 **3** bagel
小麵包 **4** bun
丹麥麵包/酥皮點心 **5** danish/pastry
小圓麵包 **6** biscuit
牛角麵包/可頌麵包 **7** croissant
雞蛋 **8** eggs
煎鬆餅/煎薄餅 **9** pancakes
格子鬆餅 **10** waffles
土司麵包 **11** toast
培根 **12** bacon
香腸 **13** sausages
自製炸薯塊 **14** home fries
咖啡 **15** coffee
低咖啡因咖啡 **16** decaf coffee
茶 **17** tea
冰茶 **18** iced tea
濃縮檸檬汁 **19** lemonade
熱巧克力 **20** hot chocolate
牛奶 **21** milk
鮪魚三明治 **22** tuna fish sandwich
蛋沙拉三明治 **23** egg salad sandwich
雞肉沙拉三明治 **24** chicken salad sandwich
火腿起司三明治 **25** ham and cheese sandwich
鹽醃牛肉三明治 **26** corned beef sandwich
培根生菜蕃茄三明治 **27** BLT/bacon, lettuce, and tomato sandwich
烤牛肉三明治 **28** roast beef sandwich
白麵包 **29** white bread
全麥麵包 **30** whole wheat bread
口袋餅 **31** pita bread
黑麥麵包 **32** pumpernickel
裸麥麵包 **33** rye bread
(一個)小麵包 **34** a roll
(一個)長條麵包 **35** a submarine roll

A. May I help you?
B. Yes. I'd like a __[1–7]__/an order of __[8–14]__, please.
A. Anything to drink?
B. Yes. I'll have a small/medium-size/large/extra-large __[15–21]__.

A. I'd like a __[22–28]__ on __[29–35]__, please.
B. What do you want on it?
A. Lettuce/tomato/mayonnaise/mustard/. . .

Do you like these foods? Which ones? Where do you get them? How often do you have them?

THE RESTAURANT

餐廳

帶位	A	seat the customers
倒水	B	pour the water
幫客人點菜	C	take the order
上菜	D	serve the meal

女(帶位)侍者	1	hostess
(帶位)侍者	2	host
用餐者/顧客/顧客	3	diner/patron/customer
雅座	4	booth
桌子	5	table
高腳椅	6	high chair
幼兒加高椅座	7	booster seat
菜單	8	menu
麵包籃	9	bread basket
企檯/侍者助手	10	busperson
女服務生/上菜者	11	waitress/server
服務生/上菜者	12	waiter/server
沙拉吧	13	salad bar
餐廳	14	dining room
廚房	15	kitchen
主廚	16	chef

[4–9]
A. Would you like a **booth**?
B. Yes, please.

[10–12]
A. Hello. My name is *Julie*, and I'll be your **waitress** this evening.
B. Hello.

[1, 2, 13–16]
A. This restaurant has a wonderful **salad bar**.
B. I agree.

清理桌子 **E** clear the table
付賬 **F** pay the check
留小費 **G** leave a tip
擺桌子 **H** set the table

洗碗室 **17** dishroom
洗碗機 **18** dishwasher
托盤 **19** tray
點心推車 **20** dessert cart
帳單 **21** check
小費 **22** tip
沙拉盤 **23** salad plate
麵包奶油盤 **24** bread-and-butter plate
主餐盤 **25** dinner plate

湯碗 **26** soup bowl
水杯 **27** water glass
酒杯 **28** wine glass
茶杯 **29** cup
淺盤 **30** saucer
餐巾 **31** napkin

銀餐具 silverware
沙拉叉 **32** salad fork
主菜叉 **33** dinner fork
餐刀 **34** knife
茶匙 **35** teaspoon
湯匙 **36** soup spoon
奶油刀 **37** butter knife

[A–H]
A. Please ______.
B. All right. I'll ______ right away.

[23–37]
A. Excuse me. Where does the ______ go?
B. It goes { to the left of the ______. / to the right of the ______. / on the ______. / between the ______ and the ______. }

[1, 2, 10–12, 16, 18]
A. Do you have any job openings?
B. Yes. We're looking for a ______.

[23–37]
A. Excuse me. I dropped my ______.
B. That's okay. I'll get you another ______ from the kitchen.

Tell about a restaurant you know. Describe the place and the people. (Is the restaurant large or small? How many tables are there? How many people work there? Is there a salad bar? . . .)

A RESTAURANT MENU

餐廳菜單

- 什錦水果 **1** fruit cup/ fruit cocktail
- 蕃茄汁 **2** tomato juice
- 雞尾酒蝦 **3** shrimp cocktail
- 雞翅 **4** chicken wings
- 墨西哥玉米片 **5** nachos
- 炸馬鈴薯皮 **6** potato skins

- 生菜沙拉/田園沙拉 **7** tossed salad/ garden salad
- 希臘沙拉 **8** Greek salad
- 菠菜沙拉 **9** spinach salad
- 義大利開胃菜(一盤) **10** antipasto (plate)
- 凱薩沙拉 **11** Caesar salad

- 肉餅 **12** meatloaf
- 烤牛肉/頂級牛排 **13** roast beef/prime rib
- 烤雞 **14** baked chicken
- 燒烤魚 **15** broiled fish
- 肉丸義大利麵 **16** spaghetti and meatballs
- 小牛排 **17** veal cutlet

- 烤洋芋(一個) **18** a baked potato
- 洋芋泥 **19** mashed potatoes
- 炸薯條 **20** french fries
- 米飯 **21** rice
- 麵 **22** noodles
- 什錦蔬菜 **23** mixed vegetables

- 巧克力蛋糕 **24** chocolate cake
- 蘋果派 **25** apple pie
- 冰淇淋 **26** ice cream
- 果凍 **27** jello
- 布丁 **28** pudding
- 冰淇淋聖代 **29** ice cream sundae

[Ordering dinner]

A. May I take your order?
B. Yes, please. For the appetizer, I'd like the __[1–6]__.
A. And what kind of salad would you like?
B. I'll have the __[7–11]__.
A. And for the main course?
B. I'd like the __[12–17]__, please.
A. What side dish would you like with that?
B. Hmm. I think I'll have __[18–23]__.

[Ordering dessert]

A. Would you care for some dessert?
B. Yes. I'll have __[24–28]__/an __[29]__.

Tell about the food at a restaurant you know. What's on the menu?

What are some typical foods on the menus of restaurants in your country?

顏色

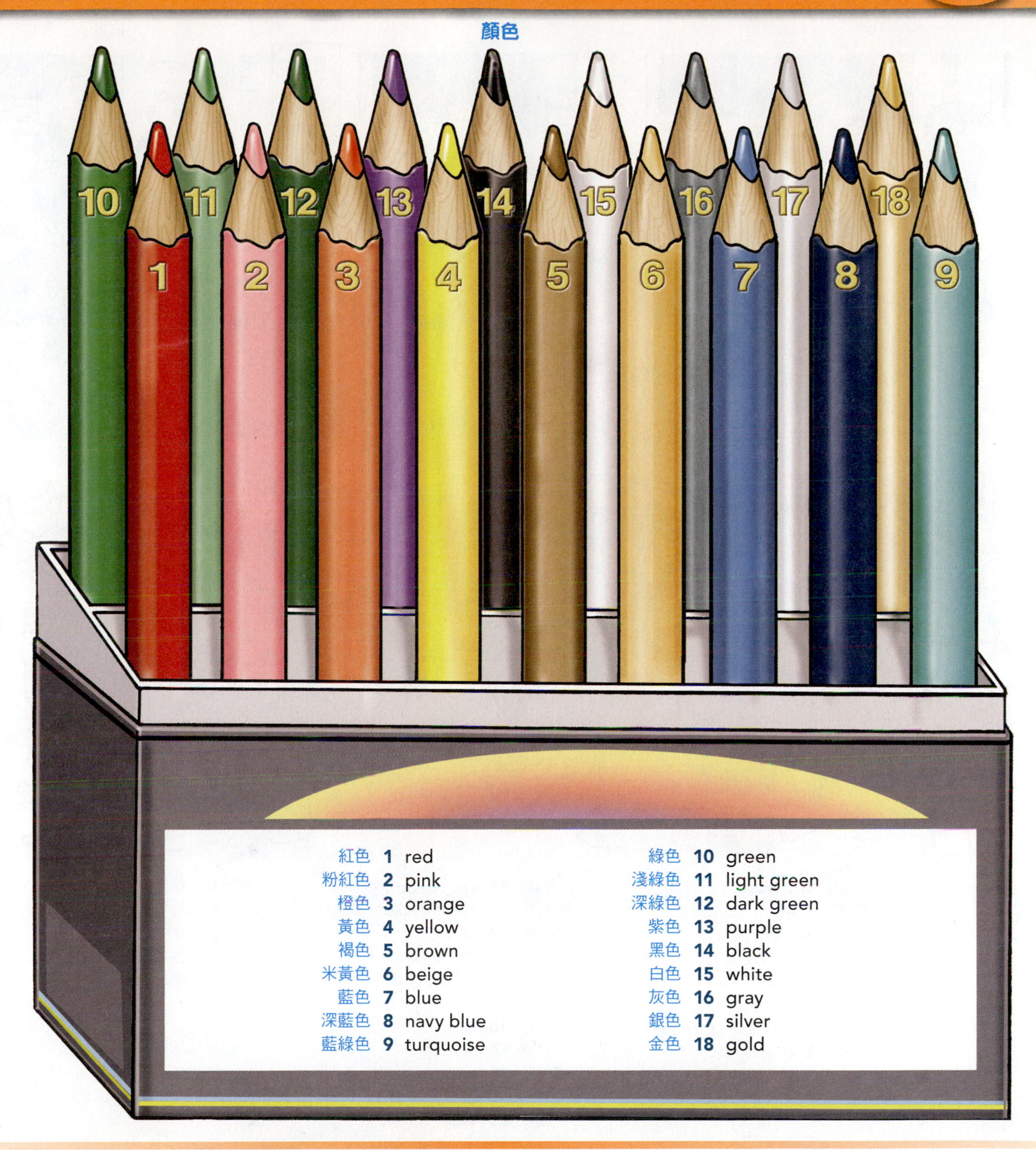

A. What's your favorite color?
B. **Red**.

A. I like your ________ shirt.
You look very good in ________.
B. Thank you. ________ is my favorite color.

A. My TV is broken.
B. What's the matter with it?
A. People's faces are ________, the sky is ________, and the grass is ________!

Do you know the flags of different countries? What are the colors of flags you know?

What color makes you happy? What color makes you sad? Why?

CLOTHING

服裝

短衫 **1** blouse
裙子 **2** skirt
襯衫 **3** shirt
長褲/(寬鬆的)長褲 **4** pants/slacks
運動衫 **5** sport shirt
牛仔褲 **6** jeans
帶領針織衫/針織衫 **7** knit shirt/jersey
洋裝 **8** dress
毛衣 **9** sweater
外套 **10** jacket
輕便外套/輕便外套/外套 **11** sport coat/sport jacket/jacket
西裝 **12** suit
三件式西裝 **13** three-piece suit
領帶 **14** tie/necktie
制服 **15** uniform
圓領運動衫 **16** T-shirt
短褲 **17** shorts
孕婦洋裝 **18** maternity dress
連身衣褲 **19** jumpsuit
背心 **20** vest
無袖背心裙 **21** jumper
西裝外套 **22** blazer
束腰外衣 **23** tunic
毛線褲襪 **24** leggings
工作褲 **25** overalls
高領毛衣 **26** turtleneck
晚禮服 **27** tuxedo
蝶形領結 **28** bow tie
(女士的)晚禮服 **29** (evening) gown

A. I think I'll wear my new **blouse** today.
B. Good idea!

A. I really like your ________.
B. Thank you.
A. Where did you get it/them?
B. At ....

A. Oh, no! I just ripped my ________!
B. What a shame!

What clothing items in this lesson do you wear?

What color clothing do you like to wear?

What do you wear at work or at school? at parties? at weddings?

OUTERWEAR

外衣

外套 **1** coat
外套 **2** overcoat
帽子 **3** hat
夾克 **4** jacket
圍巾 **5** scarf/muffler
毛衣外套 **6** sweater jacket
褲襪 **7** tights
鴨舌帽 **8** cap
皮夾克 **9** leather jacket
棒球帽 **10** baseball cap

風衣 **11** windbreaker
雨衣 **12** raincoat
雨帽 **13** rain hat
風雨衣 **14** trench coat
雨傘 **15** umbrella
南美雨披 **16** poncho
防雨夾克 **17** rain jacket
雨鞋 **18** rain boots
滑雪帽 **19** ski hat
滑雪夾克 **20** ski jacket

手套 **21** gloves
滑雪面罩 **22** ski mask
羽絨夾克 **23** down jacket
連指手套 **24** mittens
帶帽的風雪大衣 **25** parka
太陽眼鏡 **26** sunglasses
耳罩 **27** ear muffs
羽絨背心 **28** down vest

A. What's the weather like today?
B. It's cool/cold/raining/snowing.
A. I think I'll wear my _______.

[1–6, 8–17, 19, 20, 22, 23, 25, 28]
A. May I help you?
B. Yes, please. I'm looking for a/an _____.

[7, 18, 21, 24, 26, 27]
A. May I help you?
B. Yes, please. I'm looking for _____.

What do you wear outside when the weather is cool?/when it's raining?/when it's very cold?

SLEEPWEAR AND UNDERWEAR

睡衣及內衣

睡衣	1	pajamas
(女)睡袍	2	nightgown
(男)長睡衫	3	nightshirt
浴衣	4	bathrobe/robe
拖鞋	5	slippers
連身(包括腳)睡衣	6	blanket sleeper
短袖內衣/短袖圓領衫	7	undershirt/T-shirt
(男)三角內褲/內褲	8	(jockey) shorts/underpants/briefs
四角內褲	9	boxer shorts/boxers
運動縛帶/(男運動用的)護襠	10	athletic supporter/jockstrap
長內衣褲	11	long underwear/long johns
襪子	12	socks
(女)三角內褲	13	(bikini) panties
內褲	14	briefs/underpants
胸罩	15	bra
女用短袖襯衣	16	camisole
短襯裙	17	half slip
長襯裙	18	(full) slip
長統絲襪	19	stockings
連褲襪	20	pantyhose
褲襪	21	tights
中統絲襪	22	knee-highs
中統襪	23	knee socks

A. I can't find my new ________.
B. Did you look in the bureau/dresser/closet?
A. Yes, I did.
B. Then it's/they're probably in the wash.

What sleepwear items do you wear? What sleepwear items do people in your family wear?

EXERCISE CLOTHING AND FOOTWEAR

運動服裝及鞋類

- 背心 **1** tank top
- 運動短褲 **2** running shorts
- 防汗帶 **3** sweatband
- 慢跑衣褲/慢跑服/運動服 **4** jogging suit/running suit/warm-up suit
- 短袖圓領衫 **5** T-shirt
- 彈力短褲/自行車短褲 **6** lycra shorts/bike shorts
- 較厚的長袖運動衫 **7** sweatshirt
- 較厚的運動褲 **8** sweatpants
- 罩衫 **9** cover-up
- 游泳衣/泳裝 **10** swimsuit/bathing suit
- 游泳褲/游泳衣/泳裝 **11** swimming trunks/swimsuit/bathing suit
- (舞蹈、體操等穿的)緊身衣 **12** leotard
- 鞋子 **13** shoes
- 高跟鞋 **14** (high) heels
- (女)無帶便鞋 **15** pumps
- 休閒鞋 **16** loafers
- 運動鞋 **17** sneakers/athletic shoes
- 網球鞋 **18** tennis shoes
- 跑步鞋 **19** running shoes
- 高統球鞋 **20** high-tops/high-top sneakers
- 涼鞋 **21** sandals
- 夾腳鞋 **22** thongs/flip-flops
- 靴子 **23** boots
- 工作靴 **24** work boots
- 登山靴 **25** hiking boots
- 牛仔靴 **26** cowboy boots
- 軟皮鞋 **27** moccasins

[1–12]
A. Excuse me. I found this/these ________ in the dryer. Is it/Are they yours?
B. Yes. It's/They're mine. Thank you.

[13–27]
A. Are those new ________?
B. Yes, they are.
A. They're very nice.
B. Thanks.

Do you exercise? What do you do? What kind of clothing do you wear when you exercise?

What kind of shoes do you wear when you go to work or to school? when you exercise? when you relax at home? when you go out with friends or family members?

JEWELRY AND ACCESSORIES

首飾及飾物

戒指 **1** ring	可存放照片的吊墜 **10** locket	皮夾 **19** wallet
訂婚戒指 **2** engagement ring	手鐲 **11** bracelet	皮帶 **20** belt
結婚戒指 **3** wedding ring/ wedding band	條形髮夾 **12** barrette	(女用)手提包 **21** purse/ handbag/ pocketbook
耳環 **4** earrings	袖扣 **13** cuff links	肩背包 **22** shoulder bag
項鍊 **5** necklace	吊褲帶 **14** suspenders	大手提包 **23** tote bag
珍珠項鍊 **6** pearl necklace/ pearls/string of pearls	手錶 **15** watch/ wrist watch	書包 **24** book bag
項鍊 **7** chain	手帕 **16** handkerchief	背包 **25** backpack
珠子項鍊 **8** beads	鑰匙圈 **17** key ring/ key chain	化妝包 **26** makeup bag
胸針 **9** pin/brooch	零錢包 **18** change purse	公事包 **27** briefcase

A. Oh, no! I think I lost my **ring**!
B. I'll help you look for it.

A. Oh, no! I think I lost my **earrings**!
B. I'll help you look for them.

[In a store]
A. Excuse me. Is this/Are these _______ on sale this week?
B. Yes. It's/They're half price.

[On the street]
A. Help! Police! Stop that man/woman!
B. What happened?!
A. He/She just stole my _______ and my _______!

Do you like to wear jewelry? What jewelry do you have?

In your country, what do men, women, and children use to carry their things?

描述衣物

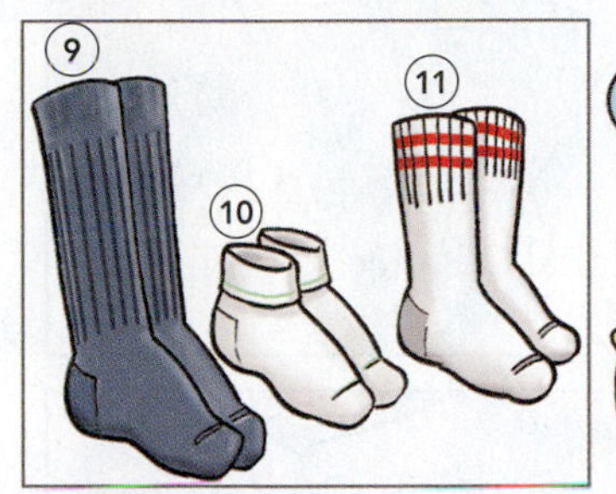

衣服類型 Types of Clothing

長袖襯衫 **1** long-sleeved shirt
短袖襯衫 **2** short-sleeved shirt
無袖襯衫 **3** sleeveless shirt
高領襯衫 **4** turtleneck (shirt)

V領毛衣 **5** V-neck sweater
無領有扣開襟的毛衣 **6** cardigan sweater
圓領毛衣 **7** crewneck sweater
高領毛衣 **8** turtleneck sweater

中統襪 **9** knee-high socks
短統襪 **10** ankle socks
運動襪 **11** crew socks

穿孔耳環 **12** pierced earrings
夾式耳環 **13** clip-on earrings

質料種類 Types of Material

燈芯絨褲 **14** corduroy *pants*
皮靴 **15** leather *boots*
尼龍絲襪 **16** nylon *stockings*
棉質短袖圓領衫 **17** cotton *T-shirt*
丁尼(一種厚棉質夾克) **18** denim *jacket*
法蘭絨襯衫 **19** flannel *shirt*
聚酯短衫 **20** polyester *blouse*
亞麻洋裝 **21** linen *dress*
絲圍巾 **22** silk *scarf*
羊毛毛衣 **23** wool *sweater*
草帽 **24** straw *hat*

花樣 Patterns

條紋 **25** striped
方格圖案 **26** checked
格子花紋 **27** plaid
圓點花紋 **28** polka-dotted
有圖案的/印花 **29** patterned/print
花卉圖案 **30** flowered/floral
渦紋圖案 **31** paisley
純藍色 **32** solid *blue*

尺寸大小 Sizes

特小 **33** extra-small
小 **34** small
中 **35** medium
大 **36** large
特大 **37** extra-large

[1–24]
A. May I help you?
B. Yes, please. I'm looking for a *shirt*.*
A. What kind?
B. I'm looking for a *long-sleeved shirt*.

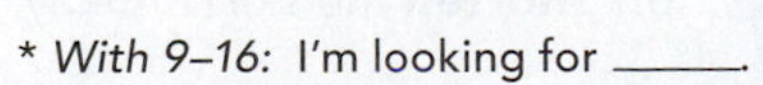

* *With 9–16:* I'm looking for _____.

[25–32]
A. How do you like this _______ tie/shirt/skirt?
B. Actually, I prefer that _______ one.

[33–37]
A. What size are you looking for?
B. _______.

Describe your favorite clothing items. For each item, tell about the color, the type of material, the size, and the pattern.

CLOTHING PROBLEMS AND ALTERATIONS

衣物問題及修改

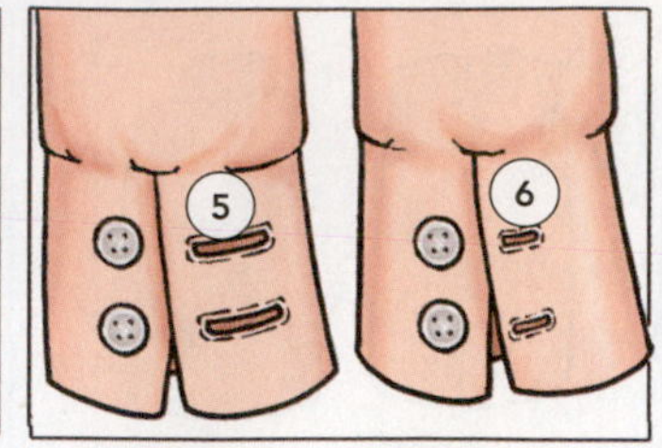

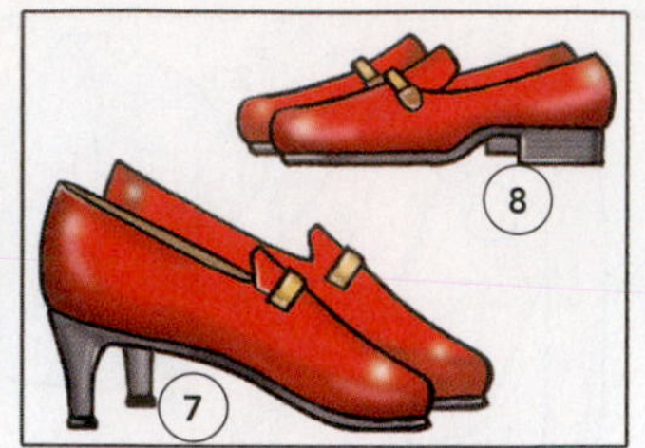

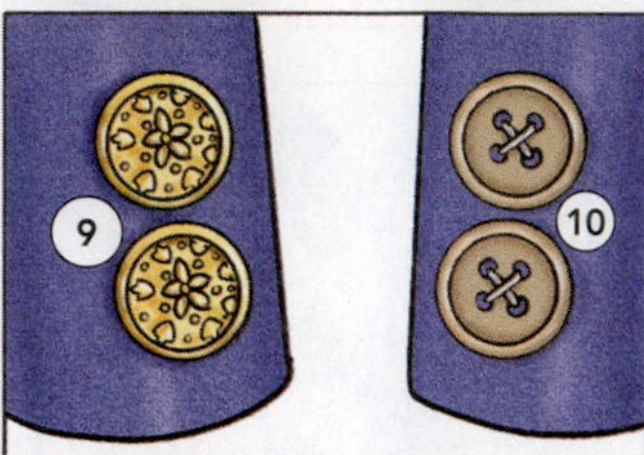

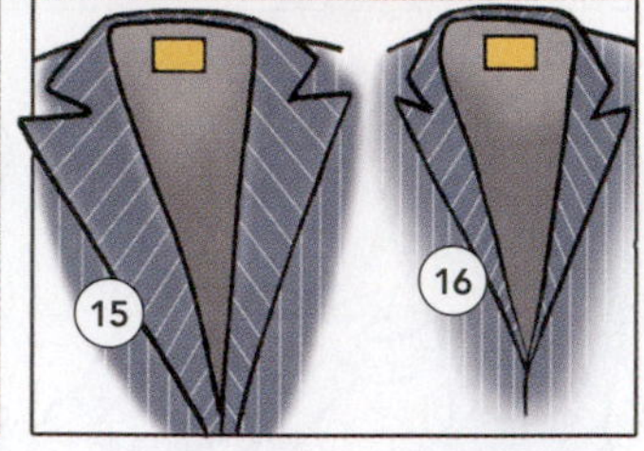

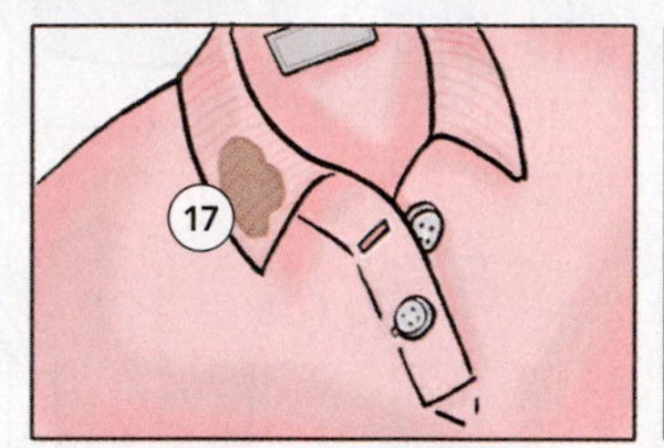

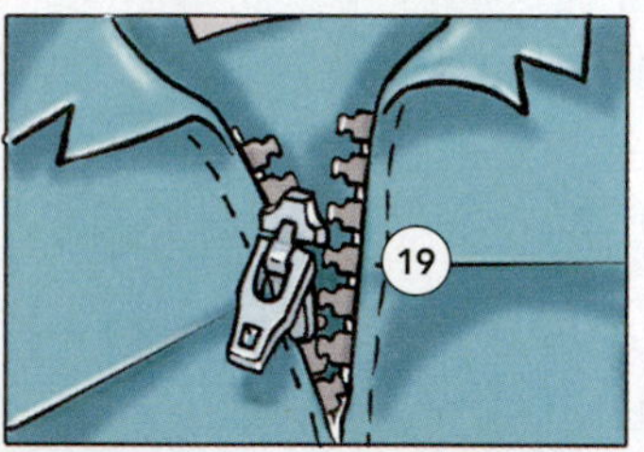

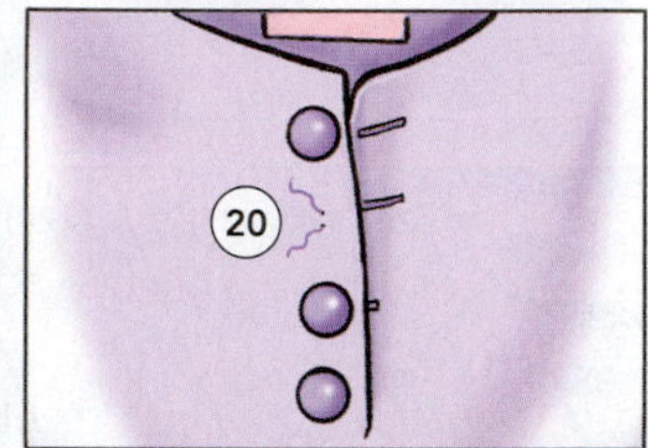

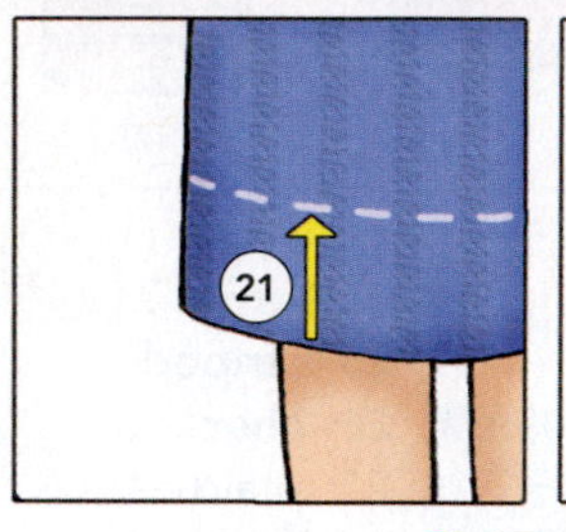

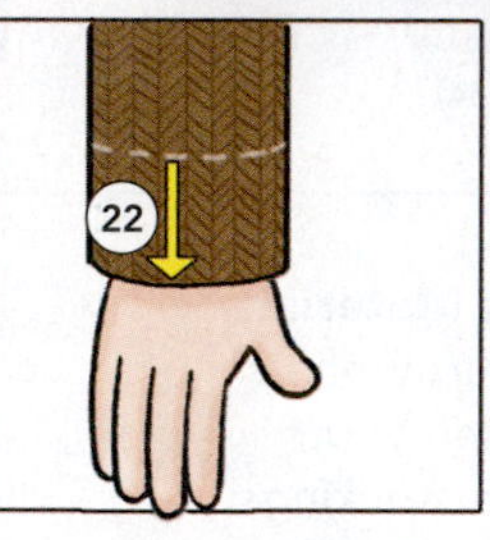

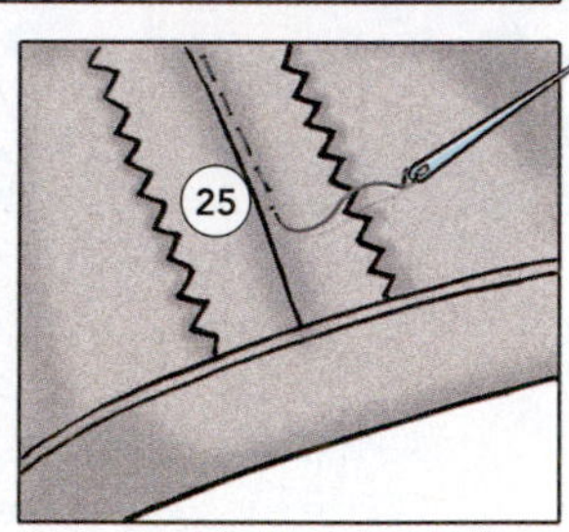

長 - 短 **1–2** long – short
緊 - 寬鬆 **3–4** tight – loose/baggy
大 - 小 **5–6** large/big – small
高 - 低 **7–8** high – low
華麗 - 樸素 **9–10** fancy – plain
重 - 輕 **11–12** heavy – light
深暗 - 明亮 **13–14** dark – light
寬 - 窄 **15–16** wide – narrow

髒衣領 **17** stained *collar*
破了的口袋 **18** ripped/torn *pocket*
壞掉的拉鍊 **19** broken *zipper*
掉了個鈕扣 **20** missing *button*
縮短裙子 **21** shorten the *skirt*
放長袖子 **22** lengthen the *sleeves*
將夾克改小 **23** take in the *jacket*
將褲子改大 **24** let out the *pants*
修補接縫 **25** fix/repair the *seam*

[1–2]
A. Are the sleeves too **long**?
B. No. They're too **short**.

1–2 Are the sleeves too ________?
3–4 Are the pants too ________?
5–6 Are the buttonholes too ________?
7–8 Are the heels too ________?

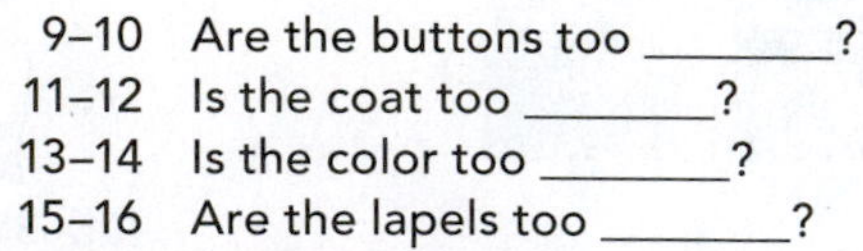
9–10 Are the buttons too ________?
11–12 Is the coat too ________?
13–14 Is the color too ________?
15–16 Are the lapels too ________?

[17–20]
A. What's the matter with it?
B. It has a **stained** *collar*.

[21–25]
A. Please **shorten** the *skirt*.
B. **Shorten** the *skirt*? Okay.

Tell about the differences between clothing people wear now and clothing people wore a long time ago.

洗衣服

- 將要洗衣物分類 **A** sort the laundry
- 將衣物放入洗衣機 **B** load the washer
- 將衣物從洗衣機取出 **C** unload the washer
- 將衣物放入乾衣機 **D** load the dryer
- 將衣服掛上曬衣繩 **E** hang clothes on the clothesline
- 燙衣服 **F** iron
- 摺疊洗好的衣物 **G** fold the laundry
- 掛衣服 **H** hang up clothing
- 收拾東西 **I** put things away

- 要洗的衣物 **1** laundry
- 淺色衣物 **2** light clothing
- 深色衣物 **3** dark clothing
- 洗衣籃 **4** laundry basket
- 洗衣袋 **5** laundry bag
- 洗衣機 **6** washer/washing machine
- 洗衣粉 **7** laundry detergent
- 衣物柔順劑 **8** fabric softener
- 漂白劑 **9** bleach
- 濕衣物 **10** wet clothing
- 乾衣機 **11** dryer
- 過濾網罩 **12** lint trap
- 除靜電紙 **13** static cling remover
- 曬衣繩 **14** clothesline
- 曬衣夾 **15** clothespin
- 熨斗 **16** iron
- 熨燙板 **17** ironing board
- 皺摺的衣物 **18** wrinkled clothing
- 燙平的衣物 **19** ironed clothing
- 熨噴漿 **20** spray starch
- 乾淨衣物 **21** clean clothing
- 衣櫥 **22** closet
- 衣架 **23** hanger
- 抽屜 **24** drawer
- 架子 - 架子(複數) **25** shelf–shelves

[A–I]
A. What are you doing?
B. I'm ________ing.

[4–6, 11, 14–17, 23]
A. Excuse me. Do you sell ________s?
B. Yes. They're at the back of the store.
A. Thank you.

[7–9, 13, 20]
A. Excuse me. Do you sell ________?
B. Yes. It's at the back of the store.
A. Thank you.

Who does the laundry in your home? What things does this person use?

THE DEPARTMENT STORE

百貨公司

商店目錄	1	(store) directory
珠寶專櫃	2	Jewelry Counter
香水專櫃	3	Perfume Counter
電扶梯	4	escalator
電梯	5	elevator
男士服裝部	6	Men's Clothing Department
顧客取貨區	7	customer pickup area
女士服裝部	8	Women's Clothing Department
兒童服裝部	9	Children's Clothing Department
家庭用品部	10	Housewares Department
家具部	11	Furniture Department/ Home Furnishings Department
家電用品部	12	Household Appliances Department
電子部門	13	Electronics Department
顧客服務處	14	Customer Assistance Counter/ Customer Service Counter
男士洗手間	15	men's room
女士洗手間	16	ladies' room
飲水機	17	water fountain
點心販賣部	18	snack bar
禮品包裝櫃檯	19	Gift Wrap Counter

A. Excuse me. Where's the **store directory**?
B. It's over there, next to the **Jewelry Counter**.
A. Thanks.
B. You're welcome.

A. Excuse me. Do you sell *ties**?
B. Yes. You can find *ties** in the ___[6, 8–13]___ /at the ___[2, 3]___ on the first/second/third/fourth floor.
A. Thank you.

**ties/bracelets/dresses/toasters/. . .*

Describe a department store you know. Tell what is on each floor.

購物

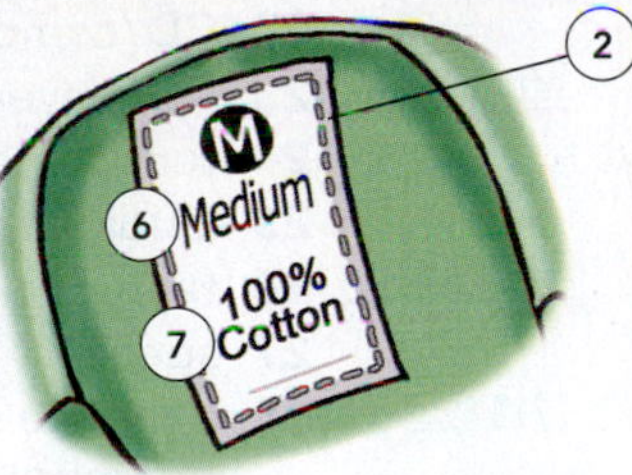

買	**A**	buy
退貨	**B**	return
換貨	**C**	exchange
試穿	**D**	try on
付錢	**E**	pay for
了解某項商品	**F**	get some information about

拍賣廣告	**1**	sale sign
標籤	**2**	label
價格標籤	**3**	price tag
收據	**4**	receipt
折扣	**5**	discount
尺寸	**6**	size
質料	**7**	material

維護說明	**8**	care instructions
原價	**9**	regular price
特價	**10**	sale price
價格	**11**	price
銷售稅	**12**	sales tax
總額/總價格	**13**	total price

A. May I help you?
B. Yes, please. I want to [A–F] this item.
A. Certainly. I'll be glad to help you.

A. {What's the [5–7, 9–13]? / What are the [8]?
B. ________.
A. Are you sure?
B. Yes. Look at the [1–4]!

Which stores in your area have sales? How often?

Tell about something you bought on sale.

VIDEO AND AUDIO EQUIPMENT

錄影及音響設備

電視	**1**	TV/television
電漿電視	**2**	plasma TV
液晶電視	**3**	LCD TV
投影電視	**4**	projection TV
攜帶型電視	**5**	portable TV
遙控器	**6**	remote (control)
數碼光碟	**7**	DVD
數碼光碟播放機	**8**	DVD player
錄影帶	**9**	video/videocassette/videotape
錄影機	**10**	VCR/videocassette recorder
攝錄像機	**11**	camcorder/video camera
電池組	**12**	battery pack
電池充電器	**13**	battery charger
收音機	**14**	radio
鬧鐘收音機	**15**	clock radio
短波收音機	**16**	shortwave radio
錄音機	**17**	tape recorder/cassette recorder
麥克風	**18**	microphone
立體音響系統/音響系統	**19**	stereo system/sound system
唱片	**20**	record
唱盤	**21**	turntable
光碟片	**22**	CD/compact disc
光碟播放機	**23**	CD player
調協器	**24**	tuner
錄音帶	**25**	(audio)tape/(audio)cassette
卡式錄音座	**26**	tape deck/cassette deck
喇叭	**27**	speakers
手提錄放音機	**28**	portable stereo system/boombox
音樂光碟隨身聽	**29**	portable/personal CD player
卡帶隨身聽	**30**	portable/personal cassette player
耳機	**31**	headphones
隨身數位音訊播放器	**32**	portable/personal digital audio player
視訊遊戲系統	**33**	video game system
視訊遊戲	**34**	video game
掌上型視訊遊戲	**35**	hand-held video game

A. May I help you?
B. Yes, please. I'm looking for a **TV**.

* *With 27 & 31, use:* I'm looking for ______.

A. I like your new ______.
Where did you get it/them?
B. At .....*(name of store)*.....

A. Which company makes the best ______?
B. In my opinion, the best ______ is/are made by ....

What video and audio equipment do you have or want?

In your opinion, which brands of video and audio equipment are the best?

電話及照相機

電話	**1**	telephone/phone
無線電話	**2**	cordless phone
行動電話/手機	**3**	cell phone/cellular phone
電池	**4**	battery
電池充電器	**5**	battery charger
答錄機	**6**	answering machine
攜帶型傳呼器	**7**	pager
個人數位助理	**8**	PDA/electronic personal organizer
傳真機	**9**	fax machine
袖珍型計算機	**10**	(pocket) calculator
桌面計算機	**11**	adding machine
穩壓器	**12**	voltage regulator
變壓器	**13**	adapter
35毫米照相機	**14**	(35 millimeter) camera
鏡頭	**15**	lens
軟片/膠捲	**16**	film
長鏡頭	**17**	zoom lens
數位照相機	**18**	digital camera
記憶硬碟	**19**	memory disk
三腳架	**20**	tripod
閃光燈	**21**	flash (attachment)
相機盒	**22**	camera case
幻燈機	**23**	slide projector
電影屏幕	**24**	(movie) screen

A. Can I help you?
B. Yes. I want to buy a **telephone**.*

** With 16, use:* I want to buy ______.

A. Excuse me. Do you sell ______s?*
B. Yes. We have a large selection of ______s.

** With 16, use the singular.*

A. Which ______ is the best?
B. This one here. It's made by ......*(company)*......

What kind of telephone do you use?

Do you have a camera? What kind is it?
What do you take pictures of?

Does anyone you know have an answering machine?
When you call, what message do you hear?

COMPUTERS

電腦

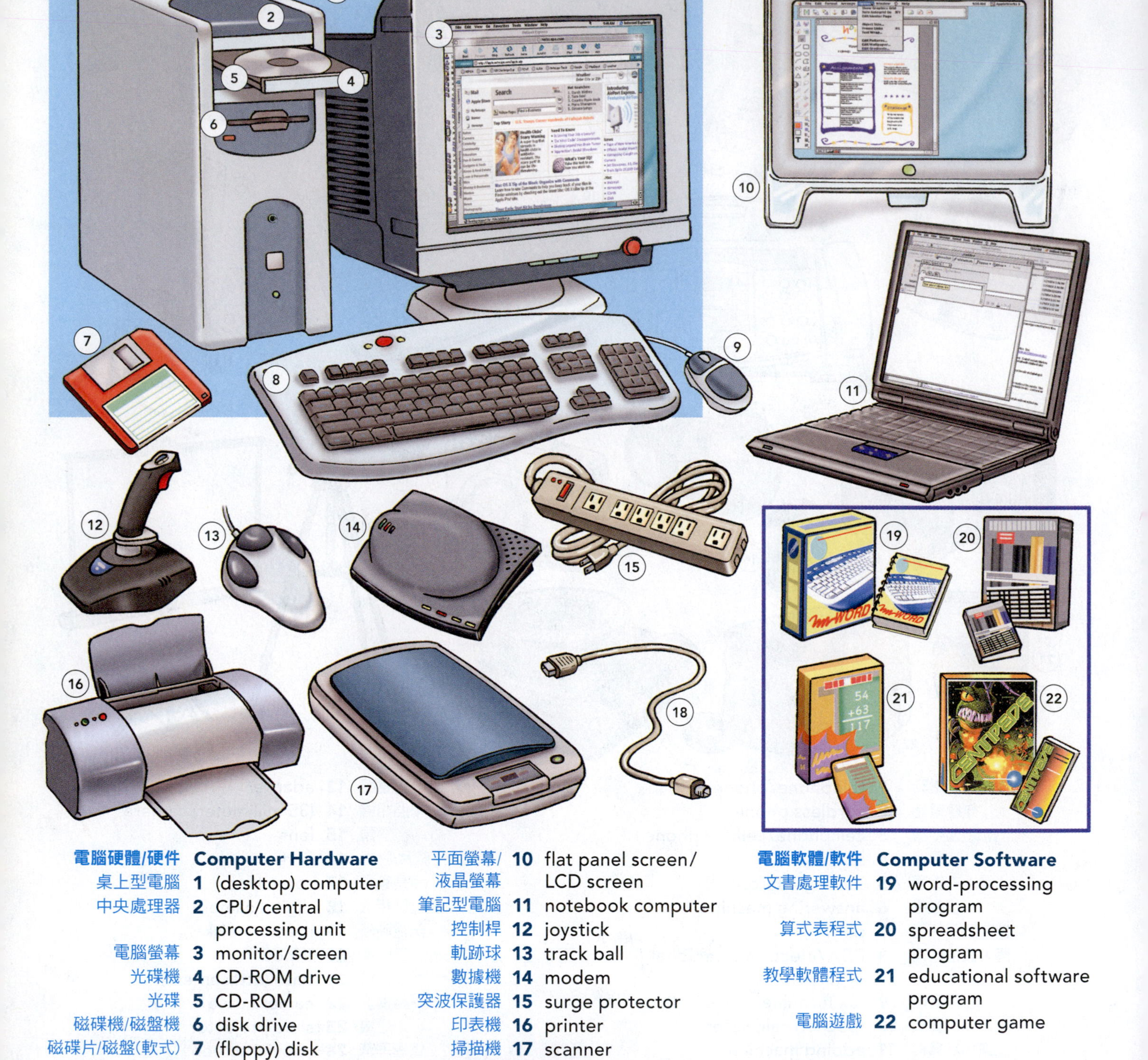

電腦硬體/硬件 Computer Hardware

桌上型電腦 **1** (desktop) computer
中央處理器 **2** CPU/central processing unit
電腦螢幕 **3** monitor/screen
光碟機 **4** CD-ROM drive
光碟 **5** CD-ROM
磁碟機/磁盤機 **6** disk drive
磁碟片/磁盤(軟式) **7** (floppy) disk
鍵盤 **8** keyboard
滑鼠 **9** mouse
平面螢幕/液晶螢幕 **10** flat panel screen/LCD screen
筆記型電腦 **11** notebook computer
控制桿 **12** joystick
軌跡球 **13** track ball
數據機 **14** modem
突波保護器 **15** surge protector
印表機 **16** printer
掃描機 **17** scanner
連接線 **18** cable

電腦軟體/軟件 Computer Software

文書處理軟件 **19** word-processing program
算式表程式 **20** spreadsheet program
教學軟體程式 **21** educational software program
電腦遊戲 **22** computer game

A. Can you recommend a good **computer**?
B. Yes. This **computer** here is excellent.

A. Is that a new ________?
B. Yes.
A. Where did you get it?
B. At ....*(name of store)*....

A. May I help you?
B. Yes, please. Do you sell ________s?
A. Yes. We carry a complete line of ________s.

Do you use a computer? When?

In your opinion, how have computers changed the world?

THE TOY STORE

玩具店

棋盤遊戲	**1**	board game
拼圖遊戲	**2**	(jigsaw) puzzle
建築玩具組合	**3**	construction set
積木	**4**	(building) blocks
皮球	**5**	rubber ball
海灘球	**6**	beach ball
桶子和鏟子	**7**	pail and shovel
洋娃娃	**8**	doll
洋娃娃衣物	**9**	doll clothing
娃娃屋	**10**	doll house
娃娃傢俱	**11**	doll house furniture
活動玩偶	**12**	action figure
毛絨玩具	**13**	stuffed animal
玩具小汽車/火柴盒小汽車	**14**	matchbox car
玩具卡車	**15**	toy truck
玩具賽車組合	**16**	racing car set
玩具火車組合	**17**	train set
模型玩具組合	**18**	model kit
科學實驗組合	**19**	science kit
對講機組合	**20**	walkie-talkie (set)
呼拉圈	**21**	hula hoop
跳繩	**22**	jump rope
吹泡泡肥皂水	**23**	bubble soap
收藏卡	**24**	trading cards
蠟筆	**25**	crayons
彩色筆	**26**	(color) markers
著色本	**27**	coloring book
彩色美工用紙	**28**	construction paper
顏料組合	**29**	paint set
黏土	**30**	(modeling) clay
貼紙	**31**	stickers
腳踏車	**32**	bicycle
三輪車	**33**	tricycle
玩具拖車	**34**	wagon
滑板	**35**	skateboard
鞦韆	**36**	swing set
遊戲屋	**37**	play house
兒童游泳池/充氣游泳池	**38**	kiddie pool/inflatable pool

A. Excuse me. I'm looking for (a/an) _______(s) for my *grandson*.*
B. Look in the next aisle.
A. Thank you.

* *grandson/granddaughter/. . .*

A. I don't know what to get my ....-year-old son/daughter for his/her birthday.
B. What about (a) _______?
A. Good idea! Thanks.

A. Mom/Dad? Can we buy this/these _______?
B. No, *Johnny*. Not today.

What toys are most popular in your country?

What were your favorite toys when you were a child?

THE BANK

銀行

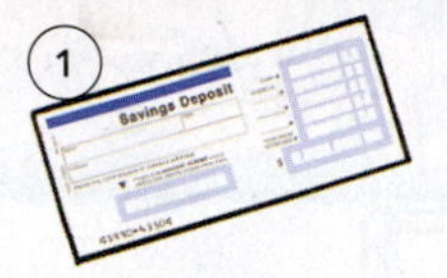

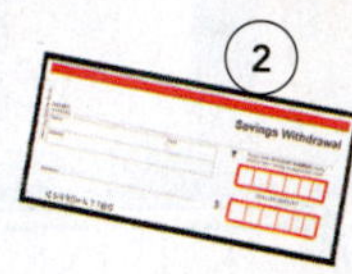

存款 **A** make a deposit
提款 **B** make a withdrawal
將支票兌換現金 **C** cash a check
買旅行支票 **D** get traveler's checks
開戶頭 **E** open an account
申請貸款 **F** apply for a loan
換貨幣 **G** exchange currency

存款單 **1** deposit slip
提款單 **2** withdrawal slip
支票 **3** check
旅行支票 **4** traveler's check
銀行存摺 **5** bankbook/passbook
金融卡/提款卡 **6** ATM card
信用卡 **7** credit card
銀行保險庫 **8** (bank) vault
保險箱 **9** safe deposit box
出納員 **10** teller
警衛 **11** security guard
自動存提款機 **12** ATM (machine)/ cash machine
銀行職員 **13** bank officer

[A–G]
A. Where are you going?
B. I'm going to the bank.
I have to ________.

[5–7]
A. What are you looking for?
B. My ________. I can't find it anywhere!

[8–13]
A. How many ________s does the State Street Bank have?
B. ....

Do you have a bank account? What kind? Where? What do you do at the bank?

Do you ever use traveler's checks? When?

Do you have a credit card? What kind? When do you use it?

金融

付款形式	**Forms of Payment**
現金	**1** cash
支票	**2** check
支票號碼	**a** check number
帳戶號碼	**b** account number
信用卡	**3** credit card
信用卡號碼	**a** credit card number
匯票	**4** money order
旅行支票	**5** traveler's check
家用帳單	**Household Bills**
房租	**6** rent
房屋貸款	**7** mortgage payment
電費單	**8** electric bill
電話帳單	**9** telephone bill
瓦斯/煤氣帳單	**10** gas bill
燃油帳單/暖氣費帳單	**11** oil bill/heating bill
水費單	**12** water bill
有線電視帳單	**13** cable TV bill
車貸	**14** car payment
信用卡帳單	**15** credit card bill

家庭理財	**Family Finances**
平衡支票本	**16** balance the checkbook
開支票	**17** write a check
使用網路銀行	**18** bank online
支票本	**19** checkbook
支票登記簿	**20** check register
月結單	**21** monthly statement
使用自動存提款機	**Using an ATM Machine**
插入金融卡	**22** insert the ATM card
輸入密碼/輸入個人身分識別碼	**23** enter your PIN number/ personal identification number
選擇交易類型	**24** select a transaction
存款	**25** make a deposit
提取現金	**26** withdraw/get cash
轉帳	**27** transfer funds
取出卡片	**28** remove your card
拿取交易收據/拿取收據	**29** take your transaction slip/receipt

A. Can I pay by __[1, 2]__/ with a __[3–5]__?
B. Yes. We accept __[1]__/ __[2–5]__s.

A. What are you doing?
B. I'm paying the __[6–15]__.
I'm __[16–18]__ing.
I'm looking for the __[19–21]__.

A. What should I do?
B. __[22–29]__.

What household bills do you receive?
How much do you pay for the different bills?

Who takes care of the finances in your household? What does that person do?

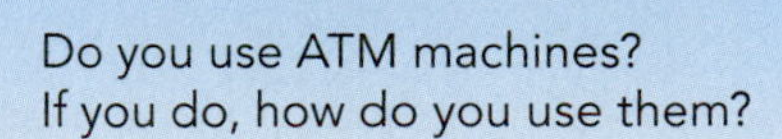

Do you use ATM machines?
If you do, how do you use them?

郵局

信 **1** letter	郵票本 **13** book of stamps	郵件口 **24** mail slot
明信片 **2** postcard	匯票 **14** money order	郵局辦事員 **25** postal worker/postal clerk
航空郵簡 **3** air letter/aerogramme	地址更換表格 **15** change-of-address form	秤 **26** scale
包裹 **4** package/parcel	入伍登記表格 **16** selective service registration form	郵票自售機 **27** stamp machine
一級郵件 **5** first class	護照申請表格 **17** passport application form	郵差 **28** letter carrier/mail carrier
優先郵件 **6** priority mail	信封 **18** envelope	郵車 **29** mail truck
特快件 隔日快件 **7** express mail/overnight mail	回郵地址 **19** return address	郵筒 **30** mailbox
包裹件 **8** parcel post	郵寄地址 **20** mailing address	
掛號信 **9** certified mail	郵遞區號 **21** zip code	
郵票 **10** stamp	郵戳 **22** postmark	
整版郵票 **11** sheet of stamps	郵票/郵資 **23** stamp/postage	
整捲郵票 **12** roll of stamps		

[1–4]
A. Where are you going?
B. To the post office. I have to mail a/an  _______.

[5–9]
A. How do you want to send it?
B. _______, please.

[10–17]
A. Next!
B. I'd like a _______, please.
A. Here you are.

[19–21, 23]
A. Do you want me to mail this letter?
B. Yes, thanks.
A. Oops! You forgot the _______!

How often do you go to the post office? What do you do there?

Tell about the postal system in your country.

圖書館

- 網上圖書目錄檢索 **1** online catalog
- 卡片目錄 **2** card catalog
- 作者 **3** author
- 書名 **4** title
- 借書証 **5** library card
- 影印機/複印機 **6** copier/photocopier/copy machine
- 書架 **7** shelves
- 兒童圖書區 **8** children's section
- 兒童圖書 **9** children's books
- 期刊室 **10** periodical section
- 期刊 **11** journals
- 雜誌 **12** magazines
- 報紙 **13** newspapers
- 視聽資料區 **14** media section
- 磁帶書 **15** books on tape
- 錄音帶 **16** audiotapes
- 光碟(複數) **17** CDs
- 錄影帶(複數) **18** videotapes
- 電腦軟體/軟件 **19** (computer) software
- 數碼光碟(複數) **20** DVDs
- 外語區 **21** foreign language section
- 外語書籍 **22** foreign language books
- 參考書閱覽室 **23** reference section
- 縮微膠捲 **24** microfilm
- 縮微膠捲閱讀機 **25** microfilm reader
- 字典 **26** dictionary
- 百科全書 **27** encyclopedia
- 地圖集 **28** atlas
- 參考諮詢台 **29** reference desk
- 圖書館參考資料諮詢員 **30** (reference) librarian
- 借書處 **31** checkout desk
- 圖書館職員 **32** library clerk

[1, 2, 6–32]

A. Excuse me. Where's/Where are the ________?

B. Over there, at/near/next to the ________.

[8–23, 26–28]

A. Excuse me. Where can I find a/an [26–28] / [9, 11–13, 15–20, 22]?

B. Look in the [8, 10, 14, 21, 23] over there.

A. I'm having trouble finding a book.

B. Do you know the [3–4]?

A. Yes. ....

A. Excuse me. I'd like to check out this [26–28]/these [11–13].

B. I'm sorry. It/They must remain in the library.

Do you go to a library? Where? What does this library have?

Tell about how you use the library.

COMMUNITY INSTITUTIONS

社區機構

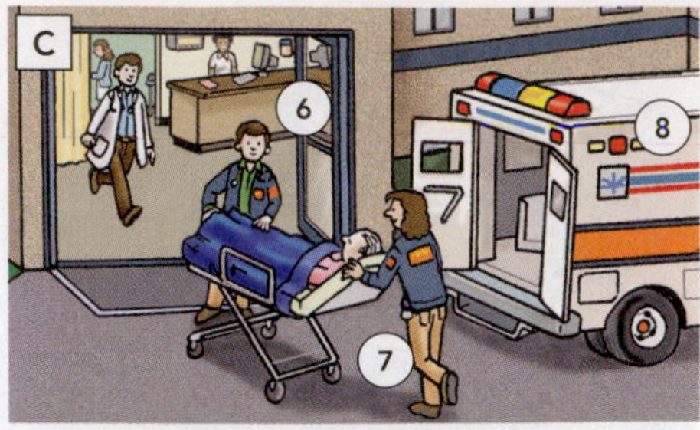

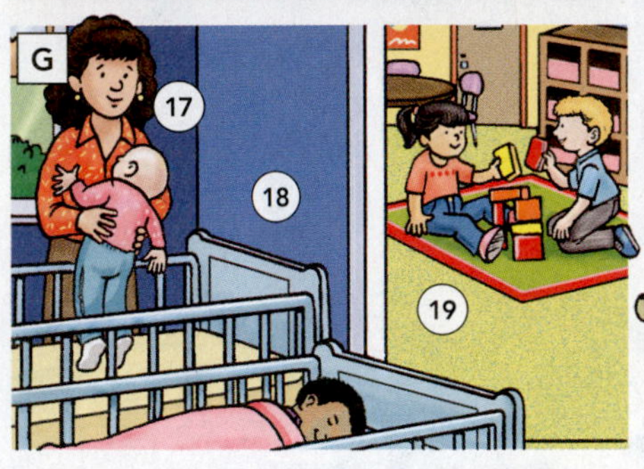

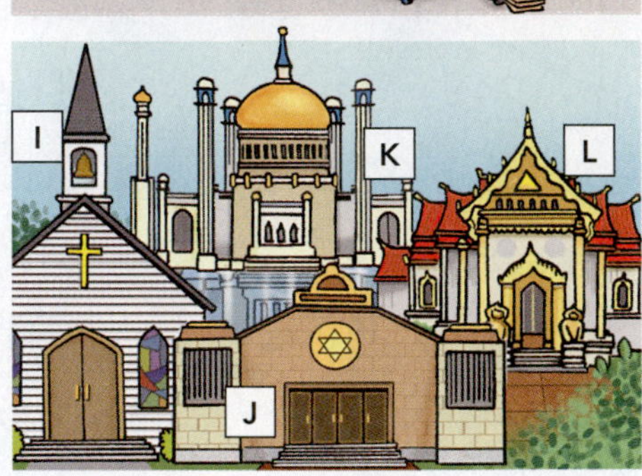

警察局 **A** police station
消防隊 **B** fire station
醫院 **C** hospital
市政廳 **D** town hall/city hall
活動中心 **E** recreation center
垃圾場 **F** dump
托兒所 **G** child-care center
老人中心 **H** senior center
教會 **I** church
猶太教堂 **J** synagogue
清真寺/回教寺院 **K** mosque
廟 **L** temple

緊急事故接線員 **1** emergency operator
警察 **2** police officer
警察車 **3** police car
救火車/消防車 **4** fire engine
救火員/消防員 **5** firefighter
急診室 **6** emergency room
緊急救護技術員/醫務助理 **7** EMT/paramedic
救護車 **8** ambulance
市長/鎮長/市行政官 **9** mayor/city manager
會議室 **10** meeting room
體育館 **11** gym
活動主任 **12** activities director
遊戲室 **13** game room
游泳池 **14** swimming pool
垃圾工 **15** sanitation worker
資源回收中心 **16** recycling center
幼兒工作員 **17** child-care worker
育兒室 **18** nursery
娛樂室 **19** playroom
老人照護人員 **20** eldercare worker/senior care worker

[A–L]
A. Where are you going?
B. I'm going to the ______.

[1, 2, 5, 7, 12, 15, 17, 20]
A. What do you do?
B. I'm a/an ______.

[3, 4, 8]
A. Do you hear a siren?
B. Yes. There's a/an ______ coming up behind us.

What community institutions are in your city or town? Where are they located?

Which community institutions do you use? When?

犯罪行為及緊急事故

車禍 **1** car accident
火 **2** fire
爆炸 **3** explosion
搶劫 **4** robbery
入屋盜竊 **5** burglary
在公共場所搶劫 **6** mugging
綁架 **7** kidnapping
迷失的孩子(單數) **8** lost child

劫車 **9** car jacking
搶銀行 **10** bank robbery
攻擊 **11** assault
兇殺 **12** murder
停電 **13** blackout / power outage
瓦斯洩漏 **14** gas leak
水管破裂 **15** water main break

電線掉落 **16** downed power line
化學品溢漏 **17** chemical spill
火車出軌 **18** train derailment
蓄意破壞公物 **19** vandalism
幫派暴力 **20** gang violence
酒後駕駛 **21** drunk driving
販賣毒品 **22** drug dealing

[1–13]
A. I want to report a/an ________.
B. What's your location?
A. ....

[14–18]
A. Why is this street closed?
B. It's closed because of a ________.

[19–22]
A. I'm very concerned about the amount of ________ in our community.
B. I agree. ________ is a very serious problem.

Is there much crime in your community? Tell about it.

Have you ever experienced a crime or emergency? What happened?

身體

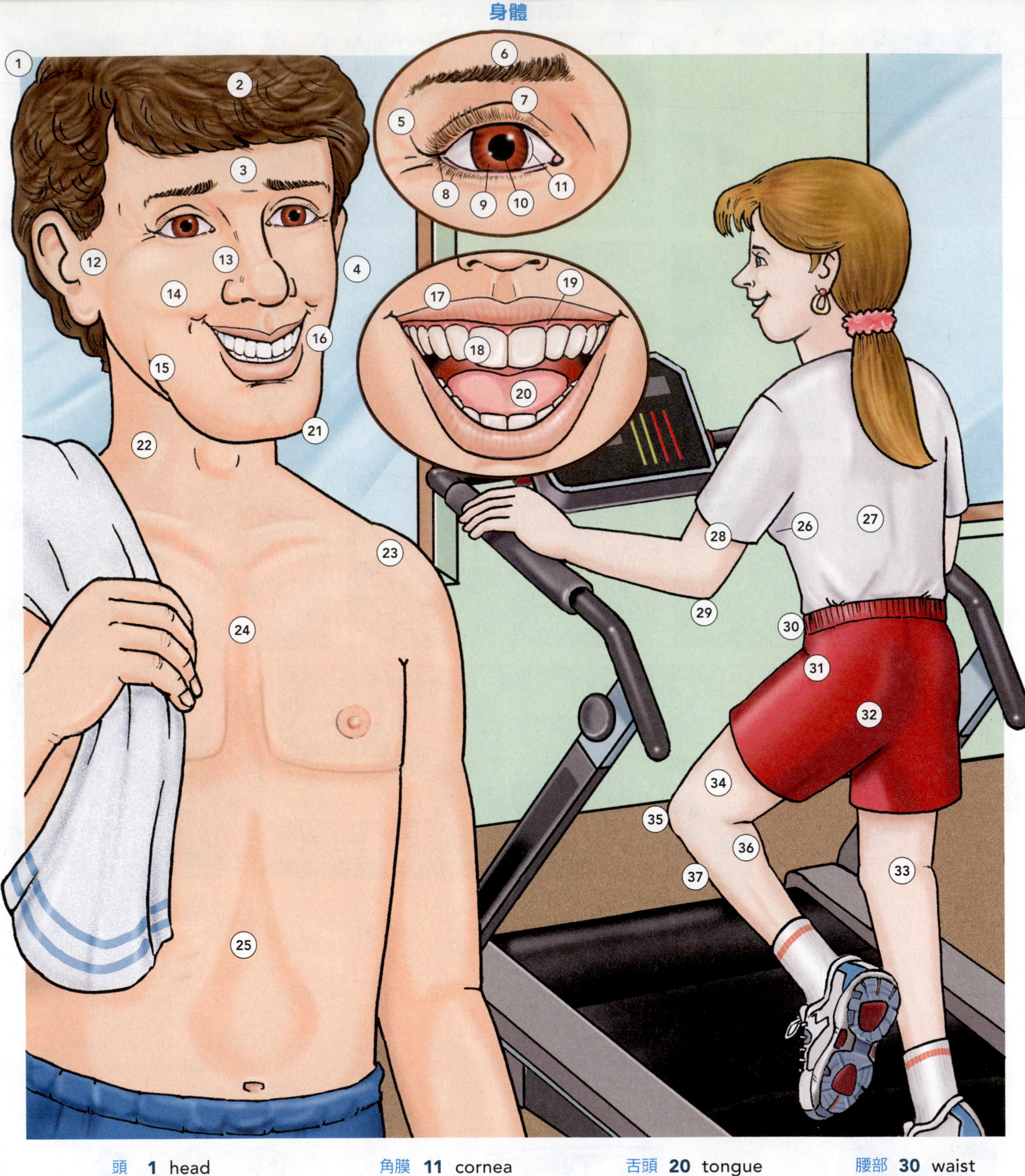

頭	1	head
頭髮	2	hair
額頭	3	forehead
臉	4	face
眼睛	5	eye
眉毛	6	eyebrow
眼瞼	7	eyelid
睫毛	8	eyelashes
(瞳孔外的)虹膜	9	iris
瞳孔	10	pupil
角膜	11	cornea
耳朵	12	ear
鼻子	13	nose
臉頰	14	cheek
下頜	15	jaw
嘴巴	16	mouth
嘴唇	17	lip
牙齒(單數) - 牙齒(複數)	18	tooth–teeth
牙齦	19	gums
舌頭	20	tongue
下巴	21	chin
頸子	22	neck
肩膀	23	shoulder
胸	24	chest
腹部	25	abdomen
乳房	26	breast
背部	27	back
手臂	28	arm
手肘	29	elbow
腰部	30	waist
臀部	31	hip
屁股	32	buttocks
腿	33	leg
大腿	34	thigh
膝蓋	35	knee
小腿	36	calf
脛	37	shin

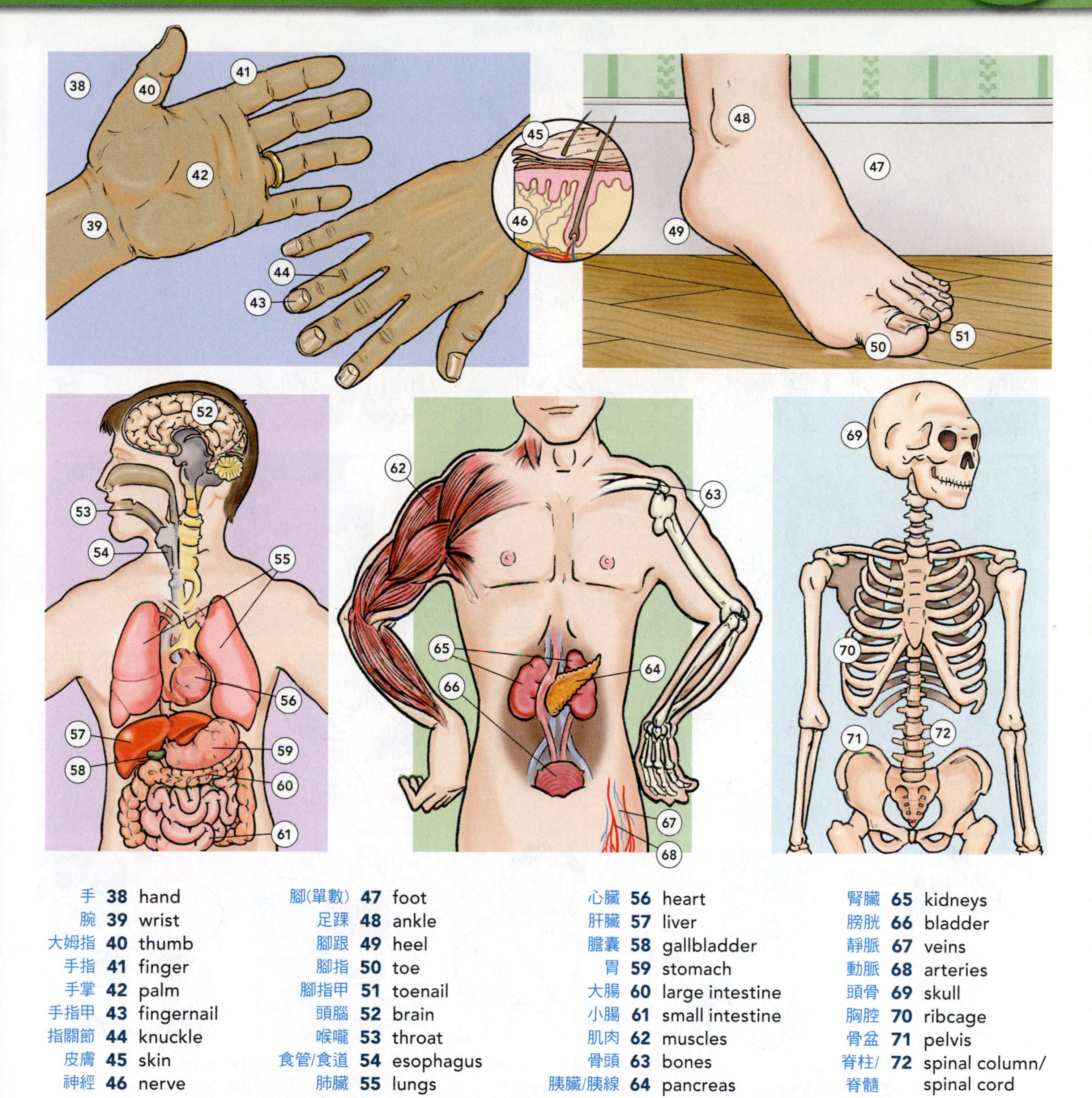

手	**38**	hand
腕	**39**	wrist
大姆指	**40**	thumb
手指	**41**	finger
手掌	**42**	palm
手指甲	**43**	fingernail
指關節	**44**	knuckle
皮膚	**45**	skin
神經	**46**	nerve
腳(單數)	**47**	foot
足踝	**48**	ankle
腳跟	**49**	heel
腳指	**50**	toe
腳指甲	**51**	toenail
頭腦	**52**	brain
喉嚨	**53**	throat
食管/食道	**54**	esophagus
肺臟	**55**	lungs
心臟	**56**	heart
肝臟	**57**	liver
膽囊	**58**	gallbladder
胃	**59**	stomach
大腸	**60**	large intestine
小腸	**61**	small intestine
肌肉	**62**	muscles
骨頭	**63**	bones
胰臟/胰線	**64**	pancreas
腎臟	**65**	kidneys
膀胱	**66**	bladder
靜脈	**67**	veins
動脈	**68**	arteries
頭骨	**69**	skull
胸腔	**70**	ribcage
骨盆	**71**	pelvis
脊柱/脊髓	**72**	spinal column/ spinal cord

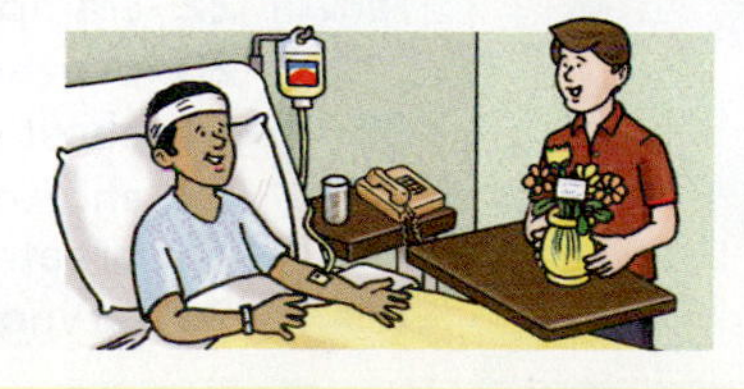

A. My doctor checked my **head** and said everything is okay.
B. I'm glad to hear that.

[1, 3–7, 12–29, 31–51]
A. Ooh!
B. What's the matter?
{ My ________ hurts!
{ My ________s hurt!

[52–72]
A. My doctor wants me to have some tests.
B. Why?
A. She's concerned about my ________.

Describe yourself as completely as you can.

Which parts of the body are most important at school? at work? when you play your favorite sport?

AILMENTS, SYMPTOMS, AND INJURIES

疾病，症狀，受傷

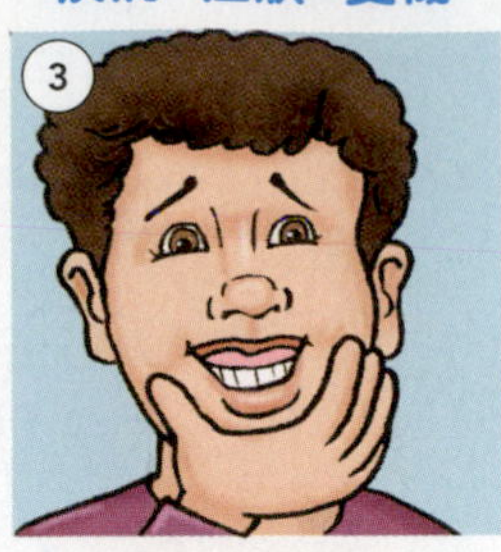

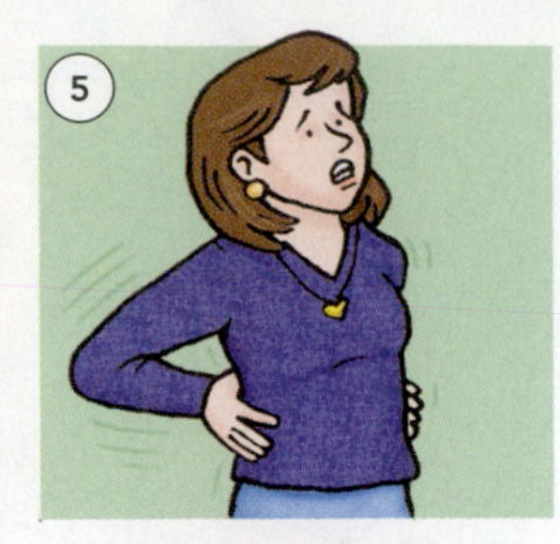

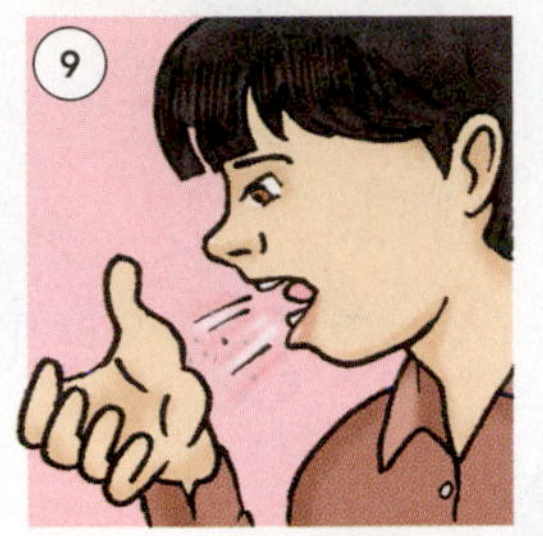
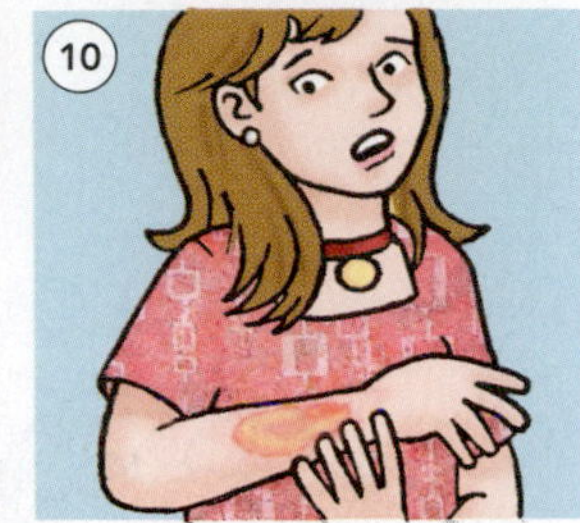
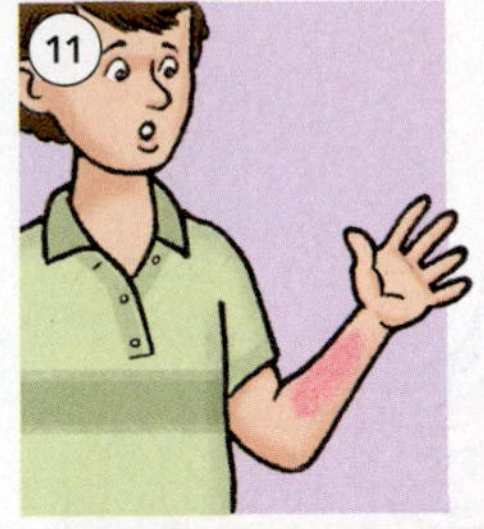

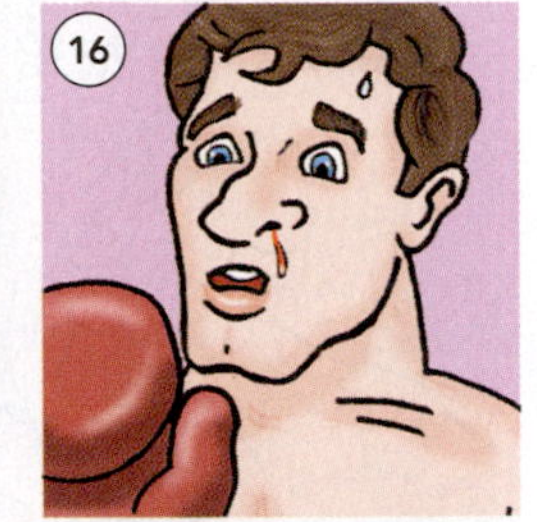
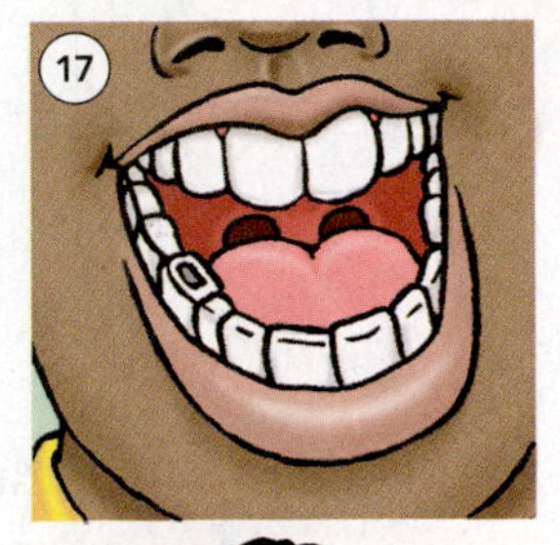
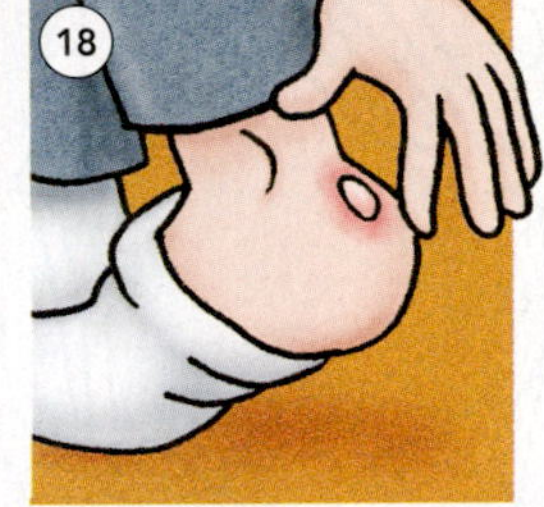
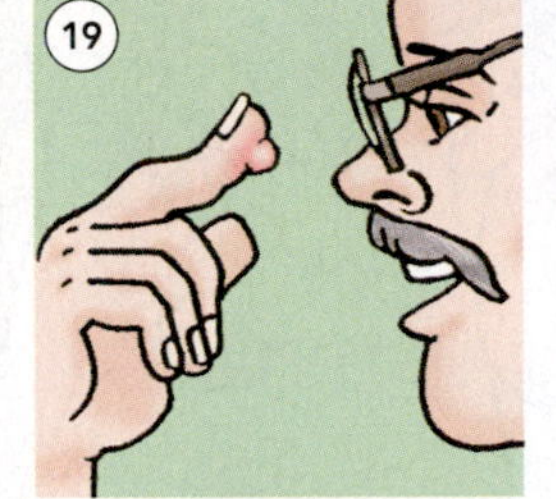

頭痛 **1** headache
耳朵痛 **2** earache
牙痛 **3** toothache
胃痛 **4** stomachache
背痛 **5** backache
喉嚨痛 **6** sore throat
發燒 **7** fever/temperature
感冒 **8** cold
咳嗽 **9** cough

感染 **10** infection
疹子 **11** rash
蟲咬 **12** insect bite
曬傷 **13** sunburn
頸僵硬 **14** stiff neck
流鼻涕 **15** runny nose
流鼻血 **16** bloody nose
蛀牙 **17** cavity
水泡 **18** blister

疣 **19** wart
打嗝 **20** (the) hiccups
發冷 **21** (the) chills
腹絞痛 **22** cramps
腹瀉 **23** diarrhea
胸口痛 **24** chest pain
氣促/呼吸短促 **25** shortness of breath
喉(頭)炎 **26** laryngitis

A. What's the matter?
B. I have a/an __[1–19]__.

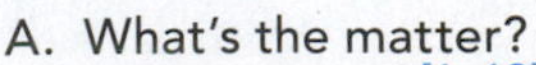

A. What's the matter?
B. I have __[20–26]__.

昏厥 **27** faint
暈眩 **28** dizzy
噁心 **29** nauseous
脹氣 **30** bloated
鼻塞 **31** congested
精疲力竭 **32** exhausted
咳嗽 **33** cough

打噴嚏 **34** sneeze
喘息 **35** wheeze
打飽嗝 **36** burp
嘔吐 **37** vomit/ throw up
流血 **38** bleed
扭(到) **39** twist

刮傷/抓傷 **40** scratch
擦傷 **41** scrape
使…瘀青 **42** bruise
燙(到) **43** burn
受傷 - 受傷(過去式) **44** hurt–hurt
切 - 切(過去式) **45** cut–cut
扭傷 **46** sprain

使…脫臼 **47** dislocate
折斷 - 折斷(過去式) **48** break–broke
腫 **49** swollen
癢 **50** itchy

A. What's the problem?
B. I feel [27–30].
I'm [31–32].
I've been [33–38] ing a lot.

A. What happened?
B. I [39–45] ed my ....
I think I [46–48] ed my ....
My .... is/are [49–50].

A. How do you feel?
B. Not so good./Not very well./Terrible!
A. What's the matter?
B. ...., ..., and ....
A. I'm sorry to hear that.

Tell about the last time you didn't feel well. What was the matter?

Tell about a time you hurt yourself. What happened? How? What did you do about it?

What do you do when you have a cold? a stomachache? an insect bite? the hiccups?

FIRST AID

急救

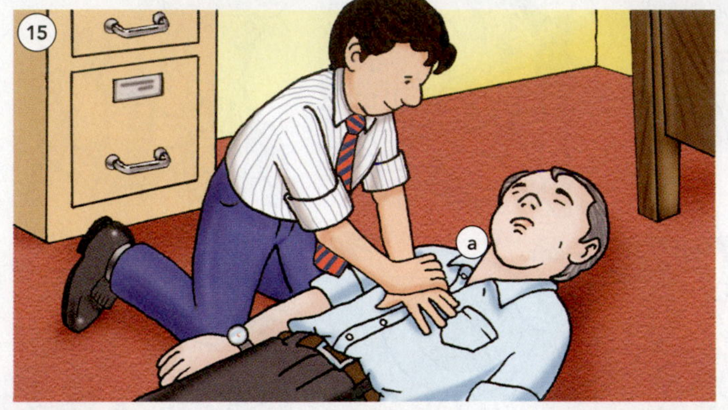

急救應變手冊 **1** first-aid manual
急救箱 **2** first-aid kit
護創膠布/OK繃 **3** (adhesive) bandage/Band-Aid™
消毒滅菌巾 **4** antiseptic cleansing wipe
消毒紗布墊 **5** sterile (dressing) pad
雙氧水 **6** hydrogen peroxide
抗生素軟膏 **7** antibiotic ointment
紗布 **8** gauze
膠帶 **9** adhesive tape
鑷子 **10** tweezers
止癢霜劑 **11** antihistamine cream
彈性繃帶 **12** elastic bandage/Ace™ bandage
阿斯匹靈(解熱鎮痛藥) **13** aspirin
不含阿斯匹靈止痛藥 **14** non-aspirin pain reliever

心肺復甦術 **15** CPR (cardiopulmonary resuscitation)
沒有脈搏 **a** has no pulse
人工呼吸 **16** rescue breathing
沒有呼吸 **b** isn't breathing
海姆利克氏操作法(使堵住喉嚨的異物吐出的急救措施) **17** the Heimlich maneuver
噎到 **c** is choking
夾板 **18** splint
手指斷了 **d** broke a finger
止血帶 **19** tourniquet
在流血 **e** is bleeding

A. Do we have any [3–5, 12] s/ [6–11, 13, 14] ?
B. Yes. Look in the first-aid kit.

A. Help! My friend [a–e] !
B. I can help!
{I know how to do [15–17] .
{I can make a [18, 19] .

Do you have a first-aid kit? If you do, what's in it? If you don't, where can you buy one?

Tell about a time when you gave or received first aid.

Where can a person learn first aid in your community?

急救與疾病

- 受傷 **1** hurt/injured
- 休克/驚愕 **2** in shock
- 不省人事 **3** unconscious
- 中暑 **4** heatstroke
- 凍傷 **5** frostbite
- 心臟病發作 **6** heart attack
- 過敏反應 **7** allergic reaction
- 喝下毒物 **8** swallow poison
- 藥物過量 **9** overdose on drugs
- 摔倒 - 摔倒(過去式) **10** fall–fell
- 觸電 **11** get–got an electric shock
- 流行性感冒 **12** the flu/influenza
- 耳朵發炎 **13** an ear infection
- 鏈球菌性喉炎 **14** strep throat
- 麻疹 **15** measles
- 腮腺炎 **16** mumps
- 水痘 **17** chicken pox
- 氣喘 **18** asthma
- 癌症 **19** cancer
- 憂鬱症 **20** depression
- 糖尿病 **21** diabetes
- 心臟病 **22** heart disease
- 高血壓 **23** high blood pressure/hypertension
- 結核病 **24** TB/tuberculosis
- 愛滋病* **25** AIDS*

*後天免疫缺乏症候群 * Acquired Immune Deficiency Syndrome

A. What happened?

B. My .... is [1–3] / has [4–5] / is having a/an [6–7] / [8–11] ed.

A. What's your location?

B. ......(address)......

A. My .... is sick.

B. What's the matter?

A. He/She has [12–25].

B. I'm sorry to hear that.

Tell about a medical emergency that happened to you or someone you know.

Which illnesses in this lesson are you familiar with?

健康檢查

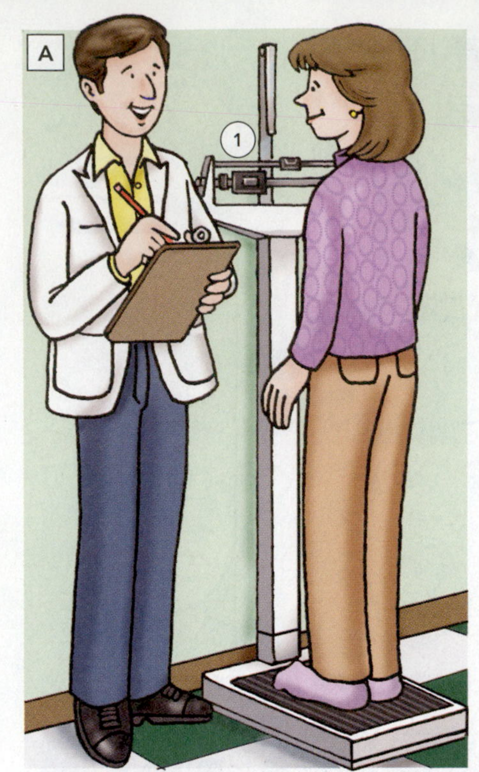

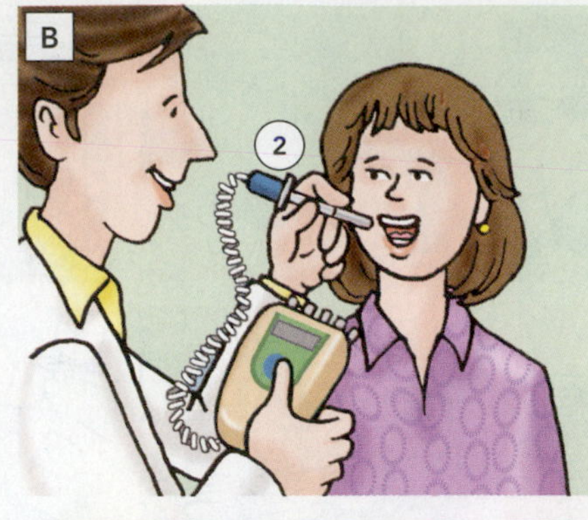

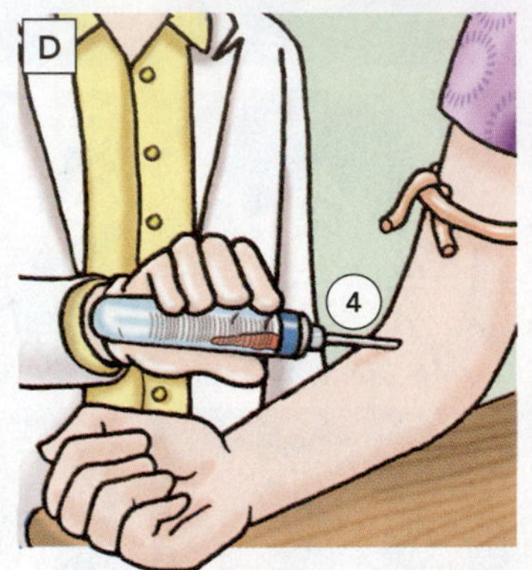

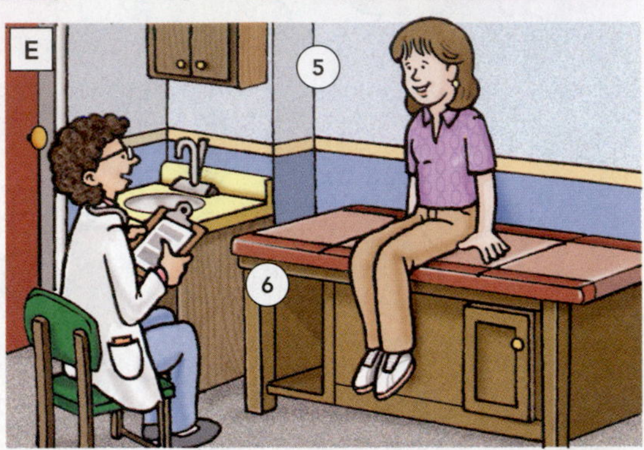

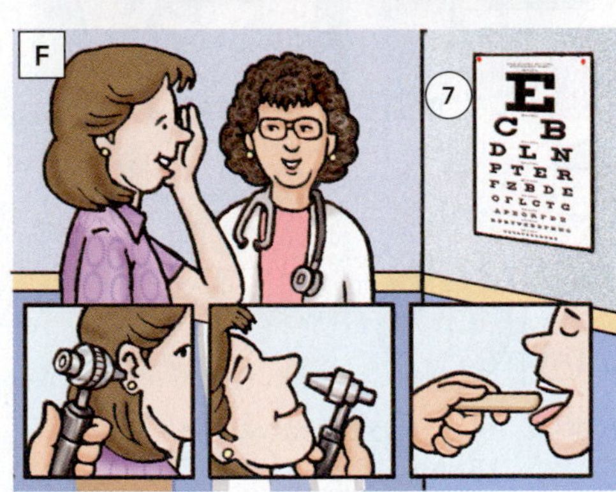

量你(妳)的身高體重	**A**	measure *your* height and weight
量你(妳)的體溫	**B**	take *your* temperature
量你(妳)的血壓	**C**	check *your* blood pressure
抽血	**D**	draw some blood
問你(妳)一些有關你(妳)的身體狀況的問題	**E**	ask *you* some questions about *your* health
檢查你(妳)的眼睛、耳朵、鼻子和喉嚨	**F**	examine *your* eyes, ears, nose, and throat
聽你(妳)的心臟	**G**	listen to *your* heart
照胸肺X光	**H**	take a chest X-ray

秤	**1**	scale
溫度計	**2**	thermometer
血壓計	**3**	blood pressure gauge
注射針	**4**	needle/syringe
檢查室	**5**	examination room
檢查台	**6**	examination table
視力檢查表	**7**	eye chart
聽診器	**8**	stethoscope
X光機	**9**	X-ray machine

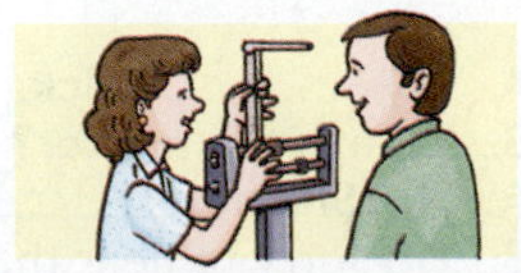

[A–H]

A. Now I'm going to **measure your height and weight**.

B. All right.

[A–H]

A. What did the doctor/nurse do during the examination?

B. She/He **measured my height and weight**.

[1–3, 5–9]

A. So, how do you like our new **scale?**

B. It's very nice, doctor.

How often do you have a medical exam? What does the doctor/nurse do?

MEDICAL AND DENTAL PROCEDURES

醫療及牙科治療過程

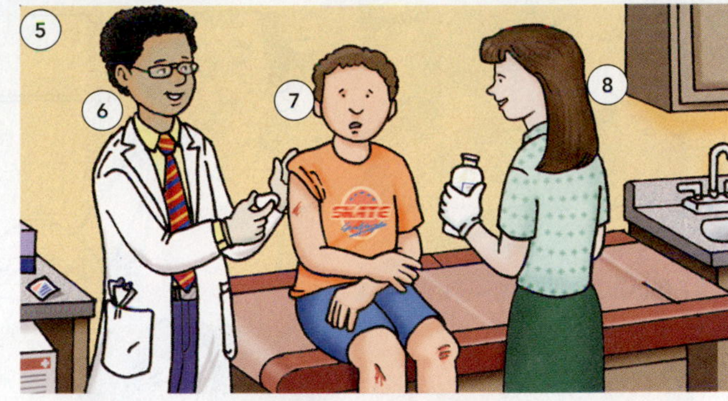

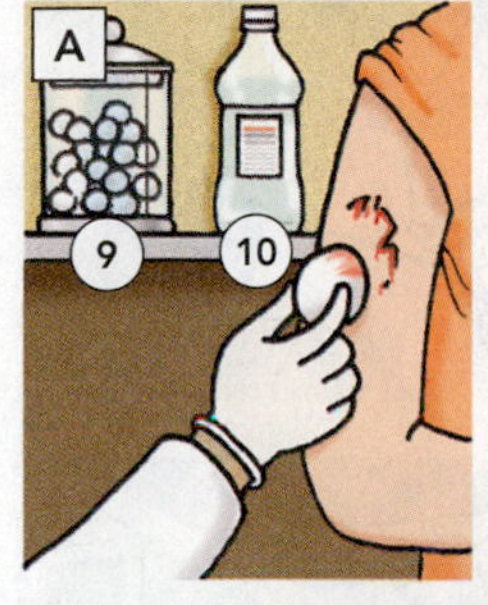

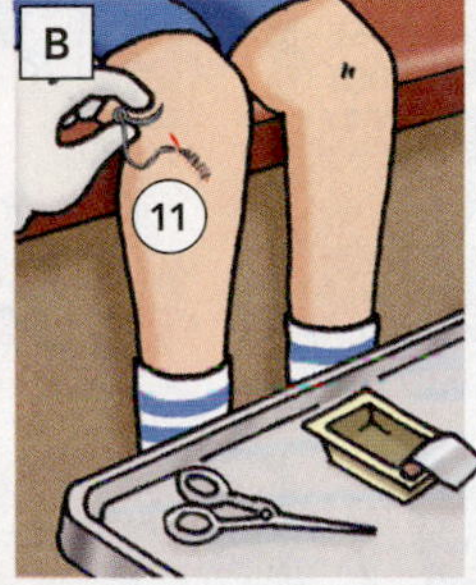

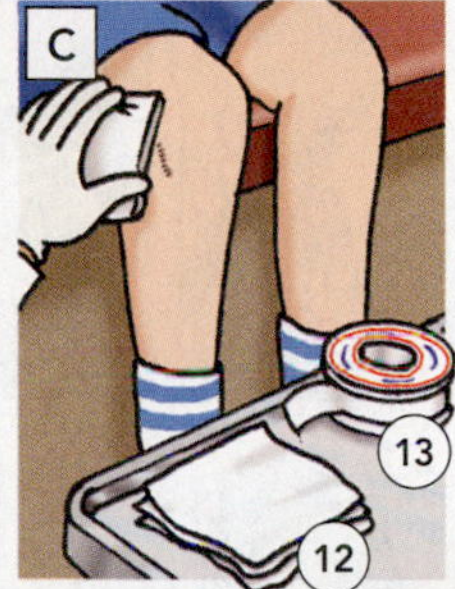

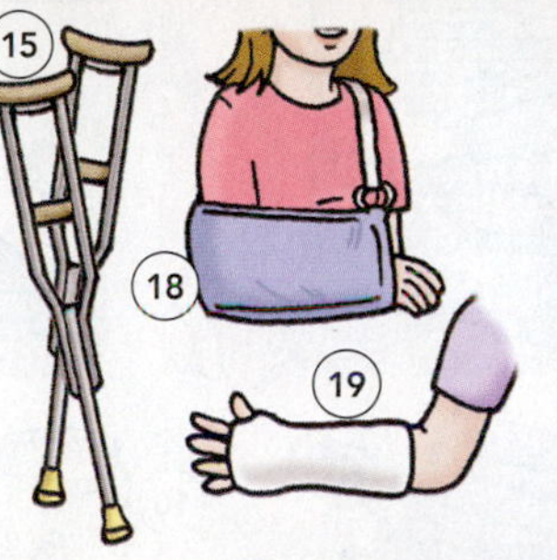

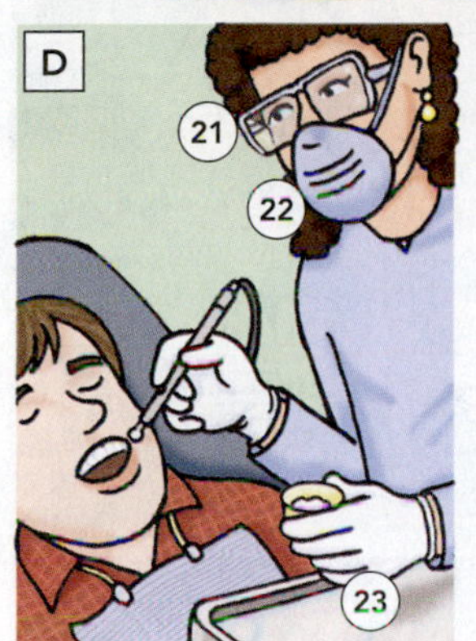

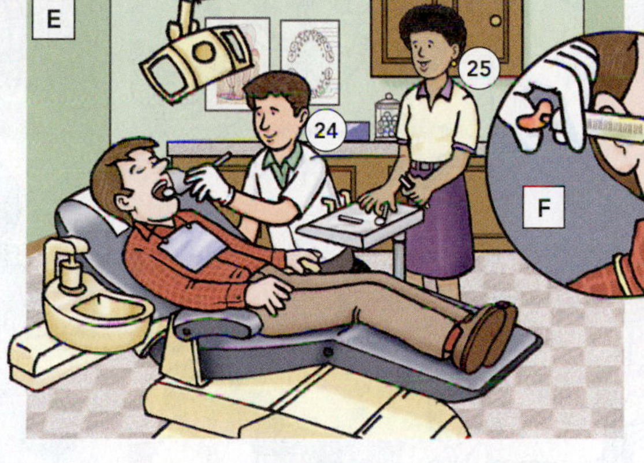

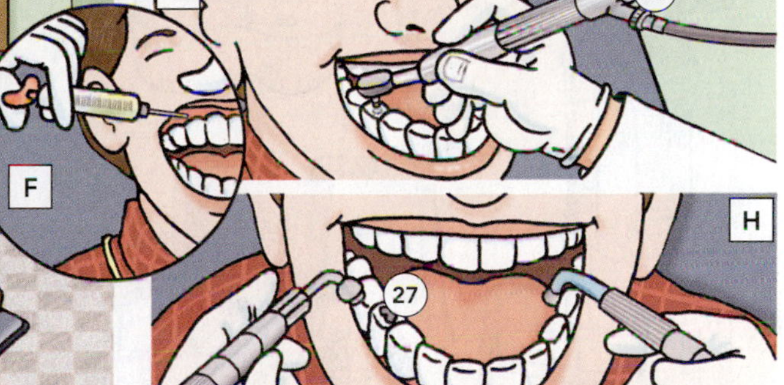

清洗傷口 **A** clean the wound
閉合傷口 **B** close the wound
包紮傷口 **C** dress the wound
洗你(妳)的牙齒 **D** clean *your* teeth
檢查你(妳)的牙齒 **E** examine *your* teeth
給你(妳)一針麻醉劑 **F** give *you* a shot of anesthetic/ Novocaine™
鑽蛀牙洞 **G** drill the cavity
補牙 **H** fill the tooth

候診室 **1** waiting room
接待員 **2** receptionist
健保卡/保險卡 **3** insurance card
醫療病史表格 **4** medical history form
檢查室 **5** examination room
醫生 **6** doctor/physician
病人 **7** patient
護士 **8** nurse
棉花球 **9** cotton balls
酒精 **10** alcohol
縫針 **11** stitches
紗布 **12** gauze
膠帶 **13** tape
打針 **14** injection/shot
丁字形枴杖 **15** crutches
冰袋 **16** ice pack
處方 **17** prescription
吊腕帶 **18** sling
固定用敷料/石膏 **19** cast
支架 **20** brace
牙科衛生員 **21** dental hygienist
口罩 **22** mask
手套 **23** gloves
牙醫 **24** dentist
牙科助理 **25** dental assistant
牙醫電鑽 **26** drill
補牙填充料 **27** filling

A. Now I'm going to { ___[A–H]___. / give you (a/an) ___[14–17]___. / put your .... in a ___[18–20]___.

B. Okay.

A. I need { ___[9, 10, 12, 13, 23]___. / a ___[22, 26]___.

B. Here you are.

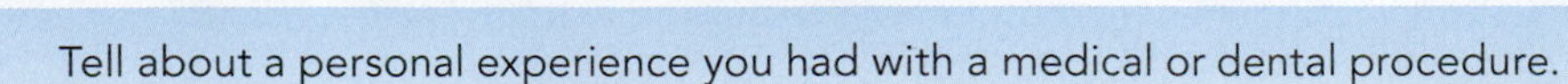

Tell about a personal experience you had with a medical or dental procedure.

MEDICAL ADVICE

醫生指示

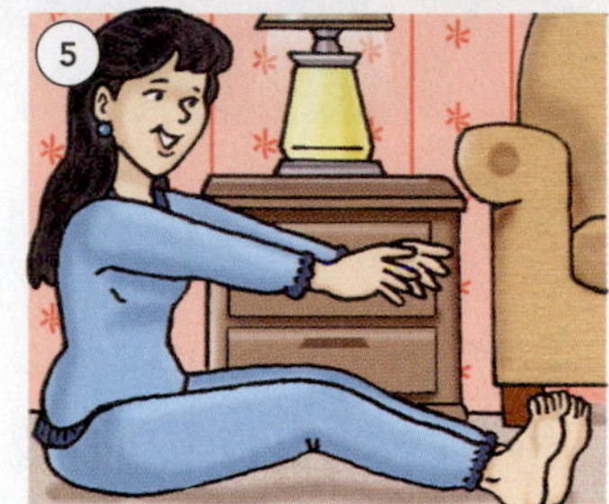

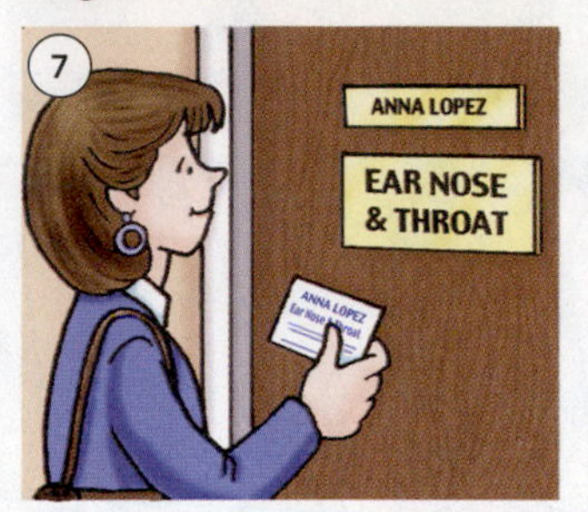

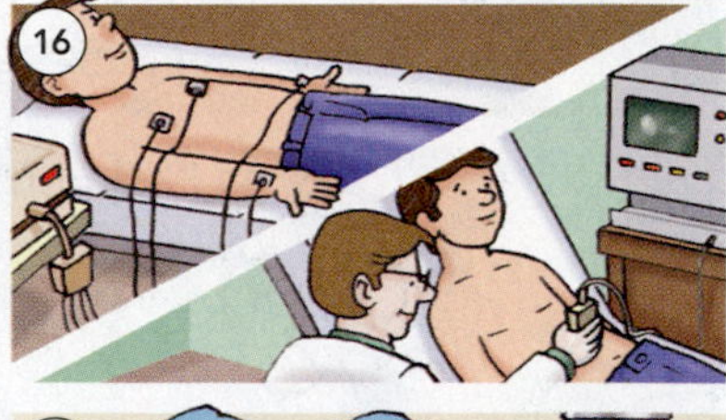
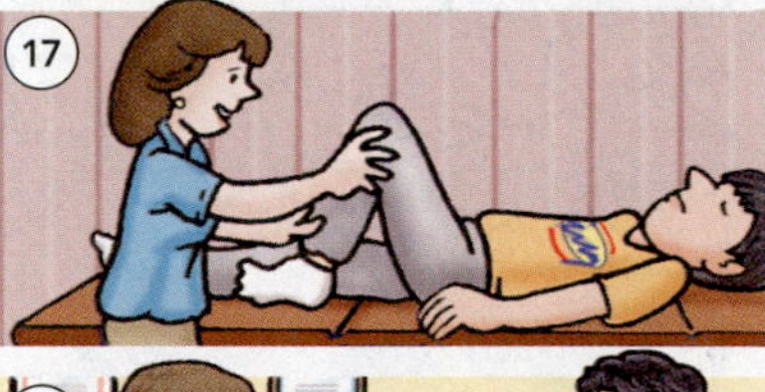
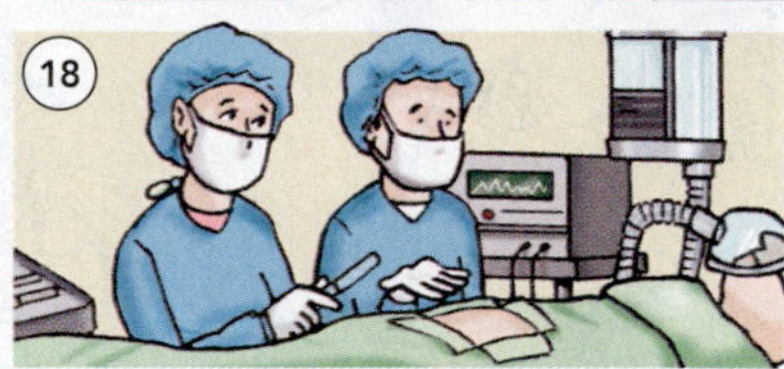

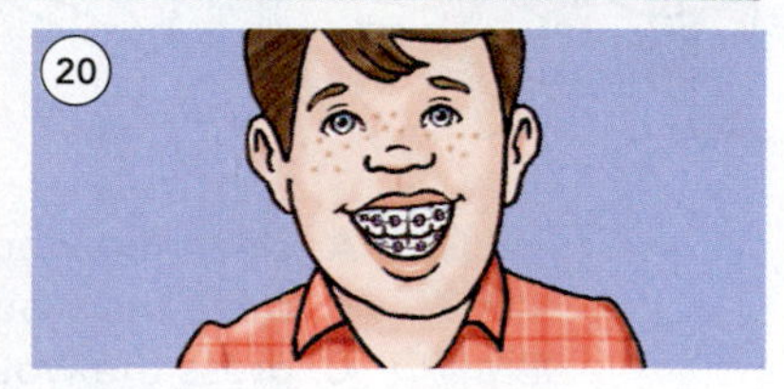

臥床休息 **1** rest in bed
喝液體 **2** drink fluids
漱口 **3** gargle
控制飲食 **4** go on a diet
作運動 **5** exercise
服用維他命 **6** take vitamins
看專科醫生 **7** see a specialist
針灸 **8** get acupuncture
熱敷墊 **9** heating pad
增濕氣 **10** humidifier

空氣清新機 **11** air purifier
柺杖 **12** cane
助行架 **13** walker
輪椅 **14** wheelchair
驗血 **15** blood work/blood tests
檢查 **16** tests
物理治療 **17** physical therapy
手術 **18** surgery
諮詢輔導 **19** counseling
牙齒矯正器 **20** braces

A. I think { you should ___[1–8]___. / you should use a/an ___[9–14]___. / you need ___[15–20]___.

B. I see.

A. What did the doctor say?

B. The doctor thinks { I should ___[1–8]___. / I should use a/an ___[9–14]___. / I need ___[15–20]___.

Tell about medical advice a doctor gave you. What did the doctor say? Did you follow the advice?

藥品

- 阿斯匹靈 **1** aspirin
- 感冒錠 **2** cold tablets
- 維他命 **3** vitamins
- 止咳糖漿 **4** cough syrup
- 不含阿斯匹靈止痛藥 **5** non-aspirin pain reliever
- 止咳糖 **6** cough drops
- 潤喉糖 **7** throat lozenges
- 健胃錠/制酸錠 **8** antacid tablets
- 鼻塞噴劑 **9** decongestant spray/nasal spray
- 眼藥水 **10** eye drops
- 軟膏 **11** ointment
- 乳霜 **12** cream/creme
- 乳液 **13** lotion
- 藥丸 **14** pill
- 藥片 **15** tablet
- 膠囊 **16** capsule
- 橢圓形藥錠 **17** caplet
- 茶匙 **18** teaspoon
- 湯匙 **19** tablespoon

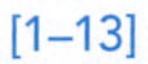

[1–13]
A. What did the doctor say?
B. She/He told me to take [1–4]/a [5].
She/He told me to use [6–13].

[14–19]
A. What's the dosage?
B. One ________ every four hours.

What medicines in this lesson do you have at home? What other medicines do you have?

What do you take or use for a fever? a headache? a stomachache? a sore throat? a cold? a cough?

Tell about any medicines in your country that are different from the ones in this lesson.

MEDICAL SPECIALISTS

醫療專家

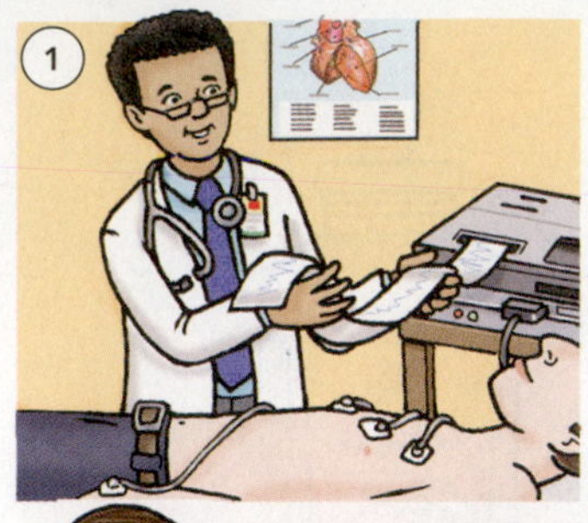

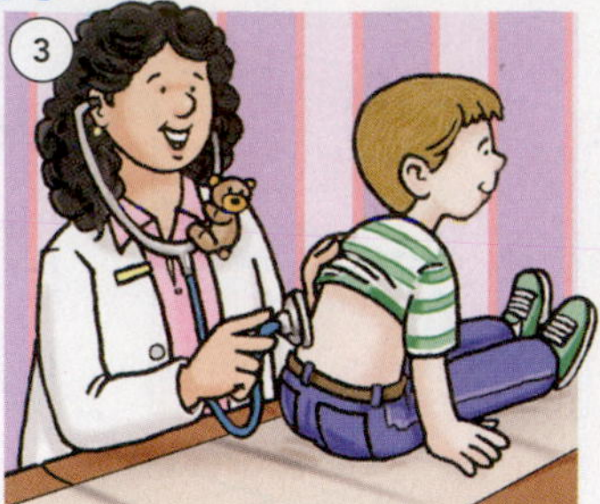

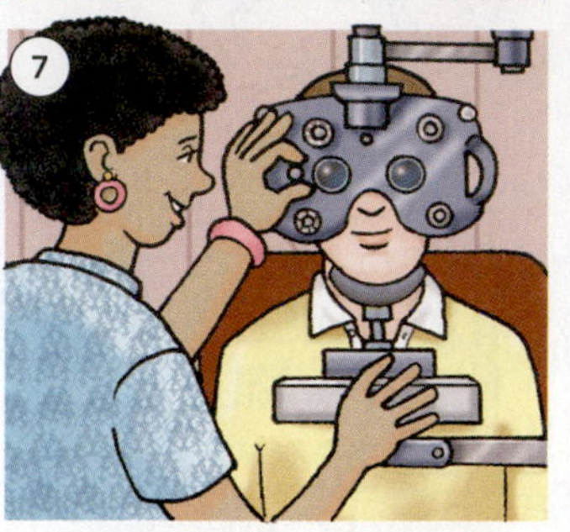

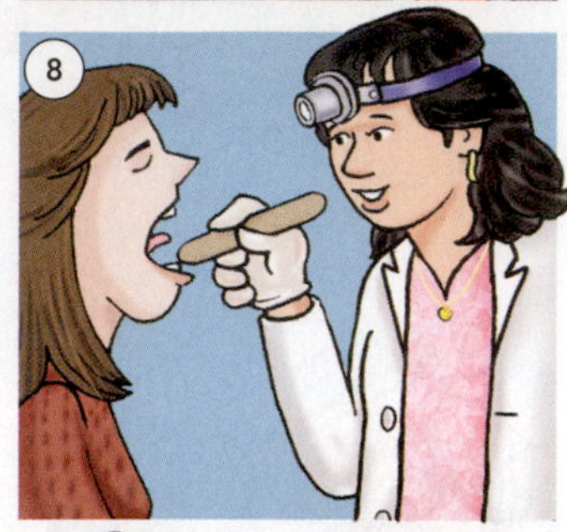

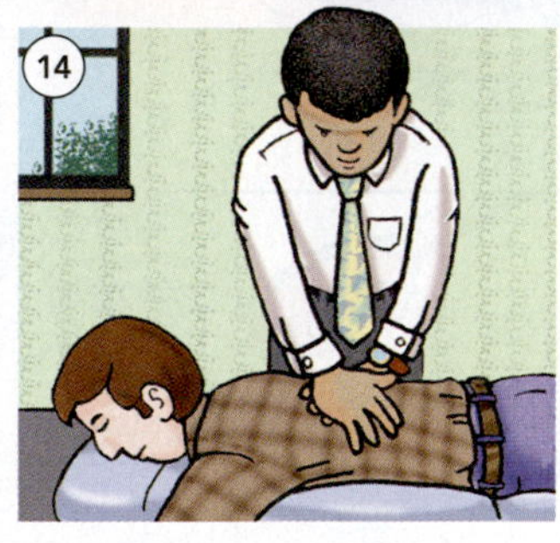

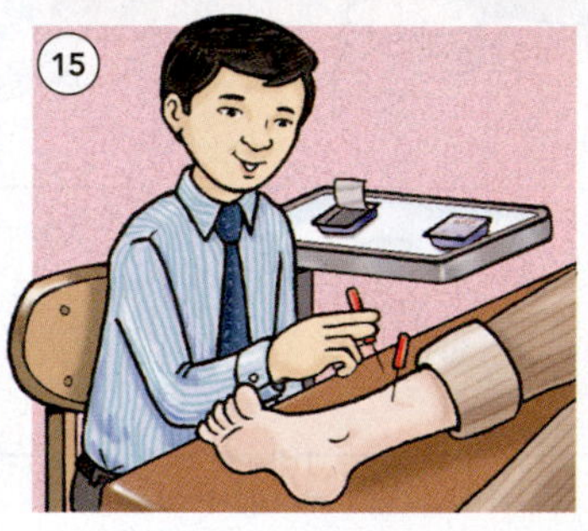

心臟病科醫師 **1** cardiologist
婦產科醫師 **2** gynecologist
小兒科醫師 **3** pediatrician
老年科醫師 **4** gerontologist
過敏症專科醫師 **5** allergist
矯形外科醫師 **6** orthopedist
眼科醫生 **7** ophthalmologist
耳鼻喉專科醫生 **8** ear, nose, and throat (ENT) specialist
聽力師/聽力檢查師 **9** audiologist
物理治療師 **10** physical therapist
諮詢輔導員/治療師 **11** counselor/therapist
精神病醫師 **12** psychiatrist
腸胃科醫生 **13** gastroenterologist
脊椎指壓治療師 **14** chiropractor
針灸醫生 **15** acupuncturist
牙齒矯正醫生 **16** orthodontist

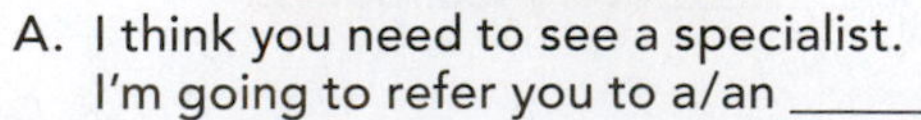

A. I think you need to see a specialist.
I'm going to refer you to a/an ______.
B. A/An ______?
A. Yes.

A. When is your next appointment with the ______?
B. It's at ......(time)...... on ......(date)......

Do you or members of your family see any of these medical specialists? Which ones?

醫院

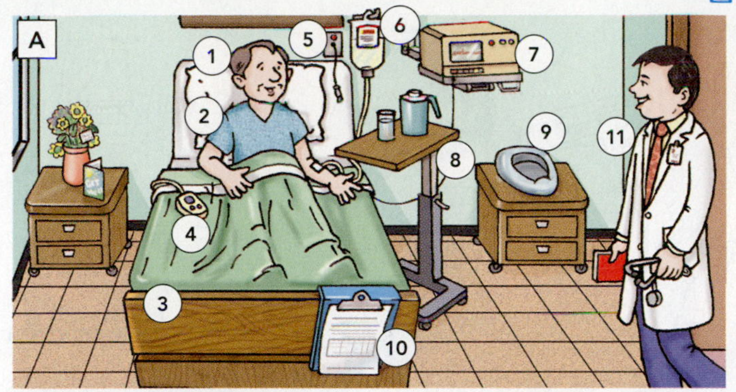

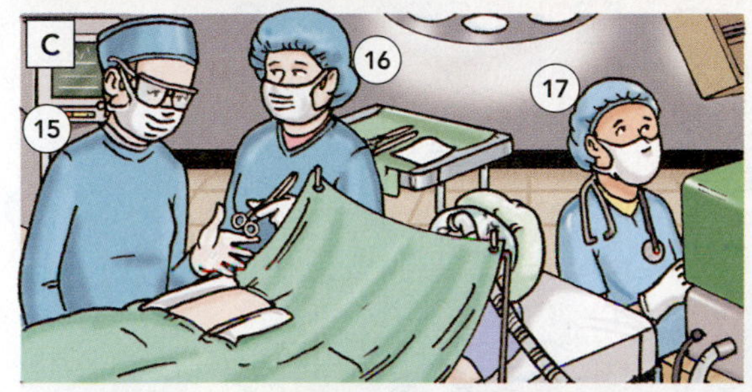

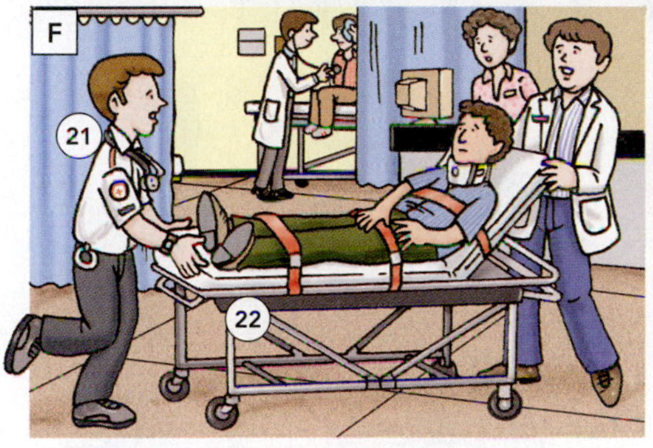

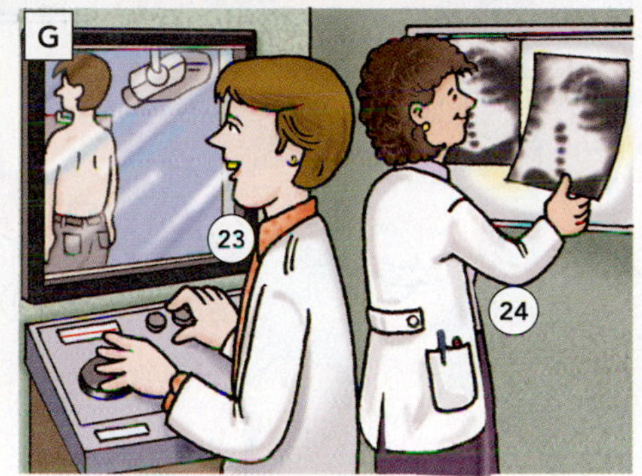

病房 **A patient's room**
- 病患 **1** patient
- 住院服 **2** hospital gown
- 病床 **3** hospital bed
- 病床控制器 **4** bed control
- 呼叫按鈕 **5** call button
- 靜脈注射 **6** I.V.
- 生命表徵監測器 **7** vital signs monitor
- 病床伸縮活動桌 **8** bed table
- (床上用)便盆 **9** bed pan
- 病歷 **10** medical chart
- 醫生 **11** doctor/physician

護士站 **B nurse's station**
- 護士 **12** nurse
- 營養學專家 **13** dietitian
- 護理員 **14** orderly

手術室 **C operating room**
- 外科醫生 **15** surgeon
- 外科護士 **16** surgical nurse
- 麻醉醫師 **17** anesthesiologist

等候室/候診室 **D waiting room**
- 義工 **18** volunteer

產房 **E birthing room/ delivery room**
- 產科醫師 **19** obstetrician
- 助產士 **20** midwife/nurse-midwife

急診室 **F emergency room/ ER**
- 緊急醫療技術人員 **21** emergency medical technician/EMT
- 輪床 **22** gurney

放射科 **G radiology department**
- X光技術員 **23** X-ray technician
- 放射線技師 **24** radiologist

檢驗室 **H laboratory/lab**
- 檢驗室技術員 **25** lab technician

A. This is your ___[2–10]___.
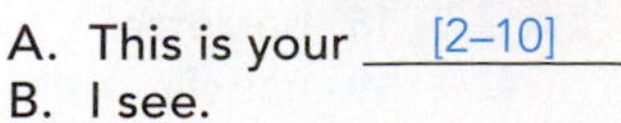
B. I see.

A. Do you work here?
B. Yes. I'm a/an ___[11–21, 23–25]___.

A. Where's the ___[11–21, 23–25]___?
B. She's/He's { in the ___[A, C–H]___. / at the ___[B]___.

Tell about an experience you or a family member had in the hospital.

個人衛生

刷我的牙齒 **A brush *my* teeth**
牙刷 1 toothbrush
牙膏 2 toothpaste

用牙線清潔我的牙齒 **B floss *my* teeth**
牙線 3 dental floss

漱口 **C gargle**
漱口水 4 mouthwash

美白我的牙齒 **D whiten *my* teeth**
牙齒美白劑 5 teeth whitener

盆浴 **E bathe/take a bath**
香皂 6 soap
泡泡沐浴露 7 bubble bath

淋浴 **F take a shower**
澡帽 8 shower cap

洗我的頭髮 **G wash *my* hair**
洗髮精 9 shampoo
潤髮乳 10 conditioner/rinse

弄乾我的頭髮 **H dry *my* hair**
吹風機 11 hair dryer/
blow dryer

梳我的頭髮 **I comb *my* hair**
尺梳 12 comb

梳我的頭髮 **J brush *my* hair**
梳子 13 (hair) brush

幫我的頭髮做造型 **K style *my* hair**
捲髮棒 14 hot comb/
curling iron
噴髮定型劑 15 hairspray
髮膠 16 hair gel
小髮夾 17 bobby pin
條狀髮夾 18 barrette
髮夾 19 hairclip

刮鬍子	**L**	**shave**
刮鬍膏	**20**	shaving cream
刮鬍刀	**21**	razor
刮鬍刀片	**22**	razor blade
電動刮鬍刀	**23**	electric shaver
止血筆	**24**	styptic pencil
刮鬍後潤膚液	**25**	aftershave (lotion)
修(塗)我的指甲	**M**	**do *my* nails**
指甲銼	**26**	nail file
指甲砂銼	**27**	emery board
剪指甲刀	**28**	nail clipper
指甲刷	**29**	nail brush
剪刀	**30**	scissors
指甲油	**31**	nail polish
去光水/洗甲水	**32**	nail polish remover
塗抹…	**N**	**put on . . .**
防臭劑	**33**	deodorant
護手乳液	**34**	hand lotion
身體潤膚乳液	**35**	body lotion
爽身粉	**36**	powder
古龍水/香水	**37**	cologne/perfume
防曬油	**38**	sunscreen
化妝	**O**	**put on makeup**
腮紅刷/腮紅	**39**	blush/rouge
粉底	**40**	foundation/base
潤膚露	**41**	moisturizer
粉餅	**42**	face powder
眼線筆	**43**	eyeliner
眼影	**44**	eye shadow
睫毛膏	**45**	mascara
眉筆	**46**	eyebrow pencil
口紅	**47**	lipstick
擦亮我的鞋	**P**	**polish *my* shoes**
鞋油	**48**	shoe polish
鞋帶	**49**	shoelaces

[A–M, N (33–38), O, P]
A. What are you doing?
B. I'm ________ing.

[1, 8, 11–14, 17–19, 21–24, 26–30, 46, 49]
A. Excuse me. Where can I find ________(s)?
B. They're in the next aisle.

[2–7, 9, 10, 15, 16, 20, 25, 31–45, 47, 48]
A. Excuse me. Where can I find ________?
B. It's in the next aisle.

Which of these personal care products do you use?

You're going on a trip. Make a list of the personal care products you need to take with you.

BABY CARE

育嬰

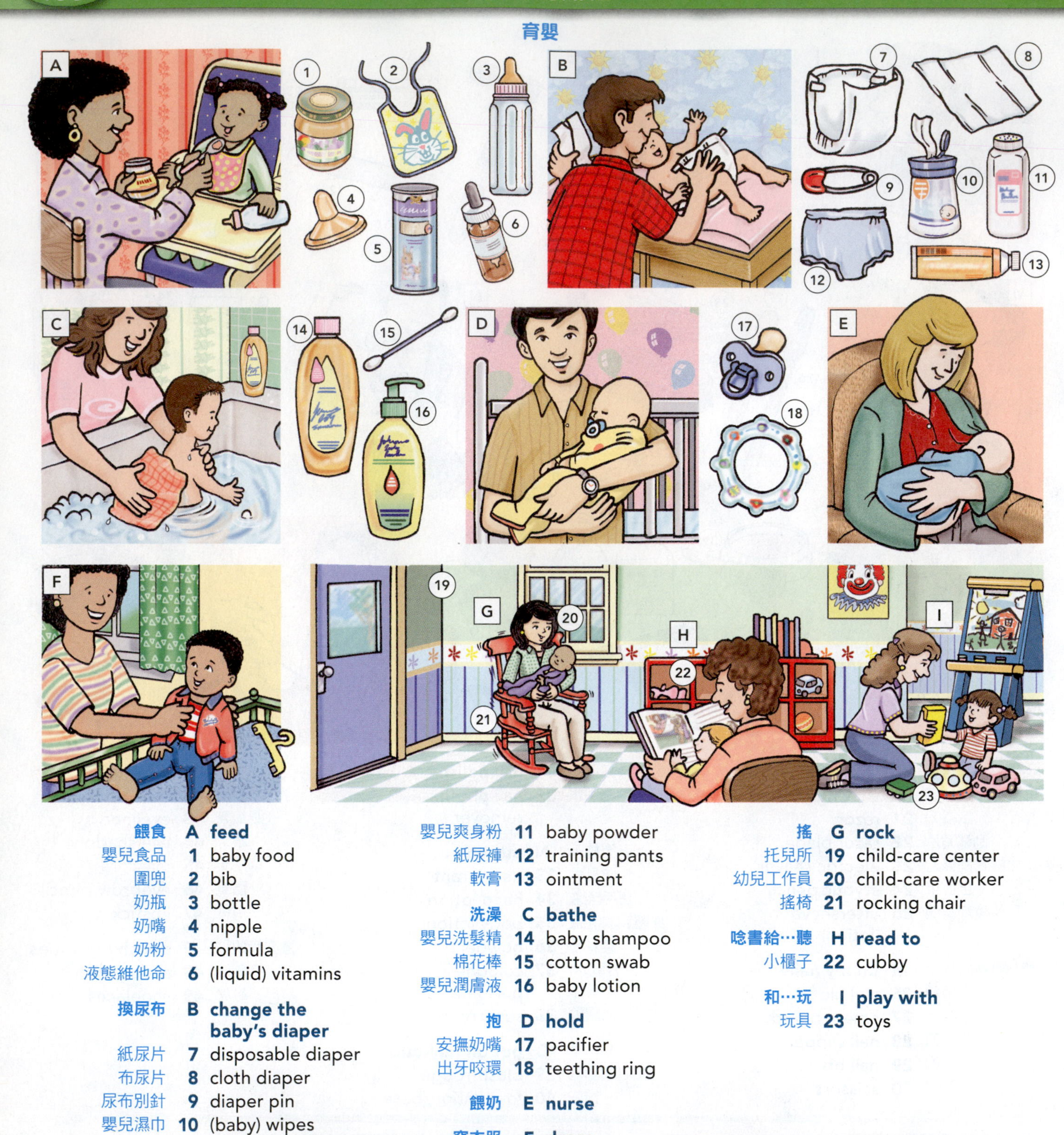

餵食	**A**	**feed**
嬰兒食品	**1**	baby food
圍兜	**2**	bib
奶瓶	**3**	bottle
奶嘴	**4**	nipple
奶粉	**5**	formula
液態維他命	**6**	(liquid) vitamins
換尿布	**B**	**change the baby's diaper**
紙尿片	**7**	disposable diaper
布尿片	**8**	cloth diaper
尿布別針	**9**	diaper pin
嬰兒濕巾	**10**	(baby) wipes
嬰兒爽身粉	**11**	baby powder
紙尿褲	**12**	training pants
軟膏	**13**	ointment
洗澡	**C**	**bathe**
嬰兒洗髮精	**14**	baby shampoo
棉花棒	**15**	cotton swab
嬰兒潤膚液	**16**	baby lotion
抱	**D**	**hold**
安撫奶嘴	**17**	pacifier
出牙咬環	**18**	teething ring
餵奶	**E**	**nurse**
穿衣服	**F**	**dress**
搖	**G**	**rock**
托兒所	**19**	child-care center
幼兒工作員	**20**	child-care worker
搖椅	**21**	rocking chair
唸書給…聽	**H**	**read to**
小櫃子	**22**	cubby
和…玩	**I**	**play with**
玩具	**23**	toys

A. What are you doing?

B. { I'm ___[A, C–I]___ing the baby.
I'm ___[B]___ing.

A. Do we need anything from the store?

B. Yes. We need some more { ___[2–4, 7–9, 15, 17, 18]___s
___[1, 5, 6, 10–14, 16]___.

In your opinion, which are better: cloth diapers or disposable diapers? Why?

Tell about baby products in your country.

TYPES OF SCHOOLS

學校種類

幼稚園/托兒所 **1** preschool/nursery school
小學 **2** elementary school
中學 **3** middle school/ junior high school
高中 **4** high school
成人學校 **5** adult school
職業學校 **6** vocational school/trade school
社區學院 **7** community college
學院 **8** college
大學 **9** university
研究所 **10** graduate school
法學院 **11** law school
醫學院 **12** medical school

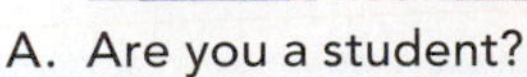

A. Are you a student?
B. Yes. I'm in [1–4, 8, 10–12].

A. Are you a student?
B. Yes. I go to a/an [5–7, 9].

A. Is this apartment building near a/an ________?
B. Yes. *(name of school)* is nearby.

A. Tell me about your previous education.
B. I went to *(name of school)*.
A. Did you like it there?
B. Yes. It was an excellent ________.

What types of schools are there in your community? What are their names, and where are they located?

What types of schools have you gone to? Where? When? What did you study?

學校

辦公室	A	(main) office
校長室	B	principal's office
護理辦公室	C	nurse's office
輔導室/訓導處	D	guidance office
教室	E	classroom
走廊	F	hallway
衣物櫃	a	locker
自然科學實驗室	G	science lab
室內體育館	H	gym/gymnasium
更衣間	a	locker room
跑道	I	track
露天看台	a	bleachers
運動場	J	field
大禮堂	K	auditorium
餐廳	L	cafeteria
圖書館	M	library
學校職員/學校秘書	1	clerk/(school) secretary
校長	2	principal
駐校護士	3	(school) nurse
學生輔導顧問/訓導員	4	(guidance) counselor
老師	5	teacher
副校長	6	assistant principal/ vice-principal
警衛人員	7	security officer
自然科學老師	8	science teacher
體育老師	9	P.E. teacher
教練	10	coach
管理員	11	custodian
餐廳工作人員	12	cafeteria worker
餐廳糾察員	13	lunchroom monitor
學校圖書館管理員	14	(school) librarian

A. Where are you going?
B. I'm going to the [A–D, G–M].
A. Do you have a hall pass?
B. Yes. Here it is.

A. Where's the [1–14]?
B. He's/She's in the [A–M].

Describe the school where you study English.
Tell about the rooms, offices, and people.

Tell about differences between the school in this lesson and schools in your country.

學科

數學	**1**	math/mathematics
英語	**2**	English
歷史	**3**	history
地理	**4**	geography
政府體制	**5**	government
自然	**6**	science
生物	**7**	biology
化學	**8**	chemistry
物理	**9**	physics
健康教育	**10**	health
電腦科學	**11**	computer science
西班牙語	**12**	Spanish
法語	**13**	French
家政	**14**	home economics
工業技術	**15**	industrial arts/shop
商業教育	**16**	business education
體育	**17**	physical education/P.E.
駕駛班	**18**	driver's education/driver's ed
藝術	**19**	art
音樂	**20**	music

A. What do you have next period?
B. **Math**. How about you?
A. **English**.
B. There's the bell. I've got to go.

What is/was your favorite subject? Why?

In your opinion, what's the most interesting subject? the most difficult subject? Why do you think so?

課外活動

High School Times
October 9, 2005
Volume 4
AMY JONES NEW CLASS PRESIDENT
Beats Sue Ross by 2 votes.

樂隊	1	band
管絃樂團	2	orchestra
合唱團	3	choir/chorus
戲劇表演	4	drama
足球	5	football
啦啦隊	6	cheerleading/pep squad
學生會	7	student government
社區服務	8	community service
校報	9	school newspaper
學校年冊	10	yearbook
文學雜誌	11	literary magazine
影音小組	12	A.V. crew
辯論社團	13	debate club
電腦社團	14	computer club
國際社團	15	international club
西洋棋社	16	chess club

A. Are you going home right after school?
B. { No. I have ___[1–6]___ practice.
  { No. I have a ___[7–16]___ meeting.

What extracurricular activities do/did you participate in?

Which extracurricular activities in this lesson are there in schools in your country? What other activities are there?

數學

Arithmetic 算數

2+1=3 8-3=5 4x2=8 10÷2=5

加法 addition	減法 subtraction	乘法 multiplication	除法 division
2 **plus** 1 **equals*** 3.	8 **minus** 3 **equals*** 5.	4 **times** 2 **equals*** 8.	10 **divided by** 2 **equals*** 5.

You can also say:* **is

A. How much is *two plus one?*
B. *Two plus one* equals/is *three.*

Make conversations for the arithmetic problems above and others.

Fractions 分數

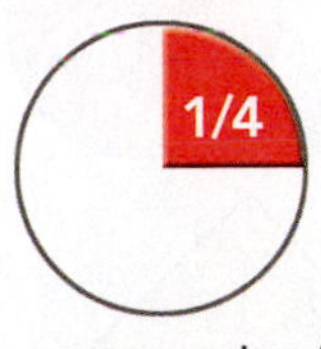

one quarter/ one fourth

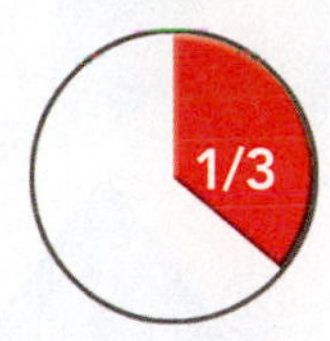

one third

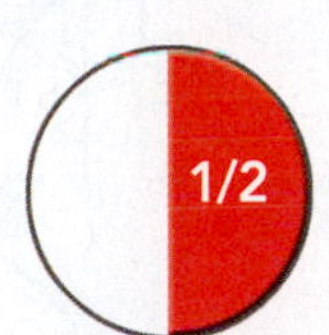

one half/ half

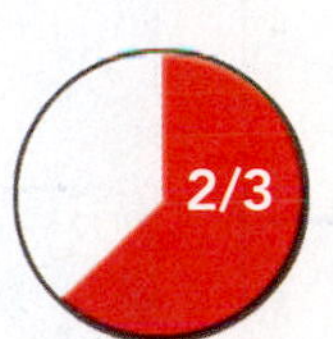

two thirds

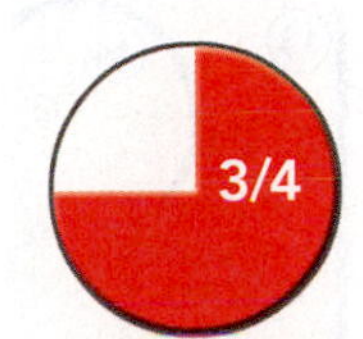

three quarters/ three fourths

A. Is this on sale?
B. Yes. It's _______ off the regular price.

A. Is the gas tank almost empty?
B. It's about _______ full.

Percents 百分比

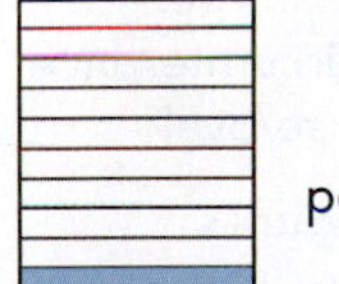
10% ten percent

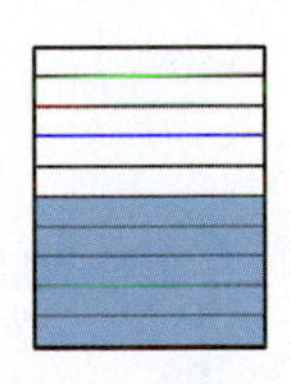
50% fifty percent

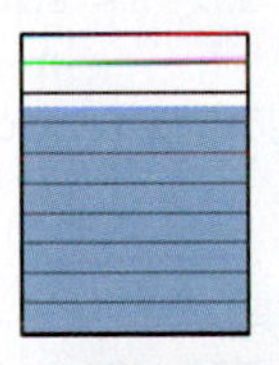
75% seventy-five percent

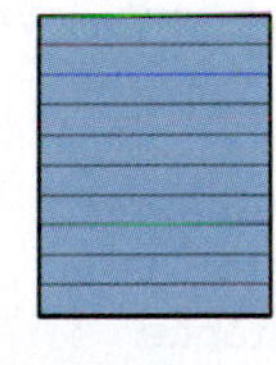
100% one-hundred percent

A. How did you do on the test?
B. I got _______ percent of the answers right.

A. What's the weather forecast?
B. There's a _______ percent chance of rain.

Types of Math 數學種類

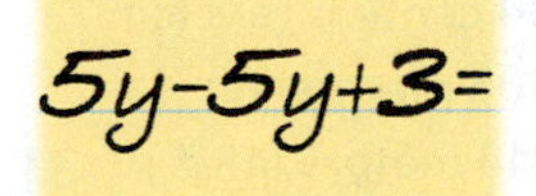

algebra 代數

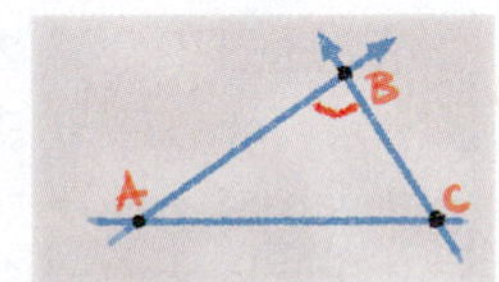

geometry 幾何

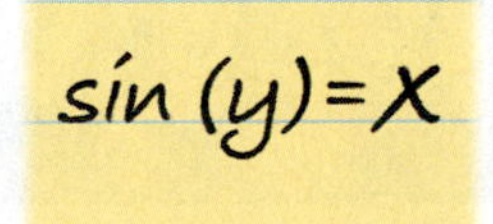

trigonometry 三角

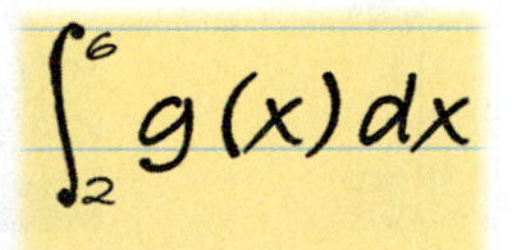

calculus 微積分

statistics 統計學

A. What math course are you taking this year?
B. I'm taking _______.

Are you good at math?

What math courses do/did you take in school?

Tell about something you bought on sale. How much off the regular price was it?

Research and discuss: What percentage of people in your country live in cities? live on farms? work in factories? vote in general elections?

測量及幾何形狀

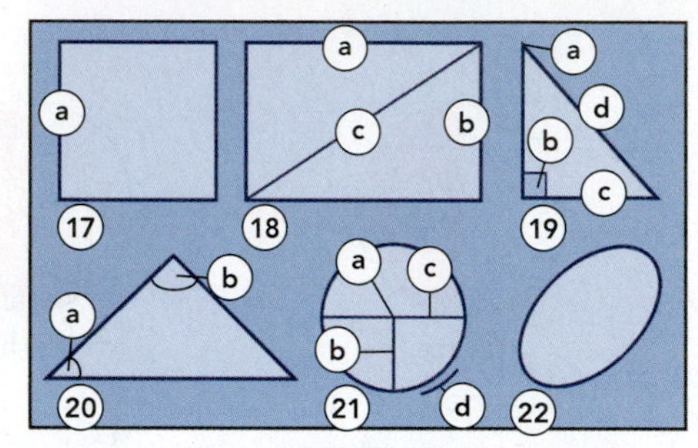

測量 Measurements

- 高度 **1** height
- 寬度 **2** width
- 深度 **3** depth
- 長度 **4** length
- 吋 **5** inch
- 英尺(單數)-英尺(複數) **6** foot–feet
- 碼 **7** yard
- 公分 **8** centimeter
- 公尺 **9** meter
- 距離 **10** distance
- 英里/哩 **11** mile
- 公里 **12** kilometer

線 Lines

- 直線 **13** straight line
- 曲線 **14** curved line
- 平行線 **15** parallel lines
- 垂直線 **16** perpendicular lines

幾何形狀 Geometric Shapes

- 正方形 **17** square
  - 邊 **a** side
- 長方形 **18** rectangle
  - 長 **a** length
  - 寬 **b** width
  - 對角線 **c** diagonal
- 直角三角形 **19** right triangle
  - 頂點 **a** apex
  - 直角 **b** right angle
  - 底邊 **c** base
  - 直角三角形之斜邊 **d** hypotenuse
- 等腰三角形 **20** isosceles triangle
  - 銳角三角形 **a** acute angle
  - 鈍角三角形 **b** obtuse angle
- 圓形 **21** circle
  - 中心 **a** center
  - 半徑 **b** radius
  - 直徑 **c** diameter
  - 圓周 **d** circumference
- 橢圓 **22** ellipse/oval

立體圖形 Solid Figures

- 立方體 **23** cube
- 圓柱體 **24** cylinder
- 球體 **25** sphere
- 圓錐體 **26** cone
- 三角椎體 **27** pyramid

[1–9]
A. What's the ___[1–4]___?
B. .... ___[5–9]___(s).

[11–12]
A. What's the distance?
B. .... ______(s).

1 inch (1″)	=	2.54 centimeters (cm)
1 foot (1′)	=	0.305 meters (m)
1 yard (1 yd.)	=	0.914 meters (m)
1 mile (mi.)	=	1.6 kilometers (km)

[17–22]
A. Who can tell me what shape this is?
B. I can. It's a/an ______.

[23–27]
A. Who knows what figure this is?
B. I do. It's a/an ______.

[13–27]
A. This painting is magnificent!
B. Hmm. I don't think so. It just looks like a lot of ______s and ______s to me!

英文與作文

Types of Sentences & Parts of Speech 句子種類及詞類

A Students(1) study(2) in(3) the(4) new(5) library.

B Do they(6) study hard(7)?

C Read page nine.

D This cake is fantastic!

敘述的 **A** declarative	名詞 **1** noun	形容詞 **5** adjective
疑問的 **B** interrogative	動詞 **2** verb	代名詞 **6** pronoun
命令式的 **C** imperative	介係詞 **3** preposition	副詞 **7** adverb
驚嘆的 **D** exclamatory	冠詞 **4** article	

A. What type of sentence is this?
B. It's a/an __[A–D]__ sentence.

A. What part of speech is this?
B. It's a/an __[1–7]__.

Punctuation Marks & the Writing Process 標點符號及寫作過程

句點 **8** period	激發構思 **16** brainstorm ideas
問號 **9** question mark	整理我的構思 **17** organize *my* ideas
驚嘆號 **10** exclamation point	寫初稿 **18** write a first draft
逗點 **11** comma	題目 **a** title
撇號 **12** apostrophe	段落 **b** paragraph
引號 **13** quotation marks	修改 **19** make corrections/revise/edit
冒號 **14** colon	得到意見 **20** get feedback
分號 **15** semi-colon	寫完成稿/重寫 **21** write a final copy/rewrite

A. Did you find any mistakes?
B. Yes. You forgot to put a/an __[8–15]__ in this sentence.

A. Are you working on your composition?
B. Yes. I'm __[16–21]__ing.

文學與寫作

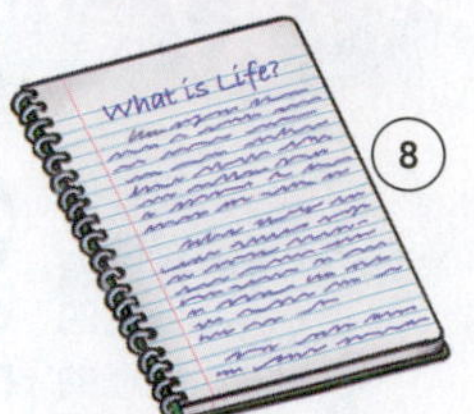

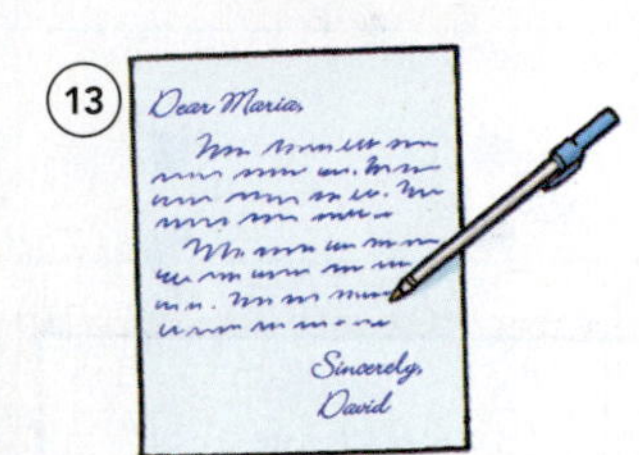

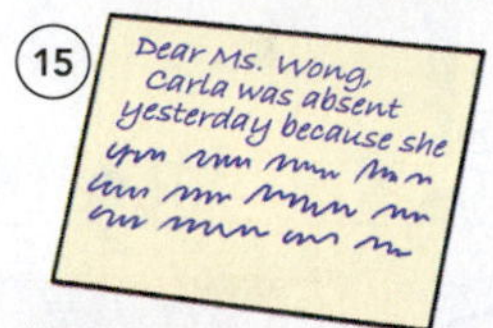

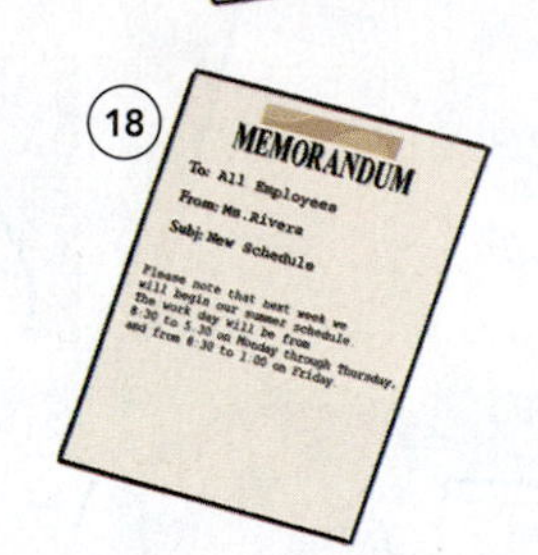

虛構小說	**1** fiction	文章/隨筆	**8** essay	紙簽/便條	**15** note
長篇小說	**2** novel	報導	**9** report	邀請函	**16** invitation
短篇故事	**3** short story	雜誌文章	**10** magazine article	感謝函	**17** thank-you note
詩歌/詩	**4** poetry/poems	報紙文章	**11** newspaper article	備忘錄	**18** memo
非虛構小說	**5** non-fiction	社論	**12** editorial	電子郵件	**19** e-mail
傳記	**6** biography	信	**13** letter	即時通訊	**20** instant message
自傳	**7** autobiography	明信片	**14** postcard		

A. What are you doing?

B. I'm writing { [1, 4, 5] . / a/an [2, 3, 6–20] .

What kind of literature do you like to read? What are some of your favorite books? Who is your favorite author?

Do you like to read newspapers and magazines? Which ones do you read?

Do you sometimes send or receive letters, postcards, notes, e-mail, or instant messages? Tell about the people you communicate with, and how.

GEOGRAPHY

地理

森林 **1** forest/woods
山丘 **2** hill
山脈 **3** mountain range
山峰 **4** mountain peak
山谷 **5** valley
湖 **6** lake
平原 **7** plains
草地 **8** meadow
小溪 **9** stream/brook
池塘 **10** pond
高原 **11** plateau
峽谷 **12** canyon
沙丘 **13** dune/sand dune
沙漠 **14** desert
叢林 **15** jungle
海岸/海濱 **16** seashore/shore
海灣 **17** bay
海洋 **18** ocean
島嶼 **19** island
半島 **20** peninsula
雨林 **21** rainforest
河流 **22** river
瀑布 **23** waterfall

A. { Isn't this a beautiful ________?!
  { Aren't these beautiful ________s?!
B. Yes. It's/They're magnificent!

Tell about the geography of your country. Describe the different geographic features.

Have you seen some of the geographic features in this lesson? Which ones? Where?

SCIENCE

自然科學

科學實驗設備 Science Equipment

顯微鏡 **1** microscope
電腦 **2** computer
(顯微鏡用)載波片/載片 **3** slide
(做細菌培養的)有蓋培養皿 **4** Petri dish
(實驗用)燒瓶/長頸瓶 **5** flask
漏斗 **6** funnel
燒杯 **7** beaker
試管 **8** test tube
鑷子 **9** forceps
坩堝鉗 **10** crucible tongs
本生燈 **11** Bunsen burner
玻璃刻度量筒 **12** graduated cylinder
磁鐵 **13** magnet
稜鏡 **14** prism
滴管 **15** dropper
化學品 **16** chemicals
天平 **17** balance
秤 **18** scale

科學方法 The Scientific Method

陳述疑問 **A** state the problem
提出假設 **B** form a hypothesis
擬定研究步驟 **C** plan a procedure
執行研究步驟 **D** do a procedure
記錄觀察 **E** make/record observations
作出結論 **F** draw conclusions

A. What do we need to do this procedure?
B. We need a/an/the [1–18].

A. How is your experiment coming along?
B. I'm getting ready to [A–F].

Do you have experience with the scientific equipment in this lesson? Tell about it.

What science courses do/did you take in school?

Think of an idea for a science experiment.
What question about science do you want to answer? State the problem.
What do you think will happen in the experiment? Form a hypothesis.
How can you test your hypothesis? Plan a procedure.

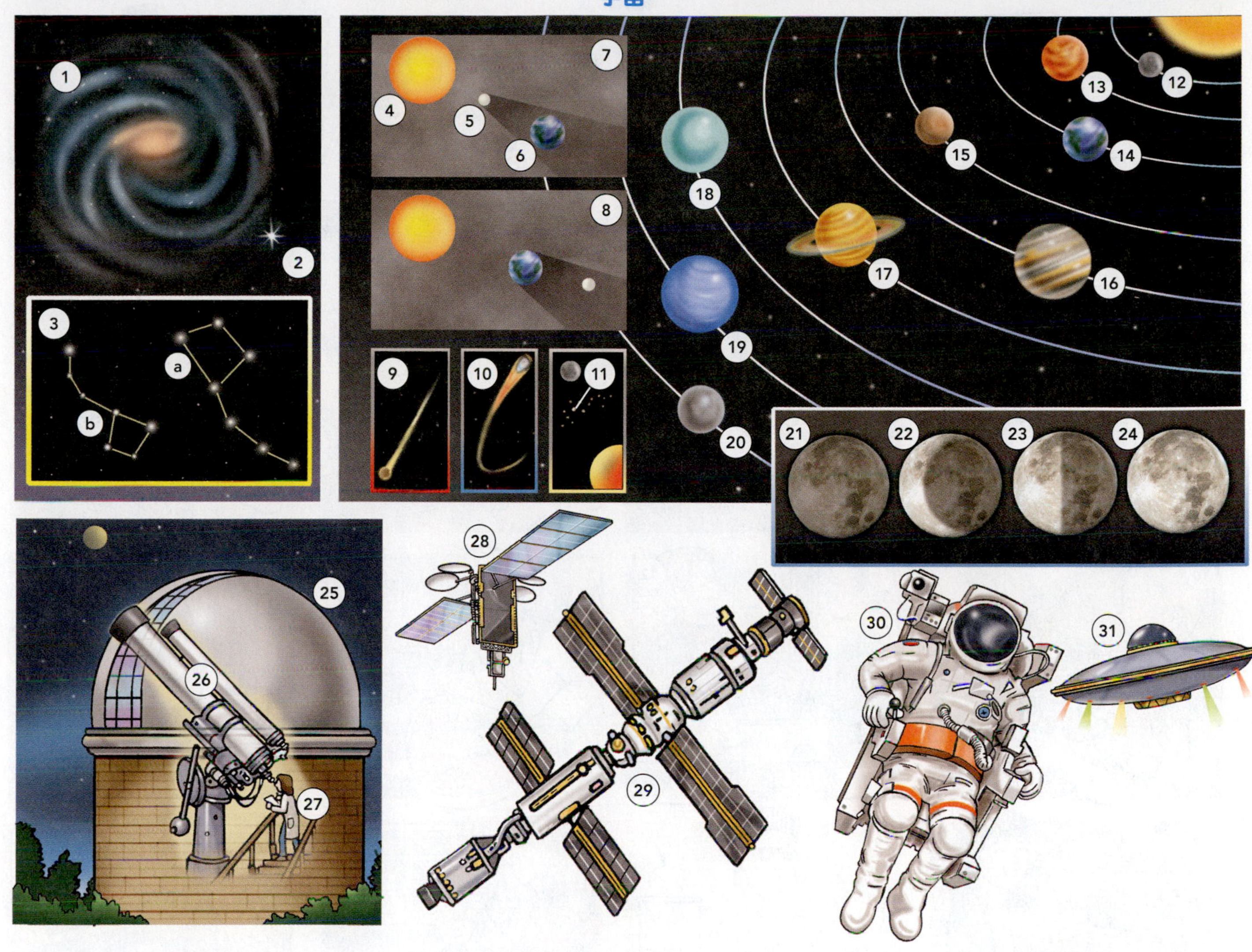

宇宙 The Universe

- 銀河系 **1** galaxy
- 恆星 **2** star
- 星座 **3** constellation
  - 大北斗星 **a** The Big Dipper
  - 小北斗星 **b** The Little Dipper

太陽系 The Solar System

- 太陽 **4** sun
- 月球 **5** moon
- 行星 **6** planet
- 日蝕 **7** solar eclipse
- 月蝕 **8** lunar eclipse
- 流星 **9** meteor
- 彗星 **10** comet
- 小行星 **11** asteroid
- 水星 **12** Mercury
- 金星 **13** Venus
- 地球 **14** Earth
- 火星 **15** Mars
- 木星 **16** Jupiter
- 土星 **17** Saturn
- 天王星 **18** Uranus
- 海王星 **19** Neptune
- 冥王星 **20** Pluto
- 新月 **21** new moon
- 娥眉月 **22** crescent moon
- 弦月 **23** quarter moon
- 滿月 **24** full moon

天文學 Astronomy

- 天文臺/觀測所 **25** observatory
- (單筒)望遠鏡 **26** telescope
- 天文學家 **27** astronomer

太空探索 Space Exploration

- 衛星 **28** satellite
- 太空站 **29** space station
- 太空人 **30** astronaut
- 幽浮/不明飛行物體/幽浮/飛碟 **31** U.F.O./Unidentified Flying Object/flying saucer

[1–24]
A. Is that (a/an/the) ________?
B. I'm not sure. I think it might be (a/an/the) ________.

[28–30]
A. Is the ________ ready for tomorrow's launch?
B. Yes. "All systems are go!"

Pretend you are an astronaut traveling in space. What do you see?

Draw and name a constellation you are familiar with.

Do you think space exploration is important? Why?

Have you ever seen a U.F.O.? Do you believe there is life in outer space? Why?

職業 1

會計	1	accountant
男演員	2	actor
女演員	3	actress
建築師	4	architect
藝術家	5	artist
裝配工	6	assembler
保姆	7	babysitter
麵包師傅	8	baker
理髮師	9	barber
砌磚匠/石匠	10	bricklayer/mason
商人	11	businessman
女商人	12	businesswoman
屠夫	13	butcher
木匠	14	carpenter
收銀員	15	cashier
廚師	16	chef/cook
托兒所工作人員	17	child day-care worker
電腦軟體工程師	18	computer software engineer
建築工人	19	construction worker
清潔工	20	custodian/janitor
客服人員	21	customer service representative
數據輸入員	22	data entry clerk

送貨員 **23** delivery person
碼頭工人 **24** dockworker
工程師 **25** engineer
工廠工人 **26** factory worker
農夫 **27** farmer
救火員 **28** firefighter
漁夫 **29** fisher

餐飲服務人員 **30** food-service worker
工頭 **31** foreman
園丁/庭院設計師 **32** gardener/landscaper
製衣工人 **33** garment worker
美髮師 **34** hairdresser
護理人員 **35** health-care aide/attendant

家庭護理人員 **36** home health aide/home attendant
家庭主婦(夫) **37** homemaker
管家/飯店客房清潔員 **38** housekeeper

A. What do you do?
B. I'm an **accountant**. How about you?
A. I'm a **carpenter**.

[At a job interview]

A. Are you an experienced ________?
B. Yes. I'm a very experienced ________.

A. How long have you been a/an ________?
B. I've been a/an ________ for .... months/years.

Which of these occupations do you think are the most interesting? the most difficult? Why?

職業 2

- 新聞記者 **1** journalist/reporter
- 律師 **2** lawyer
- 機床操作工 **3** machine operator
- 郵差 **4** mail carrier/letter carrier
- 經理 **5** manager
- 指甲修飾師 **6** manicurist
- 汽車修理員 **7** mechanic
- 醫療助理員 **8** medical assistant/ physician assistant
- 快遞人員 **9** messenger/courier
- 搬運工人 **10** mover
- 音樂家 **11** musician
- 油漆工人 **12** painter
- 藥劑師 **13** pharmacist
- 攝影師 **14** photographer
- 飛行員 **15** pilot
- 警察 **16** police officer
- 郵局辦事員 **17** postal worker
- 接待員 **18** receptionist
- 修理人員 **19** repairperson
- 推銷員 **20** salesperson

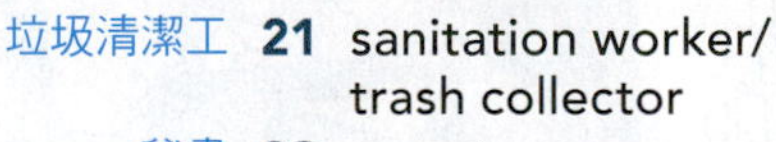

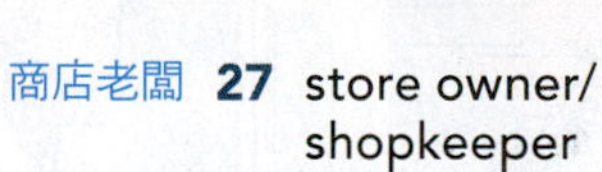

垃圾清潔工 **21** sanitation worker/trash collector
秘書 **22** secretary
警衛 **23** security guard
軍人 **24** serviceman
女軍人 **25** servicewoman
存貨管理員 **26** stock clerk
商店老闆 **27** store owner/shopkeeper
主管/督導人員 **28** supervisor
裁縫 **29** tailor
教師 **30** teacher/instructor
電話銷售員 **31** telemarketer
翻譯員/口譯員 **32** translator/interpreter
旅遊業者 **33** travel agent
卡車司機 **34** truck driver
獸醫 **35** veterinarian/vet
服務生/上菜者 **36** waiter/server
女服務生/上菜者 **37** waitress/server
焊接工 **38** welder

A. What's your occupation?
B. I'm a **journalist**.
A. A **journalist**?
B. Yes. That's right.

A. Are you still a ______?
B. No. I'm a ______.
A. Oh. That's interesting.

A. What kind of job would you like in the future?
B. I'd like to be a ______.

Do you work? What's your occupation?

What are the occupations of people in your family?

工作技能與活動

表演	**1**	act
裝配零件	**2**	assemble *components*
協助病人	**3**	assist *patients*
烘烤	**4**	bake
建造物品	**5**	build *things*/construct *things*
清掃	**6**	clean
烹調/煮	**7**	cook
送披薩餅	**8**	deliver *pizzas*
設計建築物	**9**	design *buildings*
繪(圖)	**10**	draw
開卡車	**11**	drive *a truck*
存檔	**12**	file
開飛機	**13**	fly *an airplane*
種菜	**14**	grow *vegetables*
守衛	**15**	guard *buildings*
經營餐廳	**16**	manage *a restaurant*
除草	**17**	mow *lawns*
操作器械	**18**	operate *equipment*
油漆	**19**	paint
彈鋼琴	**20**	play the *piano*

烹調食物 **21** prepare *food*
修理東西 **22** repair *things*/fix *things*
賣車 **23** sell *cars*
上菜 **24** serve *food*
縫紉 **25** sew
唱歌 **26** sing
說西班牙語 **27** speak *Spanish*
監督人員 **28** supervise *people*

照顧老人 **29** take care of *elderly people*
盤點/點清存貨 **30** take inventory
教書 **31** teach
翻譯 **32** translate
打字 **33** type
使用收銀機 **34** use *a cash register*
洗碗盤 **35** wash *dishes*
寫作 **36** write

A. Can you **act**?
B. Yes, I can.

A. Do you know how to ________?
B. Yes. I've been ________ing for years.

A. Tell me about your skills.
B. I can ________, and I can ________.

Tell about your job skills.
What can you do?

JOB SEARCH
求職

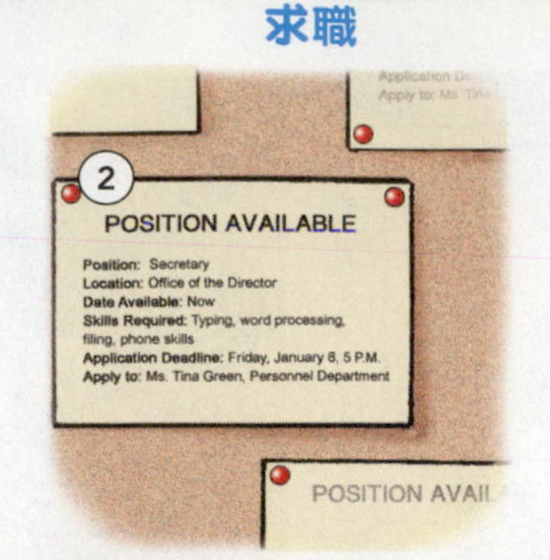

③ **CASHIERS**

FT ④ & PT ⑤ positions avail. ⑥ $11/hr. ⑦
M-F. ⑧ Days & eves. ⑨ Prev. ⑩ exper. ⑪ req. ⑫
Excel. ⑬ salary. Save-Mart, 2540 Central Ave.

各類招聘廣告 Types of Job Ads

招聘牌示	**1**	help wanted sign
招聘貼示	**2**	job notice/ job announcement
分類廣告/招聘廣告	**3**	classified ad/want ad

招聘廣告縮用語 Job Ad Abbreviations

全職	**4**	full-time
半職	**5**	part-time
有空缺	**6**	available
小時	**7**	hour
星期一至星期五	**8**	Monday through Friday
晚上	**9**	evenings
以前的	**10**	previous
經驗	**11**	experience
必須的	**12**	required
相當好的	**13**	excellent

求職 Job Search

應徵	**A**	respond to an ad
查詢資訊	**B**	request information
請求面談	**C**	request an interview
準備履歷	**D**	prepare a resume
穿著合宜	**E**	dress appropriately
填寫申請表格	**F**	fill out an application (form)
前往面試	**G**	go to an interview
談談你具備的技能與資格	**H**	talk about your skills and qualifications
描述你的經驗	**I**	talk about your experience
詢問有關薪資問題	**J**	ask about the salary
詢問有關福利問題	**K**	ask about the benefits
寫感謝函	**L**	write a thank-you note
被錄用	**M**	get hired

A. How did you find your job?
B. I found it through a ___[1–3]___.

A. How was your job interview?
B. It went very well.
A. Did you ___[D–F, H–M]___?
B. Yes, I did.

Tell about a job you are familiar with. What are the skills and qualifications required for the job? What are the hours? What is the salary?

Tell about how people you know found their jobs.

Tell about your own experience with a job search or a job interview.

THE WORKPLACE
工作場所

接待處	**A**	reception area
會議室	**B**	conference room
收發室	**C**	mailroom
辦公區	**D**	work area
辦公室	**E**	office
辦公用品儲藏室	**F**	supply room
儲藏室	**G**	storage room
員工休息室	**H**	employee lounge
衣架	**1**	coat rack
衣櫥	**2**	coat closet
接待員	**3**	receptionist
會議桌	**4**	conference table
說明圖版	**5**	presentation board
郵用秤	**6**	postal scale
郵資儀	**7**	postage meter
辦公室助理	**8**	office assistant
信箱	**9**	mailbox
小隔間	**10**	cubicle
旋轉椅	**11**	swivel chair
打字機	**12**	typewriter
臺式計算器/桌面計算機	**13**	adding machine
影印機/複印機	**14**	copier/photocopier
碎紙機	**15**	paper shredder
切紙機	**16**	paper cutter
檔案管理員	**17**	file clerk
檔案櫃	**18**	file cabinet
秘書	**19**	secretary
電腦桌	**20**	computer workstation
雇主/老闆/主管	**21**	employer/boss
行政助理	**22**	administrative assistant
辦公室經理	**23**	office manager
用品櫃	**24**	supply cabinet
儲藏櫃	**25**	storage cabinet
販賣機	**26**	vending machine
飲水機	**27**	water cooler
咖啡機	**28**	coffee machine
留言欄	**29**	message board
幫…留話	**a**	take a message
作介紹/報告	**b**	give a presentation
將信件分類	**c**	sort the mail
複印/影印	**d**	make copies
存檔	**e**	file
打一封信	**f**	type a letter

[A–H]
A. Where's .....(name).....?
B. He's/She's in the _____.

[1–29]
A. What do you think of the new _____?
B. He's/She's/It's very nice.

[a–f]
A. What's .....(name)..... doing?
B. He's/She's _____ing.

Describe a workplace you are familiar with. Tell about the rooms, the areas, and the employees.

辦公室用品及設備

書桌	1	desk
訂書機	2	stapler
文件盤	3	letter tray/ stacking tray
轉動通訊錄	4	rotary card file
桌墊	5	desk pad
預約簿	6	appointment book
夾紙板	7	clipboard
記事本	8	note pad/ memo pad
電動削鉛筆機	9	electric pencil sharpener
桌曆/檯曆	10	desk calendar
利貼便條紙本	11	Post-It note pad
萬用記事本/ 個人記事本	12	organizer/personal planner
橡皮筋	13	rubber band
迴紋針	14	paper clip
訂書機	15	staple
圖釘	16	thumbtack
長頭圖釘	17	pushpin
黃頁長便箋本	18	legal pad
文件夾	19	file folder
索引卡	20	index card
信封	21	envelope
印有信頭的信紙	22	stationery/ letterhead (paper)
氣泡信封	23	mailer
郵寄標籤	24	mailing label
打字機色帶	25	typewriter cartridge
墨水匣	26	ink cartridge
橡皮圖章	27	rubber stamp
印台	28	ink pad
膠棒	29	glue stick
膠水	30	glue
橡膠膠水	31	rubber cement
修正液	32	correction fluid
透明膠帶	33	cellophane tape/ clear tape
包裝膠帶/ 封口膠帶	34	packing tape/ sealing tape

A. My desk is a mess!
I can't find my [2–12]!
B. Here it is next to your [2–12].

A. Could you get some more [13–21, 23–29] s/ [22, 30–34] from the supply room?
B. Some more [13–21, 23–29] s/ [22, 30–34]? Sure. I'd be happy to.

Which supplies and equipment do you use? What do you use them for?

Which supplies in this lesson do you have at home? at school?

工廠

打卡鐘(上下班計時鐘)	1	time clock
工時卡	2	time cards
衣物間	3	locker room
裝配線	4	(assembly) line
工廠工人	5	(factory) worker
工作檯	6	work station
生產線主管	7	line supervisor
質量監督員	8	quality control supervisor
機器	9	machine
輸送帶	10	conveyor belt
倉庫	11	warehouse
包裝員	12	packer
鏟車/叉架起貨機	13	forklift
載貨用電梯	14	freight elevator
工會公告	15	union notice
意見箱	16	suggestion box
運輸部	17	shipping department
運務員	18	shipping clerk
搬運貨物的手推車	19	hand truck/ dolly
裝卸台	20	loading dock
財務科	21	payroll office
人事室	22	personnel office

A. Excuse me. I'm a new employee. Where's/Where are the _______?
B. Next to/Near/In/On the _______.

A. Have you seen *Tony*?
B. Yes. *He's* in/on/at/next to/near the _______.

Are there any factories where you live? What kind? What are the working conditions there?

What products do factories in your country produce?

建築工地

鐵錘	1	sledgehammer
鶴嘴鋤/十字鎬	2	pickax
鏟子	3	shovel
獨輪小推車	4	wheelbarrow
手提鑽/風鑽	5	jackhammer/ pneumatic drill
藍圖	6	blueprints
梯子	7	ladder
測量捲尺	8	tape measure
工具帶	9	toolbelt
泥刀/小鏟子	10	trowel
水泥攪拌機	11	cement mixer
水泥	a	cement
腳手架	12	scaffolding
傾卸車	13	dump truck
前卸式裝卸車	14	front-end loader
吊車	15	crane
移動升降台	16	cherry picker
推土機	17	bulldozer
挖土機	18	backhoe
混凝土攪拌車	19	concrete mixer truck
混凝土	a	concrete
敞篷載貨小卡車	20	pickup truck
汽車拖的流動屋	21	trailer
石膏板	22	drywall
木材	23	wood/lumber
三夾板	24	plywood
絕緣材料	25	insulation
電線	26	wire
磚塊	27	brick
瓦片	28	shingle
水管	29	pipe
樑	30	girder/beam

A. Could you get me that/those [1–10]?
B. Sure.

A. Watch out for that [11–21]!
B. Oh! Thanks for the warning!

A. Do we have enough [22–26]/[27–30]s?
B. I think so.

What building materials is your home made of?
When was it built?

Describe a construction site near your home or school.
Tell about the construction equipment and the materials.

工作安全

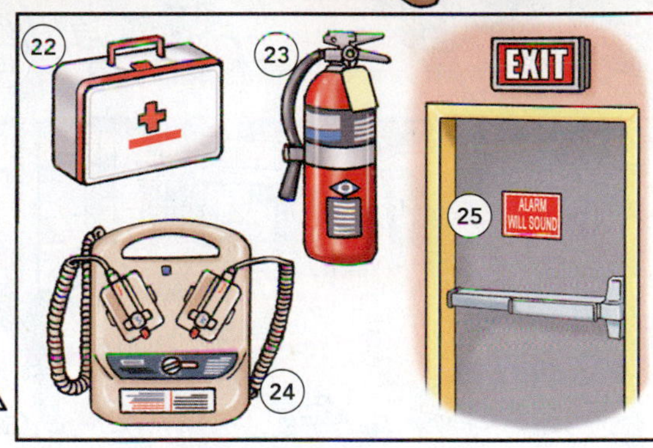

安全帽 **1** hard hat/helmet
耳塞 **2** earplugs
護目鏡 **3** goggles
安全背心 **4** safety vest
安全靴 **5** safety boots
護趾套 **6** toe guard
腰背支撐 **7** back support
安全耳罩 **8** safety earmuffs
髮網 **9** hairnet
口罩 **10** mask
乳膠手套 **11** latex gloves
呼吸防護具 **12** respirator
護目鏡 **13** safety glasses
易燃的 **14** flammable
有毒的 **15** poisonous
具侵蝕性的 **16** corrosive
具放射性的 **17** radioactive
危險的 **18** dangerous
危險的 **19** hazardous
生化危險 **20** biohazard
電力危險 **21** electrical hazard
急救箱 **22** first-aid kit
滅火器 **23** fire extinguisher
電擊器 **24** defibrillator
緊急出口 **25** emergency exit

A. Don't forget to wear your __[1–13]__!
B. Thanks for reminding me.

A. Be careful! {That material is __[14–17]__! / That machine is __[18]__! / That work area is __[19]__! / That's a __[20]__! / That's an __[21]__!}
B. Thanks for the warning.

A. Where's the __[22–25]__?
B. It's over there.

Have you ever used any of the safety equipment in this lesson? What have you used? When? Where?

Where do you see people using safety equipment in your community?

PUBLIC TRANSPORTATION

公共交通工具

公車 **A bus**
- 公車站 **1** bus stop
- 公車路線 **2** bus route
- 乘客 **3** passenger/rider
- 公車費 **4** (bus) fare
- 轉車車票 **5** transfer
- 公車司機 **6** bus driver
- 長途巴士站 **7** bus station
- 售票處 **8** ticket counter
- 車票 **9** ticket
- 行李箱 **10** baggage compartment/ luggage compartment

火車 **B train**
- 火車站 **11** train station
- 售票處 **12** ticket window
- 班機（車）抵達/離開時間看板 **13** arrival and departure board
- 服務台/詢問台 **14** information booth
- 時刻表 **15** schedule/ timetable
- 月台 **16** platform
- 軌道 **17** track
- 列車長 **18** conductor

地鐵/捷運 **C subway**
- 地鐵站/捷運站 **19** subway station
- 地鐵票/捷運票 **20** (subway) token
- 旋轉入口/十字轉門 **21** turnstile
- 儲值卡 **22** fare card
- 儲值卡自售機 **23** fare card machine

計程車 **D taxi**
- 計程車招呼站 **24** taxi stand
- 計程車 **25** taxi/cab/taxicab
- 計程車計費錶 **26** meter
- 計程車司機 **27** cab driver/taxi driver

渡輪 **E ferry**

[A–E]
A. How are you going to get there?
B. {I'm going to take the [A–C, E].
   {I'm going to take a [D].

[1, 7, 8, 10–19, 21, 23–25]
A. Excuse me. Where's the ________?
B. Over there.

How do you get to different places in your community? Describe public transportation where you live.

In your country, can you travel far by train or by bus? Where can you go? How much do tickets cost? Describe the buses and trains.

車輛種類

轎車 **1** sedan
掀背車 **2** hatchback
敞篷車 **3** convertible
跑車 **4** sports car
油電混合車 **5** hybrid
旅行車 **6** station wagon
休旅車 **7** S.U.V. (sport utility vehicle)
吉普車 **8** jeep
箱型車 **9** van
小型箱型車 **10** minivan
敞篷載貨小卡車 **11** pickup truck
加長豪華禮車 **12** limousine
拖車 **13** tow truck
露營車 **14** R.V. (recreational vehicle)/camper
搬家貨車 **15** moving van
卡車 **16** truck
聯結車 **17** tractor trailer/semi
自行車 **18** bicycle/bike
小輪摩托車 **19** motor scooter
機動腳踏兩用車 **20** moped
摩托車 **21** motorcycle

A. What kind of vehicle are you looking for?
B. I'm looking for a **sedan**.

A. Do you drive a/an ________?
B. No. I drive a/an ________.

A. I just saw an accident between a/an ________ and a/an ________!
B. Was anybody hurt?
A. No. Fortunately, nobody was hurt.

What are the most common types of vehicles in your country?

What's your favorite type of vehicle? Why? In your opinion, which company makes the best one?

汽車零件及維修

保險槓	1	bumper
前燈	2	headlight
轉彎指示燈	3	turn signal
停車燈	4	parking light
防護板/擋泥板	5	fender
輪胎	6	tire
輪蓋	7	hubcap
車蓋	8	hood
擋風玻璃	9	windshield
雨刷	10	windshield wipers
側後視鏡	11	side mirror
車頂行李架	12	roof rack
車頂天窗	13	sunroof
天線	14	antenna
後窗	15	rear window
後窗化霜器	16	rear defroster
行李箱	17	trunk
尾燈	18	taillight
煞車燈	19	brake light
倒車燈	20	backup light
汽車牌照	21	license plate
排氣管	22	tailpipe/exhaust pipe
消音器	23	muffler
變速箱	24	transmission
油箱	25	gas tank
千斤頂	26	jack
備胎	27	spare tire
十字扳手	28	lug wrench
照明燈	29	flare
汽車充電電纜	30	jumper cables
火星塞	31	spark plugs
空氣過濾器	32	air filter
引擎/發動機	33	engine
燃料噴射系統	34	fuel injection system
水箱/散熱器	35	radiator
散熱器軟管	36	radiator hose
風扇皮帶	37	fan belt
交流發電機	38	alternator
量油尺	39	dipstick
電池	40	battery
氣泵	41	air pump
油泵	42	gas pump
噴嘴	43	nozzle
加油口	44	gas cap
汽油	45	gas
機油	46	oil
冷卻劑	47	coolant
氣	48	air

安全氣袋 **49** air bag
遮陽板 **50** visor
後視鏡 **51** rearview mirror
儀表板 **52** dashboard/instrument panel
溫度表 **53** temperature gauge
油量表 **54** gas gauge/fuel gauge
時速表 **55** speedometer
里程表 **56** odometer
警告燈 **57** warning lights
轉彎指示燈 **58** turn signal
方向盤 **59** steering wheel
汽車喇叭 **60** horn
發火裝置 **61** ignition
通風孔 **62** vent
導航系統 **63** navigation system
收音機 **64** radio
光碟播放機 **65** CD player
暖氣設備 **66** heater
空調 **67** air conditioning
除霜裝置 **68** defroster
電源插座 **69** power outlet
儲物小櫃 **70** glove compartment
緊急煞車 **71** emergency brake
煞車踏板 **72** brake (pedal)
油門 **73** accelerator/gas pedal
自動排擋變速箱 **74** automatic transmission
變速桿/變速排擋 **75** gearshift
手動排擋變速箱 **76** manual transmission
手動變速桿 **77** stickshift
離合器 **78** clutch
車門鎖 **79** door lock
車門把 **80** door handle
安全肩帶 **81** shoulder harness
扶手 **82** armrest
頭枕 **83** headrest
車座 **84** seat
安全帶 **85** seat belt

[2, 3, 9–16, 24, 35–39, 49–85]
A. What's the matter with your car?
B. The ________(s) is/are broken.

[45–48]
A. Can I help you?
B. {Yes. My car needs [45–47].
Yes. My tires need [48].

[1, 2, 4–15, 17–23, 25]
A. I was just in a car accident!
B. Oh, no! Were you hurt?
A. No. But my ________(s) was/were damaged.

In your opinion, what are the most important features to look for when you buy a car?

Do you own a car? What kind? Tell about any repairs your car has needed.

HIGHWAYS AND STREETS

公路及街道

隧道	1	tunnel
橋	2	bridge
收費站	3	tollbooth
路標	4	route sign
公路	5	highway
路面	6	road
道路分隔欄/護欄	7	divider/barrier
高架橋	8	overpass
高架橋下通道	9	underpass
入口坡道	10	entrance ramp/ on ramp
州際公路	11	interstate (highway)
中間安全島	12	median
左車道	13	left lane
中央車道	14	middle lane/ center lane
右車道	15	right lane
路肩	16	shoulder
虛線	17	broken line
實線	18	solid line
限速標誌	19	speed limit sign
出口坡道	20	exit (ramp)
出口標誌	21	exit sign
街道	22	street
單行道	23	one-way street
雙黃線	24	double yellow line
行人穿越道/斑馬線	25	crosswalk
十字路口	26	intersection
交通號誌燈/紅綠燈	27	traffic light/ traffic signal
轉角	28	corner
街區	29	block

[1–28]
A. Where's the accident?
B. It's on / in / at / near the ______.

Describe a highway you travel on.

Describe an intersection near where you live.

In your area, on which highways and streets do most accidents occur? Why are these places dangerous?

PREPOSITIONS OF MOTION

動態介詞

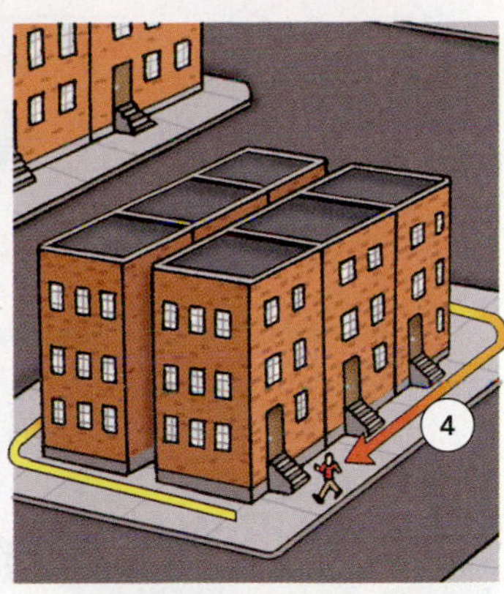
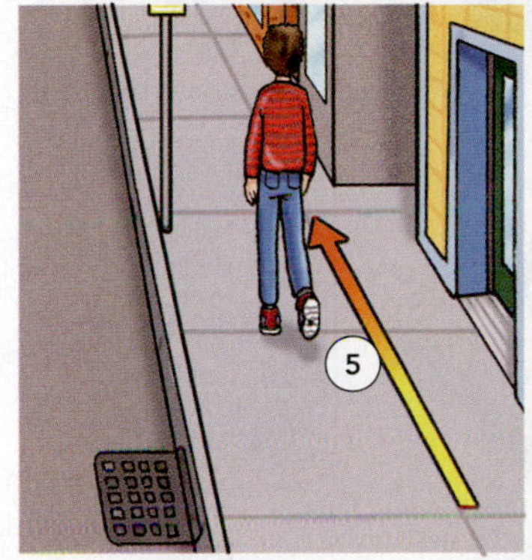

越過…的上面 **1** over
穿過…的下面 **2** under
穿過/通過 **3** through
環繞 **4** around

上 **5** up
下 **6** down
橫越/穿過 **7** across
經過 **8** past

上 **9** on
下 **10** off
進 **11** into
出 **12** out of
進入/上 **13** onto

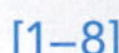
[1–8]
A. Go **over** *the bridge*.
B. **Over** *the bridge*?
A. Yes.

[9–13]
A. I can't talk right now. I'm getting **on** *a train*.
B. You're getting **on** *a train*?
A. Yes. I'll call you later.

What places do you go past on your way to school?

Tell how to get to different places from your home or your school.

交通標誌及指示

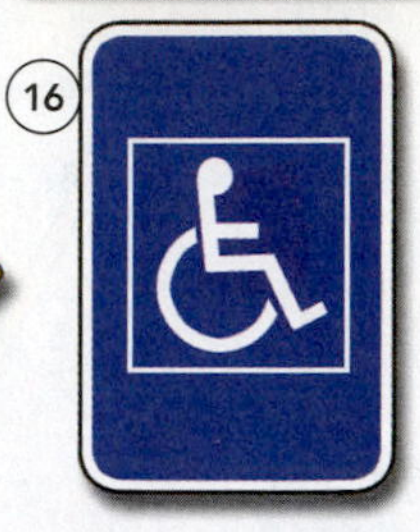

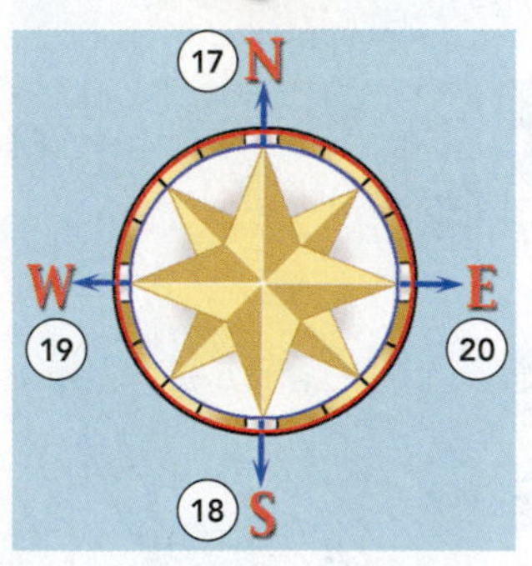

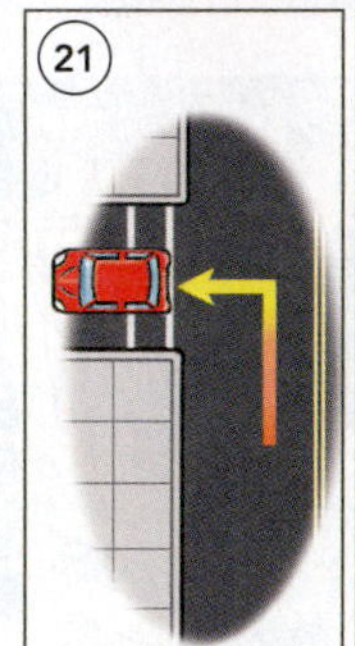
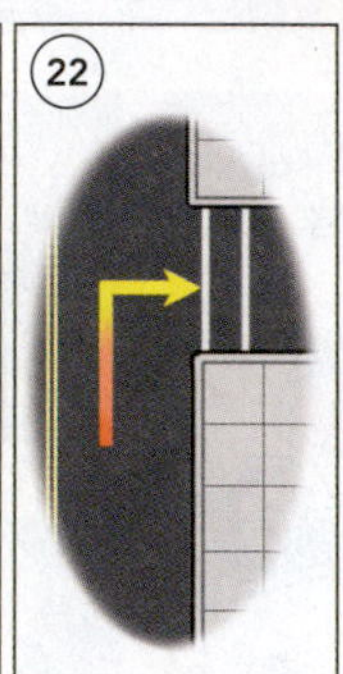
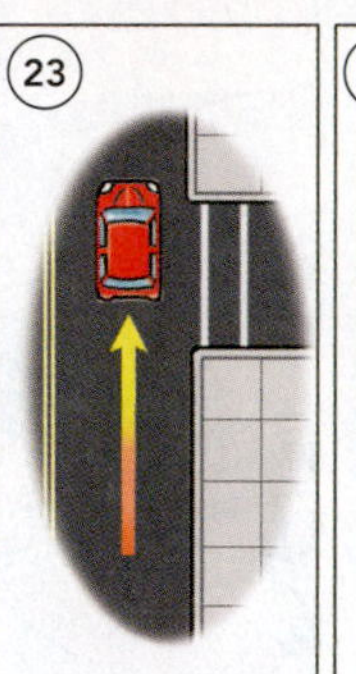
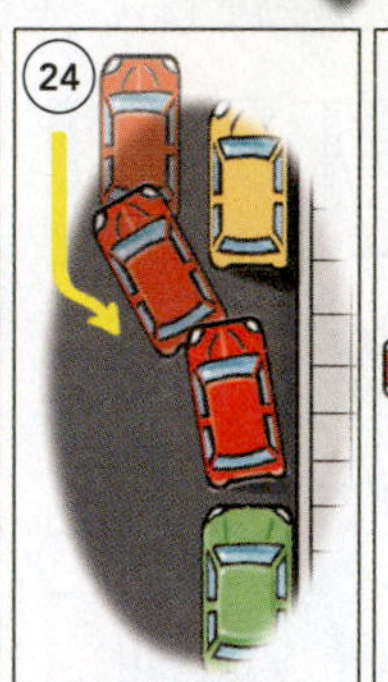
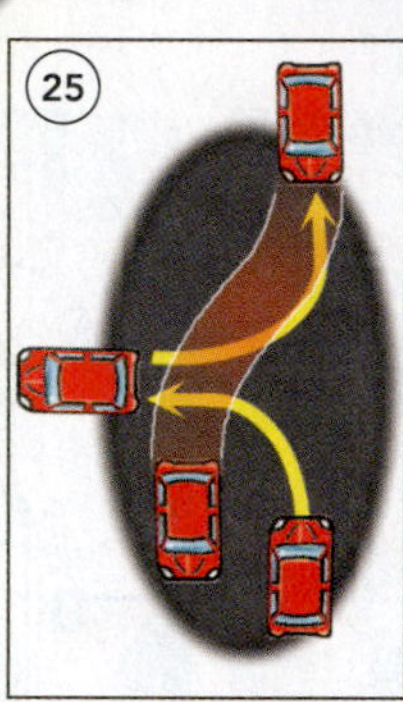

交通標誌 Traffic Signs

停 **1** stop
禁止左轉 **2** no left turn
禁止右轉 **3** no right turn
禁止回轉 **4** no U-turn
只准右轉 **5** right turn only
禁止進入 **6** do not enter
單行道 **7** one way
此路不通 **8** dead end/no outlet
行人穿越道 **9** pedestrian crossing
鐵路平交道 **10** railroad crossing
學童過路處 **11** school crossing
合流交通 **12** merging traffic
讓 **13** yield
繞道 **14** detour
路濕易滑 **15** slippery when wet
殘障停車專位 **16** handicapped parking only

方向指示 Compass Directions

北 **17** north
南 **18** south
西 **19** west
東 **20** east

路試指示 Road Test Instructions

左轉。 **21** Turn left.
右轉。 **22** Turn right.
直走。 **23** Go straight.
平行停車。 **24** Parallel park.
做三點式轉。 **25** Make a 3-point turn.
使用手勢。 **26** Use hand signals.

[1–16]
A. Careful! That sign says "**stop**"!
B. Oh. Thanks.

[17–20]
A. Which way should I go?
B. Go **north**.

[21–26]
A. Turn **right**.
B. Turn **right**?
A. Yes.

Which of these traffic signs are in your neighborhood? What other traffic signs do you usually see?

Describe any differences between traffic signs in different countries you know.

飛機場

登機手續 A Check-In

機票	1	ticket
票務櫃檯	2	ticket counter
票務員	3	ticket agent
旅行箱	4	suitcase
班機抵達／出發時間顯示螢幕	5	arrival and departure monitor

安全檢查 B Security

安全檢查關口	6	security checkpoint
金屬物品探測器	7	metal detector
安全人員	8	security officer
X光掃描機	9	X-ray machine
隨身行李	10	carry-on bag

登機門 C The Gate

驗票處	11	check-in counter
登機證	12	boarding pass
登機門	13	gate
候機室	14	boarding area

行李領取 D Baggage Claim

行李領取區	15	baggage claim (area)
行李傳送帶/行李轉盤	16	baggage carousel
行李	17	baggage
行李推車	18	baggage cart/ luggage cart
行李小拖車	19	luggage carrier
西裝袋	20	garment bag
行李牌	21	baggage claim check

海關及出入境檢查 E Customs and Immigration

海關	22	customs
海關關務員	23	customs officer
海關申報表	24	customs declaration form
出入境檢查	25	immigration
出入境檢查官	26	immigration officer
護照	27	passport
簽證	28	visa

[2, 3, 5–9, 11, 13–16, 22, 23, 25, 26]
A. Excuse me. Where's the _______?*
B. Right over there.

* *With 22 and 25, use:* Excuse me. Where's _____?

[1, 4, 10, 12, 17–21, 24, 27, 28]
A. Oh, no! I think I've lost my _______!
B. I'll help you look for it.

Describe an airport you are familiar with. Tell about the check-in area, the security area, the gates, and the baggage claim area.

Have you ever gone through Customs and Immigration? Tell about your experience.

AIRPLANE TRAVEL

航空旅行

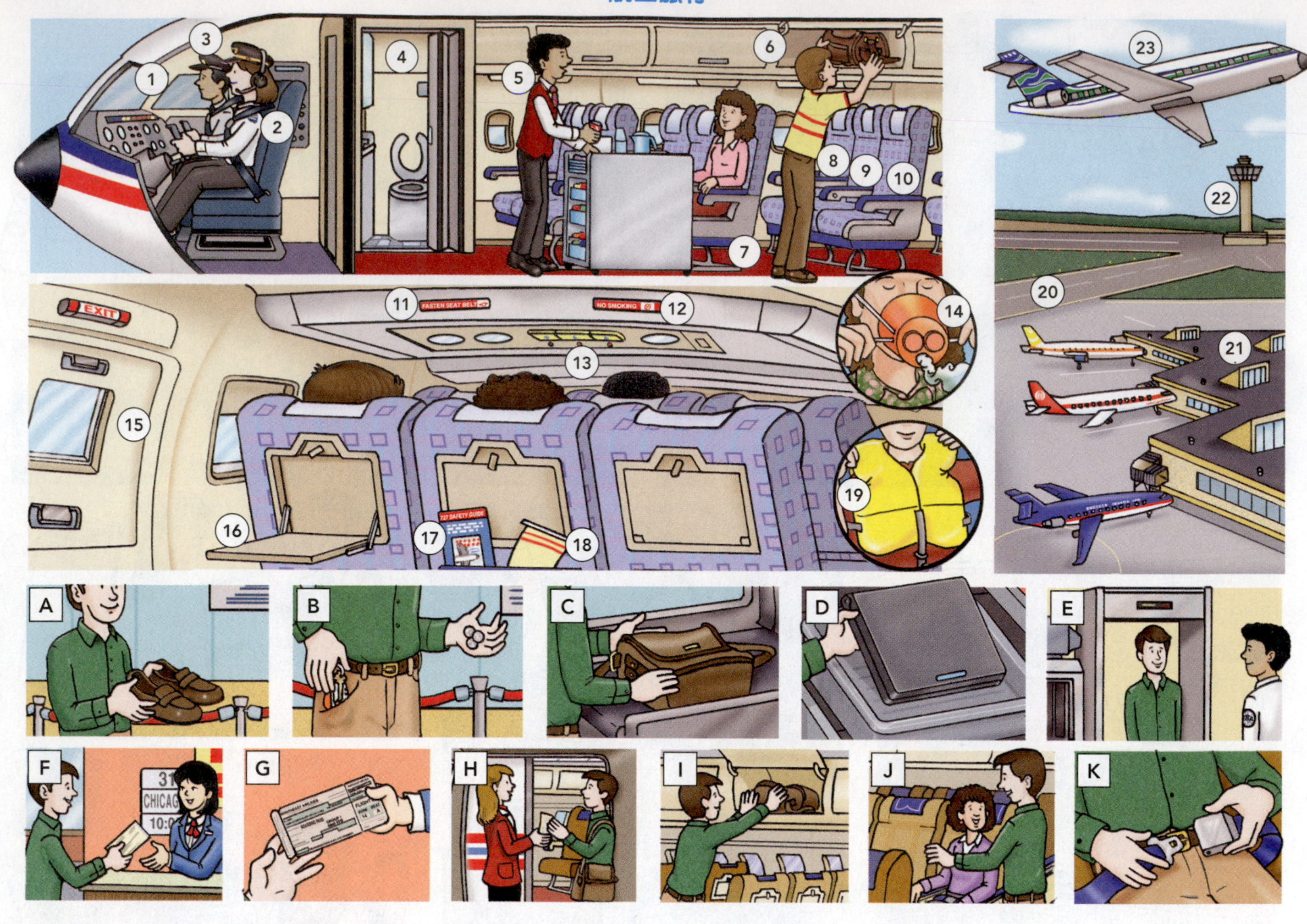

駕駛艙	**1**	cockpit
飛行員/機長	**2**	pilot/captain
副機長	**3**	co-pilot
洗手間	**4**	lavatory/bathroom
空服員	**5**	flight attendant
座位上方的行李箱	**6**	overhead compartment
走道	**7**	aisle
靠窗座位	**8**	window seat
中間座位	**9**	middle seat
靠走道座位	**10**	aisle seat
繫上安全帶指示燈	**11**	Fasten Seat Belt sign
禁止吸煙指示燈	**12**	No Smoking sign
呼叫鈕	**13**	call button
氧氣面罩	**14**	oxygen mask
緊急出口	**15**	emergency exit
(摺疊式)小桌板	**16**	tray (table)
緊急措施說明	**17**	emergency instruction card
暈機袋	**18**	air sickness bag
救生衣	**19**	life vest/life jacket
跑道	**20**	runway
航站大廈	**21**	terminal (building)
控制塔	**22**	control tower
飛機	**23**	airplane/plane/jet
脫鞋	**A**	take off your shoes
將口袋中的東西拿出來	**B**	empty your pockets
將手提袋放在輸送帶上	**C**	put your bag on the conveyor belt
將電腦放在托盤中	**D**	put your computer in a tray
通過金屬物品探測器	**E**	walk through the metal detector
在登機門辦登機手續	**F**	check in at the gate
拿登機證	**G**	get your boarding pass
登機	**H**	board the plane
藏放隨身行李	**I**	stow your carry-on bag
找座位	**J**	find your seat
繫上安全帶	**K**	fasten your seat belt

[1–23]
A. Where's the _______?
B. In/On/Next to/Behind/In front of/Above/Below the _______.

[A–K]
A. Please _______.
B. All right. Certainly.

Have you ever flown in an airplane? Tell about a flight you took.

Be an airport security officer! Give passengers instructions as they go through the security area. Now, be a flight attendant! Give passengers instructions before take-off.

旅館

看門人 **1** doorman
代客泊車 **2** valet parking
停車服務員 **3** parking attendant
行李員 **4** bellhop
行李推車 **5** luggage cart
行李員領班 **6** bell captain
一樓大廳 **7** lobby
飯店櫃檯 **8** front desk
櫃檯服務員 **9** desk clerk

客人 **10** guest
旅遊服務台 **11** concierge desk
旅遊服務台職員 **12** concierge
餐廳 **13** restaurant
會議室 **14** meeting room
禮品店 **15** gift shop
游泳池 **16** pool
健身房 **17** exercise room
電梯 **18** elevator

製冰機 **19** ice machine
走廊 **20** hall/hallway
房間鑰匙 **21** room key
客房清潔推車 **22** housekeeping cart
飯店客房清潔員 **23** housekeeper
客房 **24** guest room
客房服務 **25** room service

A. Where do you work?
B. I work at the *Grand* Hotel.
A. What do you do there?
B. I'm a/an ___[1, 3, 4, 6, 9, 12, 23]___.

A. Excuse me. Where's the ___[1–19, 22, 23]___?
B. Right over there.
A. Thanks.

Tell about a hotel you are familiar with. Describe the place and the people.

In your opinion, which hotel employee has the most interesting job? the most difficult job? Why?

嗜好，手工藝，遊戲

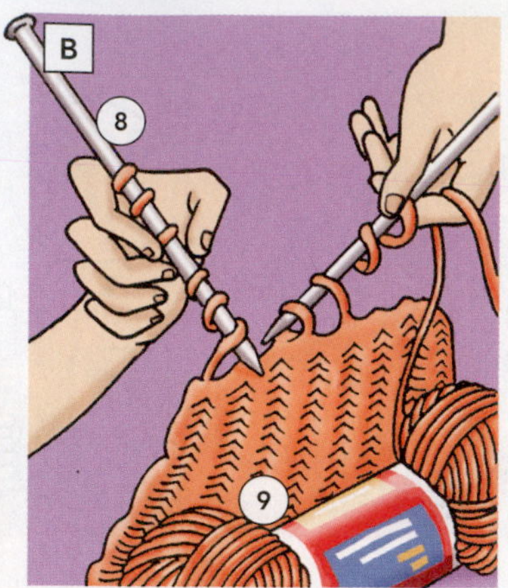

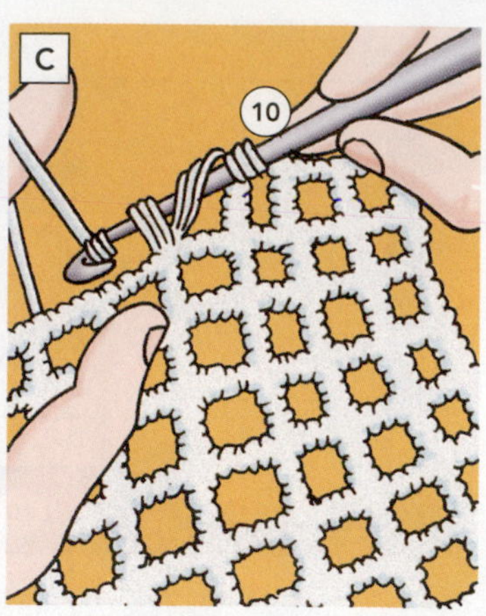

縫紉 **A sew**
縫紉機 1 sewing machine
大頭針 2 pin
針插 3 pin cushion
(一)捲線 4 (spool of) thread
縫衣針 5 (sewing) needle
頂針箍 6 thimble
安全別針 7 safety pin

毛衣編織 **B knit**
織針 8 knitting needle
毛線 9 yarn

鉤針編織 **C crochet**
鉤針 10 crochet hook

繪畫 **D paint**
畫筆 11 paintbrush
畫架 12 easel
油畫布 13 canvas
顏料 14 paint
油畫顏料 a oil paint
水彩顏料 b watercolor

畫畫 **E draw**
素描本 15 sketch book
(一套)彩色鉛筆 16 (set of) colored pencils
繪圖鉛筆 17 drawing pencil

做刺繡 **F do embroidery**
刺繡 18 embroidery

做格繡 **G do needlepoint**
格繡 19 needlepoint
圖案 20 pattern

做木工藝 **H do woodworking**
木工藝組合 21 woodworking kit

摺紙 **I do origami**
摺紙用紙 22 origami paper

製陶 **J make pottery**
陶土 23 clay
陶輪/拉胚機 24 potter's wheel

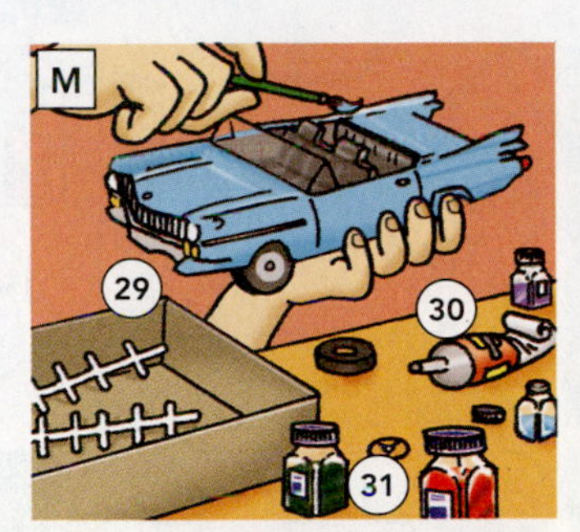

集郵	**K**	**collect stamps**
集郵冊	**25**	stamp album
放大鏡	**26**	magnifying glass
集幣	**L**	**collect coins**
錢幣目錄	**27**	coin catalog
集幣冊	**28**	coin collection
製作模型	**M**	**build models**
模型玩具組合	**29**	model kit
膠水	**30**	glue
壓克力顏料	**31**	acrylic paint
去觀鳥	**N**	**go bird-watching**
望遠鏡	**32**	binoculars
圖鑑	**33**	field guide
玩紙牌遊戲	**O**	**play cards**
(一)副紙牌	**34**	(deck of) cards
梅花	**a**	club
方塊	**b**	diamond
紅心	**c**	heart
黑桃	**d**	spade
玩棋盤遊戲	**P**	**play board games**
西洋棋	**35**	chess
西洋跳棋	**36**	checkers
西洋雙陸棋	**37**	backgammon
大富翁遊戲	**38**	Monopoly
骰子	**a**	dice
拼字遊戲	**39**	Scrabble
上網	**Q**	**go online/ browse the Web/ "surf" the net**
網頁瀏覽器	**40**	web browser
網址	**41**	web address/URL
攝影	**R**	**photography**
照相機	**42**	camera
天文學	**S**	**astronomy**
(單筒)望遠鏡	**43**	telescope

A. What do you like to do in your free time?
B. {I like to ___[A–Q]___.
   {I enjoy ___[R, S]___.

A. May I help you?
B. Yes, please. I'd like to buy (a/an) ___[1–34, 42, 43]___.

A. What do you want to do?
B. Let's play ___[35–39]___.
A. Good idea!

Do you like to do any of these activities in your free time? Which ones?

What games are popular in your country? Describe how to play one.

PLACES TO GO

遊玩去處

- 博物館 **1** museum
- 美術館 **2** art gallery
- 演唱會 **3** concert
- 戲劇 **4** play
- 遊樂園 **5** amusement park
- 古蹟 **6** historic site
- 國家公園 **7** national park
- 手工藝展覽 **8** craft fair
- 私人二手貨出售 **9** yard sale
- 廉價市場/跳蚤市場 **10** swap meet/flea market
- 公園 **11** park
- 海邊 **12** beach
- 山 **13** mountains
- 水族館 **14** aquarium
- 植物園 **15** botanical gardens
- 天文館 **16** planetarium
- 動物園 **17** zoo
- 電影院 **18** movies
- 嘉年華會 **19** carnival
- 露天遊樂場 **20** fair

A. What do you want to do today?

B. Let's go to { a/an ___[1–9]___. / the ___[10–20]___.

A. What did you do over the weekend?

B. I went to { a/an ___[1–9]___. / the ___[10–20]___.

A. What are you going to do on your day off?

B. I'm going to go to { a/an ___[1–9]___. / the ___[10–20]___.

What are some of your favorite places to go? Where are they? What do you do there?

THE PARK AND THE PLAYGROUND

公園及遊樂場

自行車道	1	bicycle path/ bike path/ bikeway
鴨池	2	duck pond
野餐區	3	picnic area
垃圾桶	4	trash can
烤肉架	5	grill
野餐桌	6	picnic table
飲水器	7	water fountain
慢跑道	8	jogging path
長凳	9	bench
網球場	10	tennis court
球場	11	ballfield
噴水池	12	fountain
腳踏車停放架	13	bike rack
旋轉木馬 / 旋轉木馬	14	merry-go-round/ carousel
滑板坡道	15	skateboard ramp
遊樂場	16	playground
攀岩牆	17	climbing wall
鞦韆	18	swings
攀爬架	19	climber
滑梯	20	slide
翹翹板	21	seesaw
沙池	22	sandbox
沙	23	sand

[1–22]
A. Excuse me. Does this park have (a) ______?
B. Yes. Right over there.

[17–23]
A. { Be careful on the [17–21]! / Be careful in the [22, 23]!
B. I will, Dad/Mom.

Describe a park and playground you are familiar with.

海邊

救生員	**1**	lifeguard
救生員看臺	**2**	lifeguard stand
救生圈	**3**	life preserver
小吃販賣部	**4**	snack bar/ refreshment stand
小販	**5**	vendor
游泳者	**6**	swimmer
海浪	**7**	wave
衝浪者	**8**	surfer
風箏	**9**	kite
沙灘躺椅	**10**	beach chair
沙灘太陽傘	**11**	beach umbrella
沙堡	**12**	sand castle
趴板	**13**	boogie board
日光浴者	**14**	sunbather
太陽眼鏡	**15**	sunglasses
沙灘巾	**16**	(beach) towel
海灘球	**17**	beach ball
衝浪板	**18**	surfboard
貝殼	**19**	seashell/shell
石頭	**20**	rock
小冷藏箱	**21**	cooler
太陽帽	**22**	sun hat
防曬油	**23**	sunscreen/ sunblock/ suntan lotion
沙灘毯	**24**	(beach) blanket
鏟子	**25**	shovel
桶子	**26**	pail

[1–26]
A. What a nice beach!
B. It is. Look at all the ______s!

[9–11, 13, 15–18, 21–26]
A. Are you ready for the beach?
B. Almost. I just have to get my ______.

Do you like to go to the beach? Describe your favorite beach. What do you take when you go there?

戶外休閒

露營 **A camping**
帳篷 **1** tent
睡袋 **2** sleeping bag
帳篷釘 **3** tent stakes
提燈 **4** lantern
短柄小斧 **5** hatchet
露營火爐 **6** camping stove
瑞士刀 **7** Swiss army knife
驅蟲劑 **8** insect repellent
火柴 **9** matches

徒步登山 **B hiking**
背包 **10** backpack
(士兵等用)水壺 **11** canteen
指南針 **12** compass
山路圖 **13** trail map
全球定位裝置 **14** GPS device
登山靴 **15** hiking boots

攀岩 **C rock climbing/ technical climbing**
安全帶 **16** harness
繩索 **17** rope

騎越野單車 **D mountain biking**
越野單車 **18** mountain bike
自行車安全帽 **19** (bike) helmet

野餐 **E picnic**
野餐毯 **20** (picnic) blanket
保溫瓶 **21** thermos
野餐籃 **22** picnic basket

A. Let's go ___[A–E]___* this weekend.
B. Good idea! We haven't gone ___[A–E]___* in a long time.

*With E, say: on a picnic.

A. Did you bring
{ the ___[1–9, 11–14, 16, 17, 20–22]___ ?
{ your ___[10, 15, 18, 19]___ ?
B. Yes, I did.
A. Oh, good.

Have you ever gone camping, hiking, rock climbing, or mountain biking? Tell about it: What did you do? Where? What equipment did you use?

Do you like to go on picnics? Where? What picnic supplies and food do you take with you?

個人運動與休閒

慢跑 A jogging
慢跑衣褲 1 jogging suit
慢跑鞋 2 jogging shoes

跑步 B running
跑步短褲 3 running shorts
跑步鞋 4 running shoes

步行 C walking
步行鞋 5 walking shoes

(溜)直排滑輪 D inline skating/rollerblading
直排滑輪 6 inline skates/rollerblades
護膝 7 knee pads

(騎)自行車/(騎)單車 E cycling/biking
自行車/單車 8 bicycle/bike
(自行車/單車)安全帽 9 (bicycle/bike) helmet

(溜)滑板運動 F skateboarding
滑板 10 skateboard
護肘 11 elbow pads

(打)保齡球 G bowling
保齡球 12 bowling ball
保齡球鞋 13 bowling shoes

騎馬 H horseback riding
馬鞍 14 saddle
韁繩 15 reins
馬鐙 16 stirrups

網球 I tennis
網球拍 17 tennis racket
網球 18 tennis ball
網球短褲 19 tennis shorts

羽毛球 J badminton
羽毛球拍 20 badminton racket
羽毛球 21 birdie/shuttlecock

短柄牆球 K racquetball
護目鏡 22 safety goggles
短柄牆球 23 racquetball
短柄牆球拍 24 racquet

乒乓球 L table tennis/ ping pong
乒乓球拍 25 paddle
乒乓球桌 26 ping pong table
乒乓球網 27 net
乒乓球 28 ping pong ball

高爾夫球 **M golf**
高爾夫球棍 **29** golf clubs
高爾夫球 **30** golf ball

飛盤 **N Frisbee**
飛盤 **31** Frisbee/ flying disc

撞球/臺球 **O billiards/pool**
撞球桌 **32** pool table
球桿 **33** pool stick
撞球 **34** billiard balls

武術 **P martial arts**
黑帶 **35** black belt

體操 **Q gymnastics**
馬 **36** horse
雙槓 **37** parallel bars
墊子 **38** mat
平衡木 **39** balance beam
蹦床/彈床 **40** trampoline

舉重 **R weightlifting**
槓鈴 **41** barbell
啞鈴 **42** weights

射箭 **S archery**
弓箭 **43** bow and arrow
靶 **44** target

拳擊 **T box**
拳擊手套 **45** boxing gloves
拳擊短褲 **46** (boxing) trunks

摔角 **U wrestle**
摔角服 **47** wrestling uniform
摔角墊子 **48** (wrestling) mat

健身運動 **V work out/exercise**
踏車 **49** treadmill
划艇機 **50** rowing machine
健身腳踏車 **51** exercise bike
多功能運動器材/運動器材 **52** universal/ exercise equipment

[A–V]
A. What do you like to do in your free time?
B. I like to go [A–H].
I like to play [I–O].
I like to do [P–S].
I like to [T–V].

[1–52]
A. I really like this/these new ______.
B. It's/They're very nice.

Do you do any of these activities? Which ones? Which are popular in your country?

團隊運動

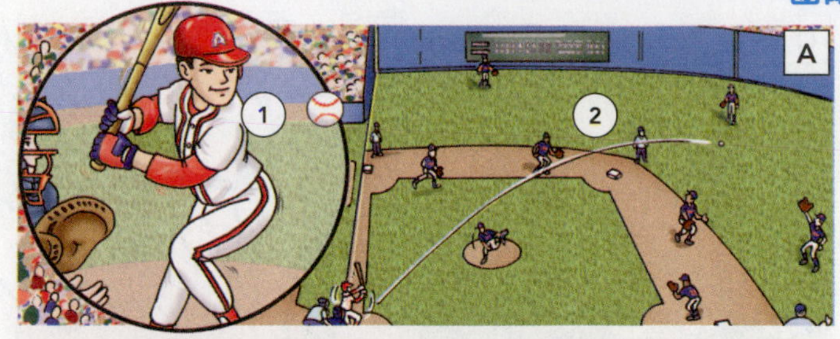

棒球 **A baseball**
棒球隊員 **1** baseball player
棒球場 **2** baseball field/ ballfield

壘球 **B softball**
壘球隊員 **3** softball player
壘球場 **4** ballfield

橄欖球 **C football**
橄欖球隊員 **5** football player
橄欖球場 **6** football field

長曲棍球 **D lacrosse**
長曲棍球隊員 **7** lacrosse player
長曲棍球場 **8** lacrosse field

冰上曲棍球 **E (ice) hockey**
曲棍球隊員 **9** hockey player
曲棍球場 **10** hockey rink

籃球 **F basketball**
籃球隊員 **11** basketball player
籃球場 **12** basketball court

排球 **G volleyball**
排球隊員 **13** volleyball player
排球場 **14** volleyball court

足球 **H soccer**
足球隊員 **15** soccer player
足球場 **16** soccer field

[A–H]
A. Do you like to play **baseball**?
B. Yes. **Baseball** is one of my favorite sports.

A. .... plays __[A–H]__ very well.
B. You're right. I think he's/she's one of the best ________s* on the team.

*Use 1, 3, 5, 7, 9, 11, 13, 15.

A. Now listen, team! I want all of you to go out on that ________† and play the best game of __[A–H]__ you've ever played!
B. All right, Coach!

† Use 2, 4, 6, 8, 10, 12, 14, 16.

Which sports in this lesson do you like to play? Which do you like to watch?

What are your favorite teams?

Name some famous players of these sports.

TEAM SPORTS EQUIPMENT

團隊運動設備

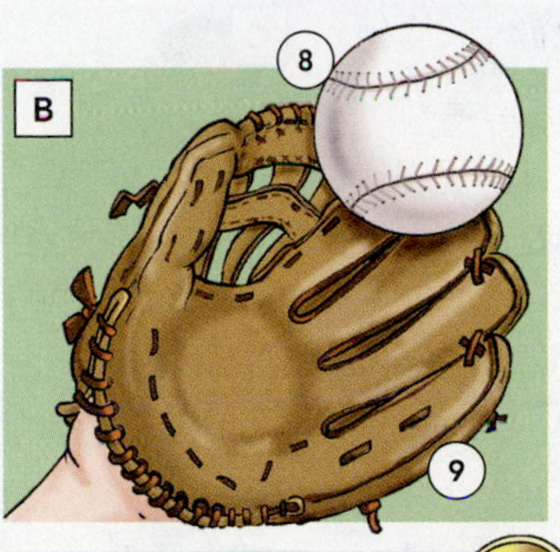

棒球 **A baseball**
棒球 **1** baseball
棒球棍 **2** bat
打擊手頭盔 **3** batting helmet
棒球制服 **4** (baseball) uniform
接球手面罩 **5** catcher's mask
棒球手套 **6** (baseball) glove
接球手套 **7** catcher's mitt

壘球 **B softball**
壘球 **8** softball
壘球手套 **9** softball glove

橄欖球 **C football**
橄欖球 **10** football
橄欖球頭盔 **11** football helmet
護肩 **12** shoulder pads

長曲棍球 **D lacrosse**
長曲棍球 **13** lacrosse ball
面具 **14** face guard
長曲棍球桿 **15** lacrosse stick

冰上曲棍球 **E (ice) hockey**
曲棍球 **16** hockey puck
曲棍球球桿 **17** hockey stick
曲棍球面罩 **18** hockey mask
曲棍球手套 **19** hockey glove
曲棍球溜冰鞋 **20** hockey skates

籃球 **F basketball**
籃球 **21** basketball
籃板 **22** backboard
籃圈 **23** basketball hoop

排球 **G volleyball**
排球 **24** volleyball
排球網 **25** volleyball net

足球 **H soccer**
足球 **26** soccer ball
護脛 **27** shinguards

[1–27]
A. I can't find my **baseball**!
B. Look in the closet.*

*closet, basement, garage

[In a store]
A. Excuse me. I'm looking for (a) [1–27] .
B. All our [A–H] equipment is over there.
A. Thanks.

[At home]
A. I'm going to play [A–H] after school today.
B. Don't forget your [1–21, 24, 26, 27] !

Which sports in this lesson are popular in your country? Which sports do students play in high school?

冬季運動與休閒

下坡滑雪 **A (downhill) skiing**
滑雪板 **1** skis
滑雪靴 **2** ski boots
滑雪板皮靴固定器 **3** bindings
滑雪撐桿 **4** (ski) poles

越野滑雪 **B cross-country skiing**
越野滑雪板 **5** cross-country skis

溜冰 **C (ice) skating**
溜冰鞋 **6** (ice) skates
冰刀 **7** blade
冰刀套 **8** skate guard

花式溜冰 **D figure skating**
花式溜冰鞋 **9** figure skates

滑雪單板 **E snowboarding**
滑雪單板 **10** snowboard

滑雪橇 **F sledding**
雪撬 **11** sled
圓雪橇 **12** sledding dish/ saucer

滑大雪橇/滑連橇 **G bobsledding**
大雪橇/連雪橇 **13** bobsled

駕雪車 **H snowmobiling**
雪車 **14** snowmobile

[A–H]
A. What's your favorite winter sport?
B. **Skiing**.

[A–H]
[At work or at school on Friday]
A. What are you going to do this weekend?
B. I'm going to go ______.

[1–14]
[On the telephone]
A. Hello. *Sally's* Sporting Goods.
B. Hello. Do you sell ______(s)?
A. Yes, we do. / No, we don't.

Have you ever done any of these activities? Which ones?

Have you ever watched the Winter Olympics? Which event do you think is the most exciting? the most dangerous?

水上運動與休閒

駕帆船	**A**	**sailing**
帆船	**1**	sailboat
救生衣	**2**	life jacket/life vest
滑獨木舟	**B**	**canoeing**
獨木舟	**3**	canoe
槳	**4**	paddles
划船	**C**	**rowing**
划船	**5**	rowboat
櫓	**6**	oars
划皮艇	**D**	**kayaking**
皮艇	**7**	kayak
槳	**8**	paddles
激流泛舟	**E**	**(white-water) rafting**
橡皮艇	**9**	raft
救生衣	**10**	life jacket/life vest
游泳	**F**	**swimming**
游泳衣	**11**	swimsuit/ bathing suit
蛙鏡	**12**	goggles
泳帽	**13**	bathing cap
浮潛	**G**	**snorkeling**
潛水鏡	**14**	mask
潛水呼吸管	**15**	snorkel
蛙鞋	**16**	fins
潛水	**H**	**scuba diving**
潛水衣	**17**	wet suit
壓縮空氣瓶	**18**	(air) tank
潛水鏡	**19**	(diving) mask
衝浪	**I**	**surfing**
衝浪板	**20**	surfboard
風帆衝浪	**J**	**windsurfing**
風帆板	**21**	sailboard
風帆	**22**	sail
滑水	**K**	**waterskiing**
滑水板/滑水橇	**23**	water skis
托纜/滑水繩	**24**	towrope
釣魚	**L**	**fishing**
釣魚桿	**25**	(fishing) rod/pole
線軸	**26**	reel
魚線	**27**	(fishing) line
魚網	**28**	(fishing) net
魚餌	**29**	bait

[A–L]
A. Would you like to go **sailing** tomorrow?
B. Sure. I'd love to.

A. Have you ever gone __[A–L]__?
B. Yes, I have. / No, I haven't.

A. Do you have everything you need to go __[A–L]__?
B. Yes. I have my __[1–29]__ (and my __[1–29]__).
A. Have a good time!

Which sports in this lesson have you tried? Which sports would you like to try?

Are any of these sports popular in your country? Which ones?

SPORT AND EXERCISE ACTIONS

運動及練習動作

打球	1	hit	運球	9	dribble	跳躍	17	jump	仰臥起坐	25	sit-up
投球	2	pitch	投籃	10	shoot	伸臂	18	reach	蹲	26	deep knee bend
擲球	3	throw	伸展	11	stretch	擺動	19	swing	開合跳	27	jumping jack
接球	4	catch	彎腰	12	bend	舉起	20	lift	翻筋斗	28	somersault
傳球	5	pass	走	13	walk	游泳	21	swim	橫翻筋斗	29	cartwheel
踢球	6	kick	跑	14	run	潛水	22	dive	手倒立	30	handstand
發球	7	serve	單腳跳	15	hop	射箭	23	shoot			
拍球	8	bounce	輕巧地跳	16	skip	伏地挺身	24	push-up			

[1–10]
A. _______ the ball!
B. Okay, Coach!

[11–23]
A. Now _______!
B. Like this?
A. Yes.

[24–30]
A. Okay, everybody. I want you to do twenty _______s!
B. Twenty _______s?!
A. That's right.

Do you exercise regularly?
Which exercises do you do?

Be an exercise instructor! Lead your friends in an exercise routine using the actions in this lesson.

娛樂

戲劇 **A play**
- 劇場 **1** theater
- 演員 **2** actor
- 女演員 **3** actress

演奏會/演唱會 **B concert**
- 音樂廳 **4** concert hall
- 管絃樂隊 **5** orchestra
- 樂師 **6** musician
- 指揮 **7** conductor
- 樂團 **8** band

歌劇 **C opera**
- 歌劇演唱者 **9** opera singer

芭蕾舞 **D ballet**
- 芭蕾舞者 **10** ballet dancer
- 女芭蕾舞者 **11** ballerina

歌廳 **E music club**
- 演唱者/歌手 **12** singer

電影院 **F movies**
- 電影院 **13** (movie) theater
- 電影屏幕 **14** (movie) screen
- 女演員 **15** actress
- 演員 **16** actor

喜劇表演俱樂部 **G comedy club**
- 喜劇家 **17** comedian

[A–G]
A. What are you doing this evening?
B. I'm going to { a [A, B, E, G]. / the [C, D, F]. }

[1–17]
A. What a magnificent ______!
B. I agree.

What kinds of entertainment in this lesson do you like?
What kinds of entertainment are popular in your country?

Who are some of your favorite actors? actresses? musicians? singers? comedians?

TYPES OF ENTERTAINMENT

娛樂種類

A

B

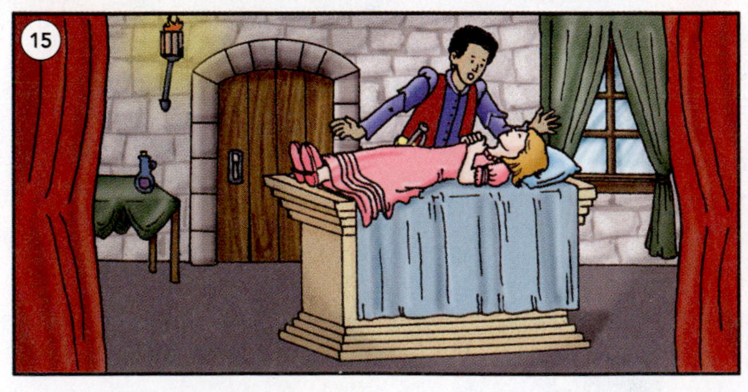

音樂 **A music**
- 古典音樂 **1** classical music
- 流行音樂 **2** popular music
- 鄉村音樂 **3** country music
- 搖滾音樂 **4** rock music
- 民俗音樂 **5** folk music
- 饒舌音樂 **6** rap music
- 福音音樂 **7** gospel music
- 爵士樂 **8** jazz
- 藍調音樂 **9** blues
- 藍草音樂(美國南方鄉村音樂) **10** bluegrass
- 嘻哈音樂 **11** hip hop
- 雷鬼/雷蓋音樂(源自牙買加) **12** reggae

戲劇 **B plays**
- 話劇/戲劇 **13** drama
- 喜劇 **14** comedy
- 悲劇 **15** tragedy
- 歌舞喜劇 **16** musical (comedy)

電影 C movies/films
劇情片 17 drama
喜劇片 18 comedy
西部片 19 western
懸疑片 20 mystery
歌舞片 21 musical
卡通片/動畫片 22 cartoon
記錄片 23 documentary
動作片/歷險片 24 action movie/adventure movie
戰爭片 25 war movie
恐怖片 26 horror movie
科幻片 27 science fiction movie
外語片 28 foreign film

電視節目 D TV programs
電視劇 29 drama
情境喜劇 30 (situation) comedy/sitcom
談話節目 31 talk show
遊戲節目/益智遊戲節目 32 game show/quiz show
實境節目 33 reality show
肥皂劇/連續劇 34 soap opera
卡通影集/動畫影集 35 cartoon
兒童節目 36 children's program
新聞節目 37 news program
體育節目 38 sports program
自然科學節目 39 nature program
購物節目 40 shopping program

A. What kind of [A–D] do you like?
B. { I like [1–12].
I like [13–40]s.

What's your favorite type of music?
Who is your favorite singer? musician? musical group?

What kind of movies do you like?
Who are your favorite movie stars?
What are the titles of your favorite movies?

What kind of TV programs do you like?
What are your favorite shows?

樂器

絃樂器 Strings

小提琴 **1** violin
中提琴 **2** viola
大提琴 **3** cello
低音提琴 **4** bass
空心吉他/ **5** (acoustic) guitar
電吉他 **6** electric guitar
班卓琴/五弦琴 **7** banjo
豎琴 **8** harp

木管樂器 Woodwinds

短笛 **9** piccolo
長笛 **10** flute
單簧管/黑管 **11** clarinet
雙簧管 **12** oboe
直笛 **13** recorder
薩克斯管 **14** saxophone
巴松笛 **15** bassoon

銅管樂器 Brass

小喇叭/小號 **16** trumpet
伸縮喇叭/長號 **17** trombone
法國號/圓號 **18** French horn
低音喇叭/大號 **19** tuba

打擊樂器 Percussion

鼓 **20** drums
鐃鈸 **a** cymbals
鈴鼓 **21** tambourine
木琴 **22** xylophone

鍵盤樂器 Keyboard Instruments

鋼琴 **23** piano
電子琴 **24** electric keyboard
風琴 **25** organ

其他樂器 Other Instruments

手風琴 **26** accordion
口琴 **27** harmonica

A. Do you play a musical instrument?
B. Yes. I play the **violin**.

A. You play the **trumpet** very well.
B. Thank you.

A. What's that noise?!
B. That's my son/daughter practicing the **drums**.

Do you play a musical instrument? Which one?

Which instruments are usually in an orchestra? a marching band? a rock group?

Name and describe typical musical instruments in your country.

農場及家畜

農舍 **1** farmhouse	公雞 **14** rooster	綿羊 **27** sheep
農夫 **2** farmer	豬圈 **15** pig pen	果樹園 **28** orchard
菜園 **3** (vegetable) garden	豬 **16** pig	果樹 **29** fruit tree
稻草人 **4** scarecrow	養雞場 **17** chicken coop	農場工人 **30** farm worker
乾草 **5** hay	雞 **18** chicken	紫花苜蓿 **31** alfalfa
雇工 **6** hired hand	母雞舍 **19** hen house	玉米 **32** corn
牲口棚/穀倉 **7** barn	母雞 **20** hen	棉花 **33** cotton
馬廄 **8** stable	農作物 **21** crop	米 **34** rice
馬 **9** horse	灌溉系統 **22** irrigation system	黃豆 **35** soybeans
穀倉旁院子 **10** barnyard	拖拉機 **23** tractor	小麥 **36** wheat
火雞 **11** turkey	農田 **24** field	
山羊 **12** goat	牧場 **25** pasture	
小羔羊 **13** lamb	牛 **26** cow	

[1–30]
A. Where's the _______?
B. In/Next to the _______.

A. The [9, 11–14, 16, 18, 20, 26] s/ [27] are loose again!
B. Oh, no! Where are they?
A. They're in the [1, 3, 7, 8, 10, 15, 17, 19, 24, 25, 28].

[31–36]
A. Do you grow _______ on your farm?
B. No. We grow _______.

Tell about farms in your country. What crops and animals are common on these farms?

動物及寵物

麋鹿 **1** moose
鹿角 **a** antler
北極熊 **2** polar bear
鹿 **3** deer
蹄(單數)-蹄(複數) **a** hoof–hooves
狼(單數)-狼(複數) **4** wolf–wolves
毛皮 **a** coat/fur
黑熊 **5** (black) bear
爪 **a** claw
美洲獅 **6** mountain lion
灰熊 **7** (grizzly) bear
北美野牛 **8** buffalo/bison
北美土狼 **9** coyote

狐狸 **10** fox
臭鼬 **11** skunk
豪豬 **12** porcupine
刺 **a** quill
兔子 **13** rabbit
河狸/海狸 **14** beaver
浣熊 **15** raccoon
負鼠 **16** possum/opossum
馬 **17** horse
尾巴 **a** tail
小馬 **18** pony
驢 **19** donkey
犰狳(中南美產) **20** armadillo

蝙蝠 **21** bat
蚯蚓 **22** worm
蛞蝓 **23** slug
猴子 **24** monkey
食蟻獸 **25** anteater
駱馬 **26** llama
美洲虎 **27** jaguar
斑點 **a** spots
小老鼠(單數)-小老鼠(複數) **28** mouse–mice
大老鼠 **29** rat
花栗鼠 **30** chipmunk
松鼠 **31** squirrel
地鼠 **32** gopher
北美的草原土撥鼠 **33** prairie dog

貓 **34** cat
鬚 **a** whiskers
小貓 **35** kitten
狗 **36** dog
小狗 **37** puppy
倉鼠 **38** hamster
沙鼠 **39** gerbil
天竺鼠 **40** guinea pig
金魚 **41** goldfish
金絲雀 **42** canary
鸚哥/小型鸚鵡 **43** parakeet

羚羊	44	antelope
狒狒	45	baboon
犀牛	46	rhinoceros
角		a horn
熊貓	47	panda
猩猩	48	orangutan
黑豹	49	panther
長臂猿	50	gibbon
老虎	51	tiger
掌		a paw
駱駝	52	camel
駱峰		a hump
大象	53	elephant
象牙		a tusk
象鼻		b trunk
土狼	54	hyena
獅子	55	lion
鬃		a mane
長頸鹿	56	giraffe
斑馬	57	zebra
條紋		a stripes
黑猩猩	58	chimpanzee
河馬	59	hippopotamus
豹	60	leopard
大猩猩	61	gorilla
袋鼠	62	kangaroo
肚袋		a pouch
無尾熊	63	koala (bear)
鴨嘴獸	64	platypus

[1–33, 44–64]
A. Look at that ________!
B. Wow! That's the biggest ________ I've ever seen!

[34–43]
A. Do you have a pet?
B. Yes. I have a ________.
A. What's your ________'s name?
B. ....

What animals are there where you live?

Is there a zoo near where you live? What animals does it have?

What are some common pets in your country?

If you could be an animal, which animal would you like to be? Why?

Does your culture have any popular folk tales or children's stories about animals? Tell a story you know.

BIRDS AND INSECTS

鳥類及昆蟲類

鳥類 Birds

- 知更鳥 **1** robin
  - 鳥窩 **a** nest
  - 鳥蛋 **b** egg
- 冠藍鴉 **2** blue jay
  - 翅膀 **a** wing
  - 尾巴 **b** tail
  - 羽毛 **c** feather
- 紅衣鳳頭鳥 **3** cardinal
- 烏鴉 **4** crow
- 海鷗 **5** seagull
- 啄木鳥 **6** woodpecker
  - 鳥嘴 **a** beak
- 鴿子 **7** pigeon
- 貓頭鷹 **8** owl
- 蒼鷹 **9** hawk
- 老鷹 **10** eagle
  - 爪 **a** claw
- 天鵝 **11** swan
- 蜂鳥 **12** hummingbird
- 鴨子 **13** duck
  - 鴨嘴 **a** bill
- 麻雀 **14** sparrow
- 鵝(單數)-鵝(複數) **15** goose-geese
- 企鵝 **16** penguin
- 紅鶴 **17** flamingo
- 鶴 **18** crane
- 鸛 **19** stork
- 鵜鶘 **20** pelican
- 孔雀 **21** peacock
- 鸚鵡 **22** parrot
- 鴕鳥 **23** ostrich

昆蟲類 Insects

- 蒼蠅 **24** fly
- 瓢蟲 **25** ladybug
- 螢火蟲 **26** firefly/lightning bug
- 蛾 **27** moth
- 毛毛蟲 **28** caterpillar
  - 繭 **a** cocoon
- 蝴蝶 **29** butterfly
- 扁蝨 **30** tick
- 蚊子 **31** mosquito
- 蜻蜓 **32** dragonfly
- 蜘蛛 **33** spider
  - 蜘蛛網 **a** web
- 螳螂 **34** praying mantis
- 黃蜂 **35** wasp
- 蜜蜂 **36** bee
  - 蜂窩 **a** beehive
- 蚱蜢 **37** grasshopper
- 甲蟲 **38** beetle
- 蠍子 **39** scorpion
- 蜈蚣 **40** centipede
- 蟋蟀 **41** cricket

[1–41]
A. Is that a/an ______?
B. No. I think it's a/an ______.

[24–41]
A. Hold still! There's a ______ on your shirt!
B. Oh! Can you get it off me?
A. There! It's gone!

What birds and insects are there where you live?

Does your culture have any popular folk tales or children's stories about birds or insects? Tell a story you know.

魚類，海洋動物，爬行動物

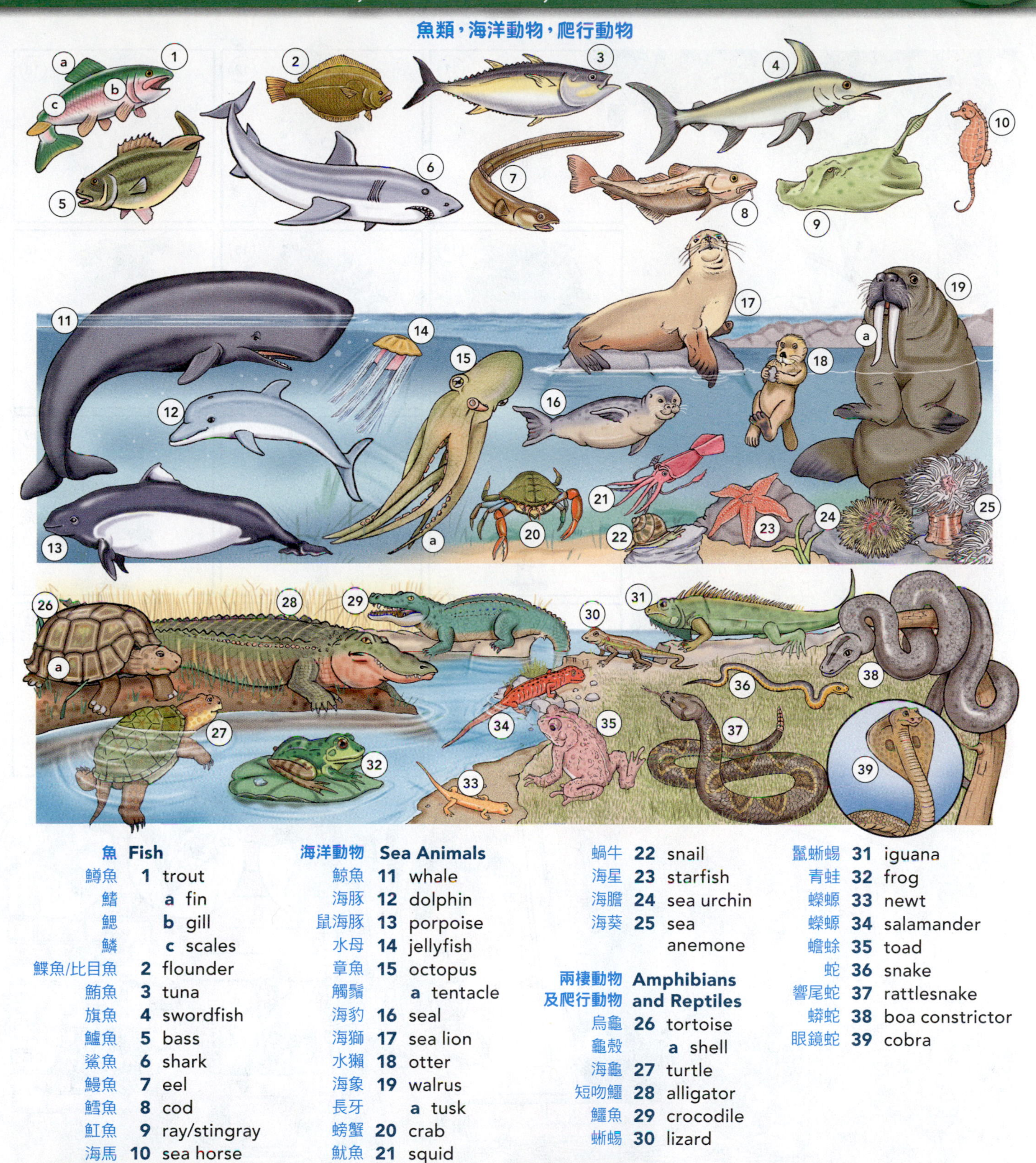

魚 Fish

- 鱒魚 **1** trout
  - 鰭 **a** fin
  - 鰓 **b** gill
  - 鱗 **c** scales
- 鰈魚/比目魚 **2** flounder
- 鮪魚 **3** tuna
- 旗魚 **4** swordfish
- 鱸魚 **5** bass
- 鯊魚 **6** shark
- 鰻魚 **7** eel
- 鱈魚 **8** cod
- 魟魚 **9** ray/stingray
- 海馬 **10** sea horse

海洋動物 Sea Animals

- 鯨魚 **11** whale
- 海豚 **12** dolphin
- 鼠海豚 **13** porpoise
- 水母 **14** jellyfish
- 章魚 **15** octopus
  - 觸鬚 **a** tentacle
- 海豹 **16** seal
- 海獅 **17** sea lion
- 水獺 **18** otter
- 海象 **19** walrus
  - 長牙 **a** tusk
- 螃蟹 **20** crab
- 魷魚 **21** squid
- 蝸牛 **22** snail
- 海星 **23** starfish
- 海膽 **24** sea urchin
- 海葵 **25** sea anemone

兩棲動物及爬行動物 Amphibians and Reptiles

- 烏龜 **26** tortoise
  - 龜殼 **a** shell
- 海龜 **27** turtle
- 短吻鱷 **28** alligator
- 鱷魚 **29** crocodile
- 蜥蜴 **30** lizard
- 鬣蜥蜴 **31** iguana
- 青蛙 **32** frog
- 蠑螈 **33** newt
- 蠑螈 **34** salamander
- 蟾蜍 **35** toad
- 蛇 **36** snake
- 響尾蛇 **37** rattlesnake
- 蟒蛇 **38** boa constrictor
- 眼鏡蛇 **39** cobra

[1–39]
A. Is that a/an _______?
B. No. I think it's a/an _______.

[26–39]
A. Are there any _______s around here?
B. No. But there are lots of _______!

What fish, sea animals, and reptiles can be found in your country? Which ones are endangered and need to be protected? Why?

In your opinion, which ones are the most interesting? the most beautiful? the most dangerous?

樹木，植物，花卉

樹	1	tree
葉子(單數)－葉子(複數)	2	leaf–leaves
細枝	3	twig
樹枝	4	branch
大樹枝/主枝	5	limb
樹幹	6	trunk
樹皮	7	bark
樹根	8	root
針葉	9	needle
松果/松球	10	pine cone
山茱萸	11	dogwood
冬青樹	12	holly
木蘭	13	magnolia
榆樹	14	elm
櫻桃樹	15	cherry
棕櫚樹	16	palm
白樺	17	birch
楓樹	18	maple
橡樹	19	oak
松樹	20	pine
紅杉	21	redwood
垂柳	22	(weeping) willow
灌木叢	23	bush
冬青樹	24	holly
漿果	25	berries
灌木	26	shrub
蕨類植物	27	fern
植物	28	plant
仙人掌(單數)－仙人掌(複數)	29	cactus–cacti
藤蔓	30	vine
毒葛	31	poison ivy
(毒)鹽膚木	32	poison sumac
毒櫟	33	poison oak

花 **34** flower
花瓣 **35** petal
莖 **36** stem
花蕾 **37** bud
刺 **38** thorn
球莖 **39** bulb
菊花 **40** chrysanthemum
水仙花 **41** daffodil
雛菊 **42** daisy
萬壽菊/金盞花 **43** marigold
康乃馨 **44** carnation
梔子花 **45** gardenia
百合花 **46** lily
鳶尾花 **47** iris
三色堇/三色紫羅蘭 **48** pansy
矮牽牛 **49** petunia
蘭花 **50** orchid
玫瑰 **51** rose
太陽花 **52** sunflower
番紅花 **53** crocus
鬱金香 **54** tulip
天竺葵 **55** geranium
紫羅蘭 **56** violet
聖誕紅 **57** poinsettia
茉莉花 **58** jasmine
木槿 **59** hibiscus

[11–22]
A. What kind of tree is that?
B. I think it's a/an _______ tree.

[31–33]
A. Watch out for the _______ over there!
B. Oh. Thanks for the warning.

[40–57]
A. Look at all the _________s!*
B. They're beautiful!

**With 58 and 59, use:* Look at all the ___!

Describe your favorite tree and your favorite flower.

What kinds of trees and flowers grow where you live?

In your country, what flowers do you see at weddings? at funerals? during holidays? in hospital rooms? Tell which flowers people use for different occasions.

ENERGY, CONSERVATION, AND THE ENVIRONMENT

能源，環保，環境

能源 Sources of Energy

- 石油 **1** oil/petroleum
- 天然氣 **2** (natural) gas
- 煤 **3** coal
- 核能 **4** nuclear energy
- 太陽能 **5** solar energy
- 水力發電 **6** hydroelectric power
- 風 **7** wind
- 地熱能 **8** geothermal energy

環保 Conservation

- 資源回收 **9** recycle
- 節約能源 **10** save energy/ conserve energy
- 節約用水 **11** save water/ conserve water
- 汽車共乘 **12** carpool

環境問題 Environmental Problems

- 空氣污染 **13** air pollution
- 水污染 **14** water pollution
- 危險廢物/有毒廢物 **15** hazardous waste/ toxic waste
- 酸雨 **16** acid rain
- 放射物 **17** radiation
- 全球暖化 **18** global warming

[1–8]
A. In my opinion, _______ will be our best source of energy in the future.
B. I disagree. I think our best source of energy will be _______.

[9–12]
A. Do you _______?
B. Yes. I'm very concerned about the environment.

[13–18]
A. Do you worry about the environment?
B. Yes. I'm very concerned about _______.

What kind of energy do you use to heat your home? to cook? In your opinion, which will be the best source of energy in the future?

Do you practice conservation? What do you do to help the environment?

In your opinion, what is the most serious environmental problem in the world today? Why?

自然災害

地震 **1** earthquake	洪水 **6** flood	山崩 **11** landslide
颶風 **2** hurricane	海嘯 **7** tsunami	塌方 **12** mudslide
颱風 **3** typhoon	乾旱 **8** drought	雪崩 **13** avalanche
暴風雪 **4** blizzard	森林大火 **9** forest fire	火山爆發 **14** volcanic eruption
龍捲風 **5** tornado	野火 **10** wildfire	

A. Did you hear about the ______ in ......(country)......?
B. Yes, I did. I saw it on the news.

Have you or someone you know ever experienced a natural disaster? Tell about it.

Which natural disasters sometimes happen where you live? How do people prepare for them?

FORMS OF IDENTIFICATION

身份證明種類

1
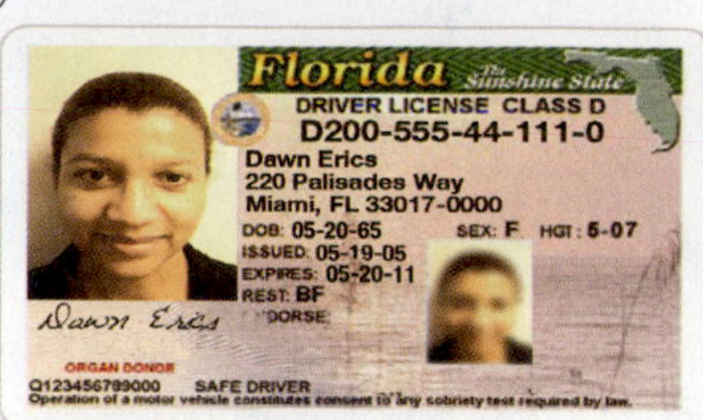

2

3

4

5
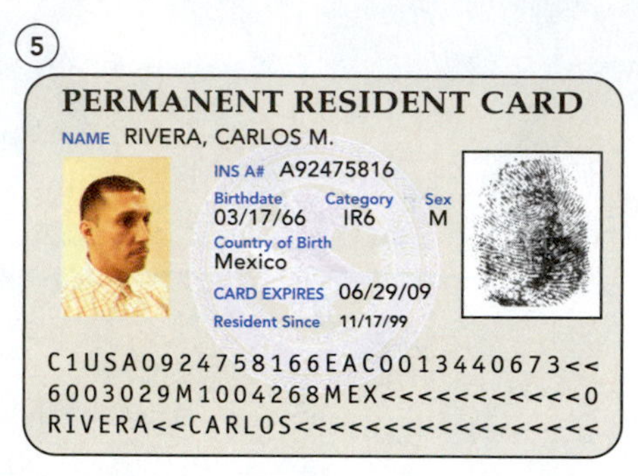

6 7

8
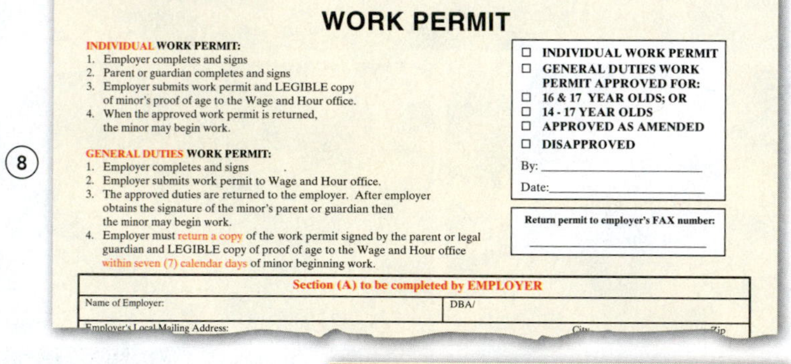

WORK PERMIT

INDIVIDUAL WORK PERMIT:
1. Employer completes and signs
2. Parent or guardian completes and signs
3. Employer submits work permit and LEGIBLE copy of minor's proof of age to the Wage and Hour office.
4. When the approved work permit is returned, the minor may begin work.

GENERAL DUTIES WORK PERMIT:
1. Employer completes and signs
2. Employer submits work permit to Wage and Hour office.
3. The approved duties are returned to the employer. After employer obtains the signature of the minor's parent or guardian then the minor may begin work.
4. Employer must return a copy of the work permit signed by the parent or legal guardian and LEGIBLE copy of proof of age to the Wage and Hour office within seven (7) calendar days of minor beginning work.

☐ INDIVIDUAL WORK PERMIT
☐ GENERAL DUTIES WORK PERMIT APPROVED FOR:
☐ 16 & 17 YEAR OLDS; OR
☐ 14 - 17 YEAR OLDS
☐ APPROVED AS AMENDED
☐ DISAPPROVED
By: ____________
Date: ____________

Return permit to employer's FAX number:

Section (A) to be completed by EMPLOYER

Name of Employer: DBA/

9
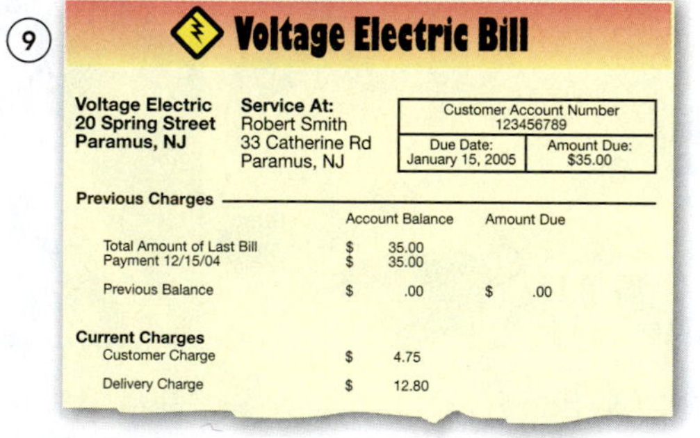

Voltage Electric Bill

Voltage Electric
20 Spring Street
Paramus, NJ

Service At:
Robert Smith
33 Catherine Rd
Paramus, NJ

Customer Account Number	
123456789	
Due Date: January 15, 2005	Amount Due: $35.00

Previous Charges

	Account Balance	Amount Due
Total Amount of Last Bill	$ 35.00	
Payment 12/15/04	$ 35.00	
Previous Balance	$ .00	$ .00

Current Charges

Customer Charge	$ 4.75
Delivery Charge	$ 12.80

10
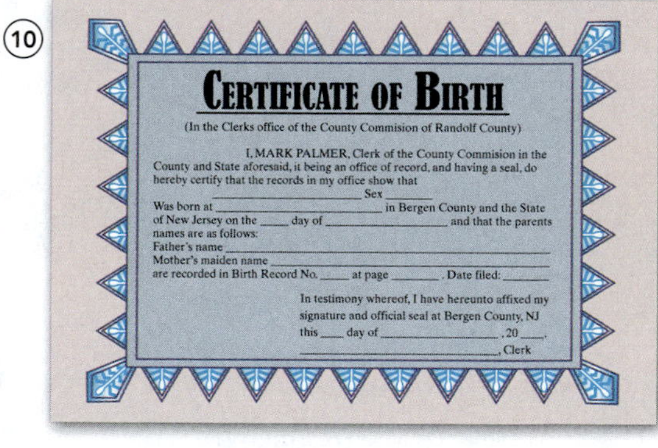

CERTIFICATE OF BIRTH

(In the Clerks office of the County Commision of Randolf County)

I, MARK PALMER, Clerk of the County Commission in the County and State aforesaid, it being an office of record, and having a seal, do hereby certify that the records in my office show that ____ Sex ____ Was born at ____ in Bergen County and the State of New Jersey on the ____ day of ____ and that the parents names are as follows:
Father's name ____
Mother's maiden name ____
are recorded in Birth Record No. ____ at page ____ Date filed: ____

In testimony whereof, I have hereunto affixed my signature and official seal at Bergen County, NJ this ____ day of ____, 20 ____.
____, Clerk

駕駛執照	1	driver's license
社會安全卡	2	social security card
學生證	3	student I.D. card
員工識別證	4	employee I.D. badge
永久居留卡	5	permanent resident card
護照	6	passport
簽證	7	visa
工作許可證	8	work permit
居住證明	9	proof of residence
出生證明書	10	birth certificate

A. May I see your ________?
B. Yes. Here you are.

A. Oh, no! I can't find my ________!
B. I'll help you look for it.
A. Thanks.

Which forms of identification do you have? When do you need to show them?

美國政府

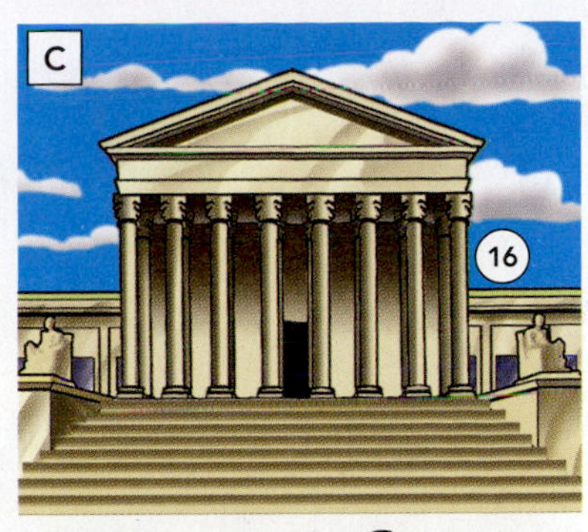

立法部門 **A legislative branch**
制定法律/立法 **1** makes the laws
國會眾議員/眾議院議員及眾議院女議員 **2** representatives/congressmen and congresswomen
眾議院 **3** house of representatives
參議員 **4** senators
參議院 **5** senate
國會大廈 **6** Capitol Building

行政部門 **B executive branch**
執行法律 **7** enforces the laws
總統 **8** president
副總統 **9** vice-president
內閣 **10** cabinet
白宮 **11** White House

司法部門 **C judicial branch**
解釋法律/司法審查 **12** explains the laws
最高法院法官 **13** Supreme Court justices
首席法官 **14** chief justice
最高法院 **15** Supreme Court
最高法院大樓 **16** Supreme Court Building

A. Which branch of government [1, 7, 12]?
B. The [A, B, C].

A. Who works in the [A, B, C] of the government?
B. The [2, 4, 8–10, 13, 14].

A. Where do/does the [2, 4, 8–10, 13, 14] work?
B. In the [6, 11, 16].

A. In which branch of the government is the [3, 5, 10, 15]?
B. In the [A, B, C].

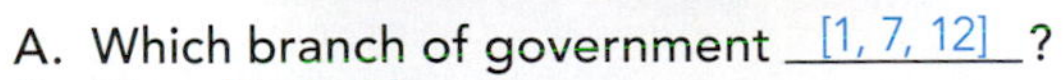

Compare the governments of different countries you are familiar with. What are the branches of government? Who works there? What do they do?

憲法及人權法案

A 1 B 3

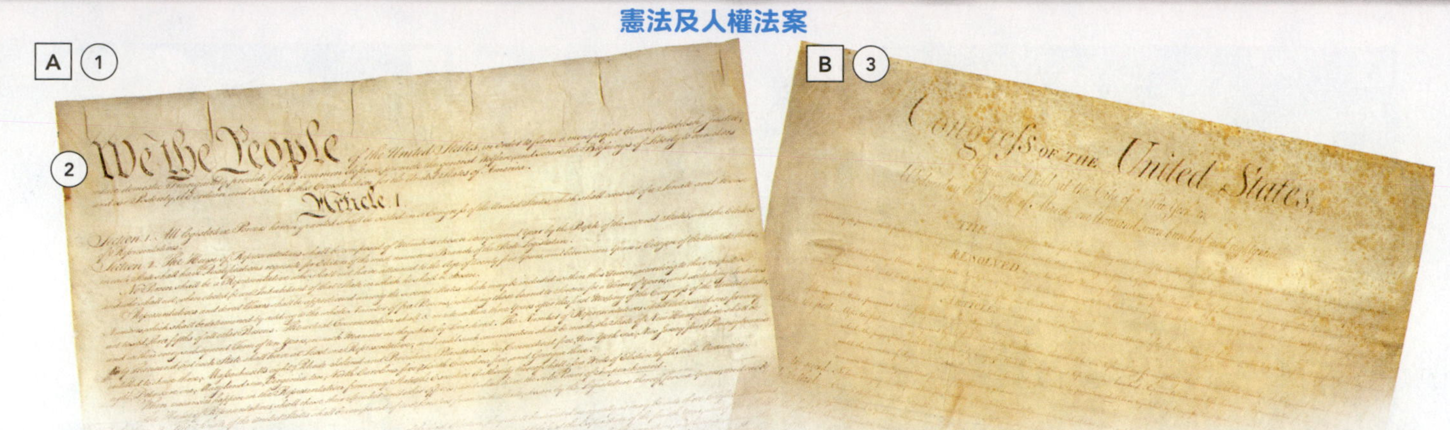

C

D

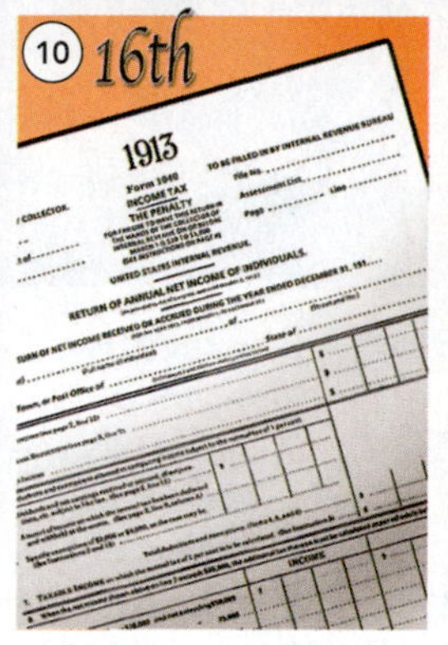

憲法 **A The Constitution**

“國家最高法律” **1** “the supreme law of the land”

憲法序言 **2** the Preamble

人權法案 **B The Bill of Rights**

憲法修正案第一至第十條 **3** the first 10 amendments to the Constitution

美國憲法第一修正案 **C The 1st Amendment**

言論自由 **4** freedom of speech

出版自由 **5** freedom of the press

宗教自由 **6** freedom of religion

集會自由 **7** freedom of assembly

其他修正案 **D Other Amendments**

終結奴役制 **8** ended slavery

給非裔美國人投票權 **9** gave African-Americans the right to vote

建立所得稅制度 **10** established income taxes

給予婦女投票權 **11** gave women the right to vote

給予滿十八歲以上的公民投票權 **12** gave citizens eighteen years and older the right to vote

A. What is [A ,B]?
B. [1 ,3].

A. Which amendment guarantees people [4–7]?
B. The 1st Amendment.

A. Which amendment [8–12]?
B. The ______ Amendment.

A. What did the ______ Amendment do?
B. It [8–12].

Describe how people in your community exercise their 1st Amendment rights. What are some examples of freedom of speech? the press? religion? assembly?

Do you have an idea for a new amendment? Tell about it and why you think it's important.

EVENTS IN UNITED STATES HISTORY

美國歷史上的大事

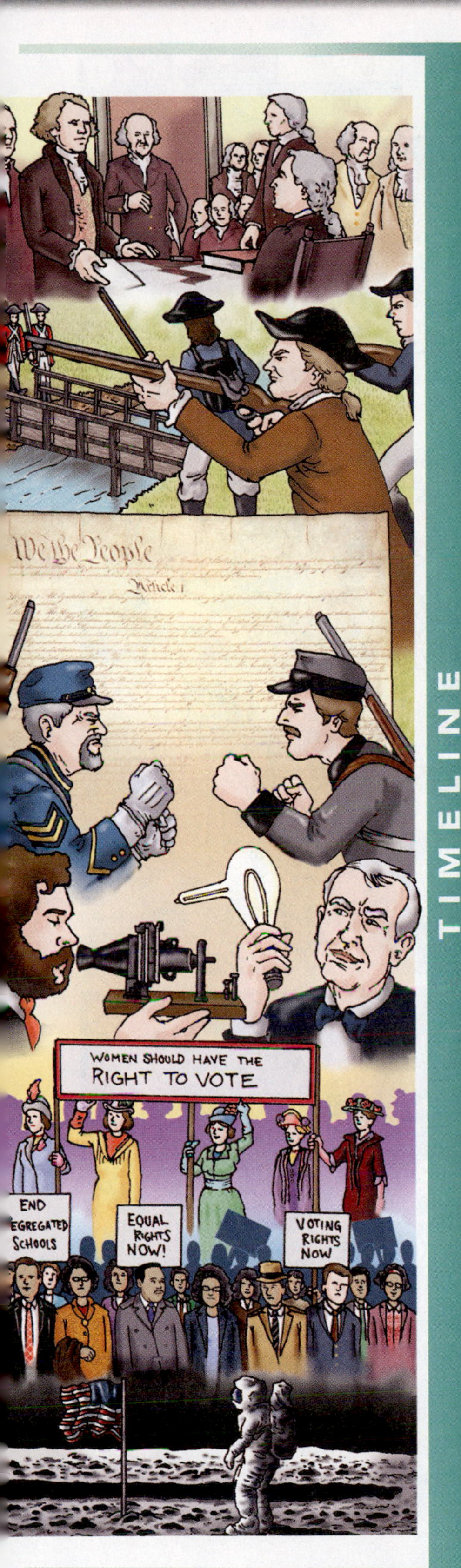

TIMELINE

1607	Colonists come to Jamestown, Virginia. 殖民地開拓者來到維吉尼亞的詹姆士鎮。
1620	Pilgrims come to the Plymouth Colony. 英國清教徒來到普利茅斯殖民地。
1775	The Revolutionary War begins. 革命戰爭爆發。
1776	The colonies declare their independence. 殖民地宣佈獨立。
1783	The Revolutionary War ends. 革命戰爭結束。
1787	Representatives write the United States Constitution. 國會眾議員撰寫美國憲法。
1789	George Washington becomes the first president. 喬治・華盛頓成為美國第一任總統。
1791	The Bill of Rights is added to the Constitution. 憲法中加入人權法案。.
1861	The Civil War begins. 南北戰爭爆發。
1863	President Lincoln signs the Emancipation Proclamation. 林肯總統簽頒解放宣言。
1865	The Civil War ends. 南北戰爭結束。
1876	Alexander Graham Bell invents the telephone. 亞歷山大・格雷翰・貝爾發明電話。
1879	Thomas Edison invents the lightbulb. 湯瑪斯・愛迪生發明燈泡。
1914	World War I (One) begins. 第一次世界大戰爆發。
1918	World War I (One) ends. 第一次世界大戰結束。
1920	Women get the right to vote. 婦女獲得投票權。
1929	The stock market crashes, and the Great Depression begins. 股市崩盤，經濟大蕭條開始。
1939	World War II (Two) begins. 第二次世界大戰爆發。
1945	World War II (Two) ends. 第二次世界大戰結束。
1950	The Korean War begins. 朝鮮戰爭爆發。
1953	The Korean War ends. 朝鮮戰爭結束。
1954	The civil rights movement begins. 民權運動開始。
1963	The March on Washington takes place. 舉行向華盛頓進軍大遊行。
1964	The Vietnam War begins. 越南戰爭爆發。
1969	Astronaut Neil Armstrong lands on the moon. 太空人尼爾・阿姆斯壯登陸月球。
1973	The Vietnam War ends. 越南戰爭結束。
1991	The Persian Gulf War occurs. 波斯灣戰爭爆發。
2001	The United States is attacked by terrorists. 美國受到恐部分子襲擊。

A. What happened in ......(year)......?
B. ......(Event)...... ed.

A. When did ......(event)......?
B. In ......(year)......

In your opinion, which event in this lesson is the most important? Why?

Tell about important events in the history of your country.

HOLIDAYS

節日

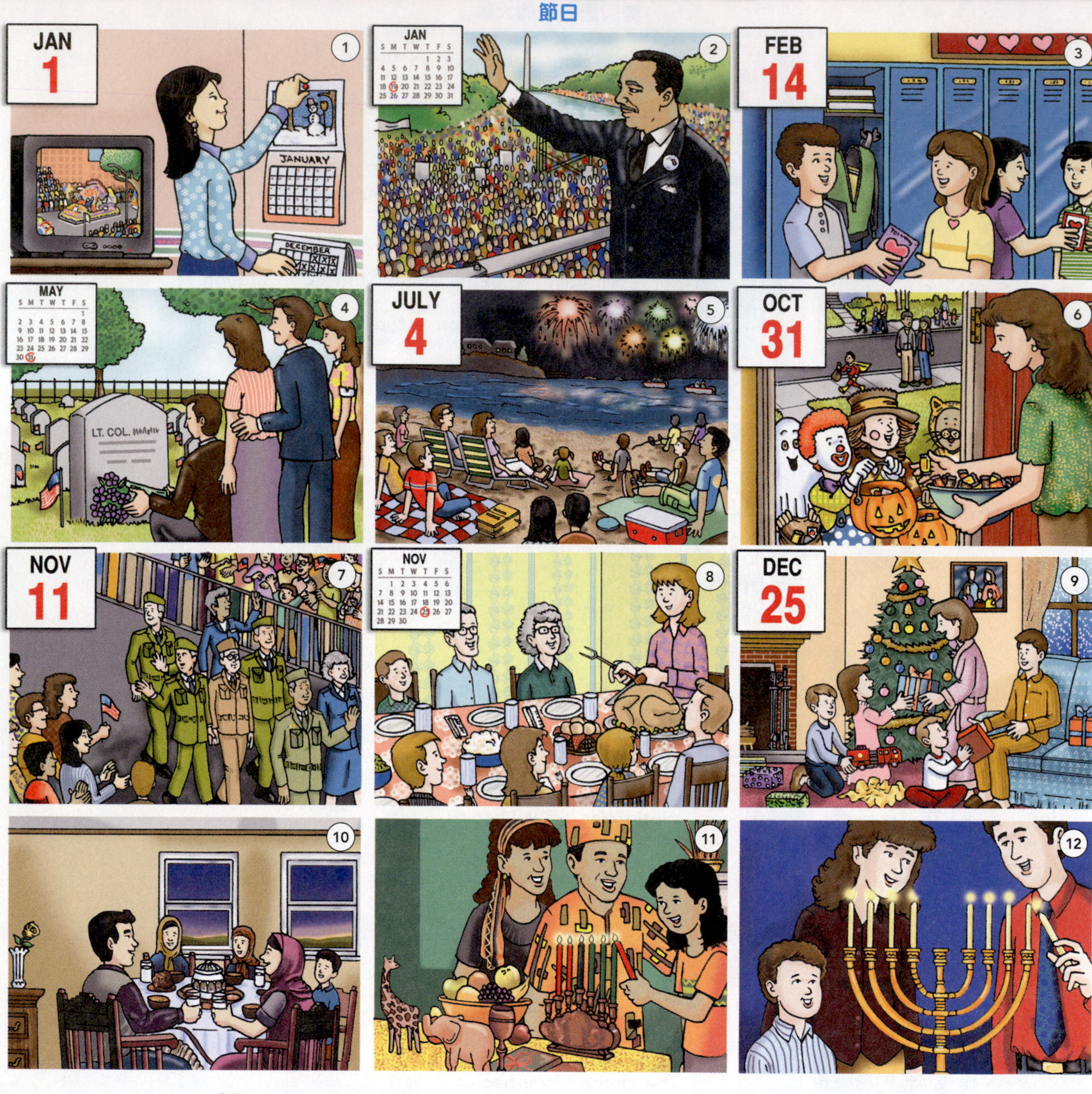

新年 1 New Year's Day
馬丁路德·金紀念日 2 Martin Luther King, Jr.* Day
情人節 3 Valentine's Day
陣亡將士紀念日 4 Memorial Day
(美國)獨立紀念日/(美國)國慶日 5 Independence Day/ the Fourth of July
萬聖節 6 Halloween

* Jr. = Junior

退伍軍人節 7 Veterans Day
感恩節 8 Thanksgiving
聖誕節 9 Christmas
回教齋月 10 Ramadan
(非裔美國人的)寬扎節 11 Kwanzaa
(猶太教的)光明節 12 Hanukkah

A. When is [1, 3, 5, 6, 7, 9]?
B. It's on (date).

A. When is [2, 4, 8]?
B. It's in (month).

A. When does [10–12] begin this year?
B. It begins on (date).

Which of these holidays do you celebrate? How?

What holidays do people celebrate in your country?

THE LEGAL SYSTEM

司法制度

被逮捕 **A** be arrested
在警察局被登記為案犯 **B** be booked at the police station
請律師 **C** hire a lawyer/ hire an attorney
出庭 **D** appear in court
受審 **E** stand* trial
被宣告無罪 **F** be acquitted
被宣告有罪 **G** be convicted
被判決 **H** be sentenced
監禁/入獄 **I** go to jail/prison
被釋放 **J** be released
嫌疑犯 **1** suspect
警察 **2** police officer

*stand–stood

手銬 **3** handcuffs
米蘭達權力(犯罪嫌疑人保持沉默的權利) **4** Miranda rights
指紋 **5** fingerprints
(嫌犯檔案)面部照片 **6** mug shot/ police photo
律師 **7** lawyer/attorney
法官 **8** judge
被告 **9** defendant
保釋金 **10** bail
法庭 **11** courtroom
檢察官 **12** prosecuting attorney
證人 **13** witness

法庭記錄員 **14** court reporter
辯護律師 **15** defense attorney
證據 **16** evidence
(在法庭上的)法警 **17** bailiff
陪審團 **18** jury
(陪審團的)裁決 **19** verdict
清白/無罪 **20** innocent/ not guilty
有罪 **21** guilty
判決 **22** sentence
罰金 **23** fine
獄警 **24** prison guard
囚犯 **25** convict/prisoner/ inmate

[A–J]
A. Did you hear about ......(name)......?
B. No, I didn't.
A. He/She ________ed.
B. Really? I didn't know that.

[A–J]
A. What happened in the last episode?
B. ......(name of character)...... ________ed.

[1, 2, 7–9, 12–15, 17, 24, 25]
A. Are you the ________?
B. No. I'm the ________.

Tell about the legal system in your country.
Describe what happens after a person is arrested.

Do you watch any crime shows on TV? Which ones?
Tell about an episode you remember.

CITIZENSHIP

公民身份

公民的權利與責任 Citizens' Rights and Responsibilities

投票	1	vote
遵守法律	2	obey laws
付稅	3	pay taxes
陪審	4	serve on a jury
加入社區生活	5	be part of community life
關注新聞明瞭時事	6	follow the news to know about current events
向選徵兵役體系登記*	7	register with the Selective Service System

*美國國內凡18到26歲的男子都必須向選徵兵役體系登記。

成為公民的途徑 The Path to Citizenship

申請公民身份/申請公民權	8	apply for citizenship
認識和學習有關美國政府和歷史知識	9	learn about U.S. government and history
參加公民入籍考試	10	take a citizenship test
接受歸化面談	11	have a naturalization interview
出席歸化典禮	12	attend a naturalization ceremony
朗誦忠誠宣誓	13	recite the Oath of Allegiance

A. Can you name one responsibility of United States citizens?
B. Yes. Citizens should [1–7].

A. How is your citizenship application coming along?
B. Very well. I [8–11]ed, and now I'm preparing to [9–13].
A. Good luck!

In your opinion, what are the most important rights and responsibilities of all people in their communities?

In your opinion, should non-citizens have all the same rights as citizens? Why or why not?

美國及加拿大

RUSSIA
ARCTIC OCEAN
Chukchi Sea
Bering Sea
Beaufort Sea
Norwegian Sea
ICELAND
GREENLAND
Baffin Bay
Alaska
(US)
Gulf of Alaska
Yukon Territory
Northwest Territories
Nunavut
Hudson Bay
CANADA
British Columbia
Alberta
Saskatchewan
Manitoba
Ontario
Québec
Newfoundland and Labrador
Prince Edward Island
New Brunswick
Nova Scotia
Ottawa
PACIFIC OCEAN
Washington
Oregon
Idaho
Montana
North Dakota
South Dakota
Wyoming
Minnesota
Wisconsin
Michigan
Maine
Vermont
New Hampshire
Massachusetts
Rhode Island
Connecticut
New Jersey
Delaware
Maryland
Washington, DC
New York
Pennsylvania
Nevada
California
Utah
Colorado
Nebraska
Iowa
Illinois
Indiana
Ohio
West Virginia
Virginia
Kansas
Missouri
Kentucky
UNITED STATES of AMERICA
Arizona
New Mexico
Oklahoma
Arkansas
Tennessee
North Carolina
South Carolina
ATLANTIC OCEAN
BERMUDA
Texas
Alabama
Georgia
Mississippi
Louisiana
Florida
Hawaii
(US)
Gulf of Mexico
THE BAHAMAS
CUBA
PUERTO RICO
MEXICO
HAITI
DOMINICAN REPUBLIC
JAMAICA
N
W
E
S
0
0
1000 Miles
1000 KM

墨西哥，中美洲，加勒比海

UNITED STATES of AMERICA
BAJA CALIFORNIA
SONORA
CHIHUAHUA
Gulf of California
BAJA CALIFORNIA SUR
COAHUILA
MEXICO
NUEVO LEÓN
DURANGO
SINALOA
ZACATECAS
TAMAULIPAS
Gulf of Mexico
ATLANTIC OCEAN
PACIFIC OCEAN
NAYARIT
SAN LUIS POTOSÍ
QUERÉTARO
HIDALGO
DISTRITO FEDERAL
TLAXCALA
VERACRUZ
AGUASCALIENTES
JALISCO
GUANAJUATO
COLIMA
MICHOACÁN
MÉXICO
MORELOS
Mexico City
PUEBLA
GUERRERO
OAXACA
TABASCO
CAMPECHE
YUCATÁN
QUINTANA ROO
CHIAPAS
Gulf of Tehuantepec
GUATEMALA
Guatemala City
San Salvador
EL SALVADOR
BELIZE
Belmopan
HONDURAS
Tegucigalpa
NICARAGUA
Managua
San José
COSTA RICA
Panama City
PANAMA
COLOMBIA
VENEZUELA
Caracas
Havana
CUBA
CAYMAN ISLANDS
JAMAICA
Kingston
Nassau
THE BAHAMAS
TURKS AND CAICOS ISLANDS
Port-au-Prince
HAITI
DOMINICAN REPUBLIC
Santo Domingo
PUERTO RICO
San Juan
VIRGIN ISLANDS (US & UK)
ANGUILLA
SAINT KITTS AND NEVIS
ANTIGUA AND BARBUDA
MONTSERRAT
GUADELOUPE
DOMINICA
MARTINIQUE
SAINT LUCIA
SAINT VINCENT AND THE GRENADINES
GRENADA
BARBADOS
Caribbean Sea
NETHERLANDS ANTILLES
ARUBA
Port of Spain
TRINIDAD AND TOBAGO
N
W
E
S
0
500 Miles
0
500 KM

南美洲

Caribbean Sea
Barranquilla
Cartagena
Maracaibo
Valencia
Barquisimeto
Caracas
VENEZUELA
Georgetown
Paramaribo
Cayenne
GUYANA
SURINAME
FRENCH GUIANA
ATLANTIC OCEAN
Medellín
Bogotá
Cali
COLOMBIA
Equator
Quito
ECUADOR
Guayaquil
Gulf of Guayaquil
Belém
Manaus
Fortaleza
Teresina
Recife
PERU
BRAZIL
Lima
Salvador
Brasília
Goiânia
La Paz
BOLIVIA
Sucre
Belo Horizonte
Rio de Janeiro
Campinas
São Paulo
CHILE
PARAGUAY
Asuncion
Curitiba
PACIFIC OCEAN
ARGENTINA
Pôrto Alegre
Córdoba
Rosario
URUGUAY
Santiago
Buenos Aires
Montevideo
Gulf of San Matías
ATLANTIC OCEAN
N
W
E
S
Gulf of San Jorge
FALKLAND ISLANDS
Port Stanley
Strait of Magellan
SOUTH GEORGIA ISLAND
0
500 Miles
0
500 KM

世界

ARCTIC OCEAN
Baffin Bay
GREENLAND
ICELAND
Hudson Bay
Bering Sea
CANADA
ALEUTIAN ISLANDS
NORTH AMERICA
UNITED STATES OF AMERICA
AZORES (Portugal)
ATLANTIC OCEAN
MOROCCO
BERMUDA
CANARY ISLANDS (Spain)
WESTERN SAHARA
Gulf of Mexico
THE BAHAMAS
HAWAIIAN ISLANDS (US)
MEXICO
CUBA
DOMINICAN REPUBLIC
JAMAICA
PUERTO RICO
BELIZE
HAITI
MAURITANIA
SENEGAL
CAPE VERDE
GAMBIA
GUINEA-BISSAU
GUINEA
SIERRA LEONE
LIBERIA
GHANA
EQUATORIAL GUINEA
PACIFIC OCEAN
GUATEMALA
HONDURAS
NICARAGUA
EL SALVADOR
COSTA RICA
PANAMA
GUYANA
SURINAME
FRENCH GUIANA
VENEZUELA
COLOMBIA
LINE ISLANDS
PHOENIX ISLANDS
Equator
GALÁPAGOS ISLANDS
ECUADOR
SOUTH AMERICA
KIRIBATI
AMERICAN SAMOA
MARQUESAS ISLANDS
PERU
BRAZIL
COOK ISLANDS
WESTERN SAMOA
FRENCH POLYNESIA
TAHITI
BOLIVIA
TONGA
SOCIETY ISLANDS
PARAGUAY
AUSTRAL ISLANDS
CHILE
URUGUAY
ARGENTINA
FALKLAND/MALVINAS ISLANDS
N
W
E
S

ARCTIC OCEAN
Barents Sea
RUSSIA
ASIA
EUROPE
North Sea
Bering Sea
Sea of Okhotsk
KAZAKHSTAN
MONGOLIA
GEORGIA
Black Sea
Caspian Sea
UZBEKISTAN
KYRGYZSTAN
ARMENIA
AZERBAIJAN
TURKMENISTAN
TAJIKISTAN
TURKEY
NORTH KOREA
Sea of Japan
SOUTH KOREA
JAPAN
CHINA
CYPRUS
SYRIA
LEBANON
ISRAEL
IRAQ
IRAN
AFGHANISTAN
TUNISIA
Mediterranean Sea
JORDAN
PAKISTAN
NEPAL
BHUTAN
East China Sea
PACIFIC OCEAN
ALGERIA
LIBYA
EGYPT
KUWAIT
QATAR
UNITED ARAB EMIRATES
INDIA
MYANMAR
TAIWAN
DAITO ISLANDS (Japan)
VOLCANO ISLANDS (Japan)
SAUDI ARABIA
AFRICA
NIGER
CHAD
ERITREA
SUDAN
YEMEN
OMAN
DJIBOUTI
SOCOTRA
Arabian Sea
LAOS
THAILAND
BANGLADESH
VIETNAM
South China Sea
PARECE VELA (Japan)
NORTHERN MARIANA ISLANDS
WAKE ISLAND (US)
PHILIPPINES
GUAM
MARSHALL ISLANDS
NIGERIA
BENIN
CENTRAL AFRICAN REPUBLIC
CAMEROON
ETHIOPIA
SOMALIA
CAMBODIA
SRI LANKA
BRUNEI
YAP
PALAU
FEDERATED STATES OF MICRONESIA
UGANDA
GABON
CONGO
KENYA
DEMOCRATIC REPUBLIC OF CONGO
RWANDA
BURUNDI
TANZANIA
SEYCHELLES
MALAYSIA
SINGAPORE
Equator
NAURU
INDONESIA
PAPUA NEW GUINEA
SOLOMON ISLANDS
TUVALU
MALAWI
COMOROS
INDIAN OCEAN
EAST TIMOR
Coral Sea
VANUATU
FIJI
ANGOLA
ZAMBIA
NAMIBIA
ZIMBABWE
MADAGASCAR
MAURITIUS
BOTSWANA
AUSTRALIA
NEW CALEDONIA
MOZAMBIQUE
SOUTH AFRICA
SWAZILAND
LESOTHO
ATLANTIC OCEAN
NORWAY
FINLAND
SWEDEN
RUSSIA
ESTONIA
North Sea
IRELAND
DENMARK
LATVIA
Baltic Sea
LITHUANIA
UNITED KINGDOM
BELARUS
NETHERLANDS
BELGIUM
GERMANY
POLAND
LUXEMBOURG
CZECH REPUBLIC
UKRAINE
SLOVAKIA
FRANCE
SWITZERLAND
AUSTRIA
HUNGARY
MOLDOVA
SLOVENIA
ROMANIA
CROATIA
ANDORRA
PORTUGAL
BOSNIA and HERZEGOVINA
SERBIA and MONTENEGRO
BULGARIA
Black Sea
SPAIN
MONACO
ITALY
MACEDONIA
ALBANIA
GREECE
TURKEY
Mediterranean Sea
MALTA
TASMANIA (Australia)
NEW ZEALAND
ANTARCTICA

時區

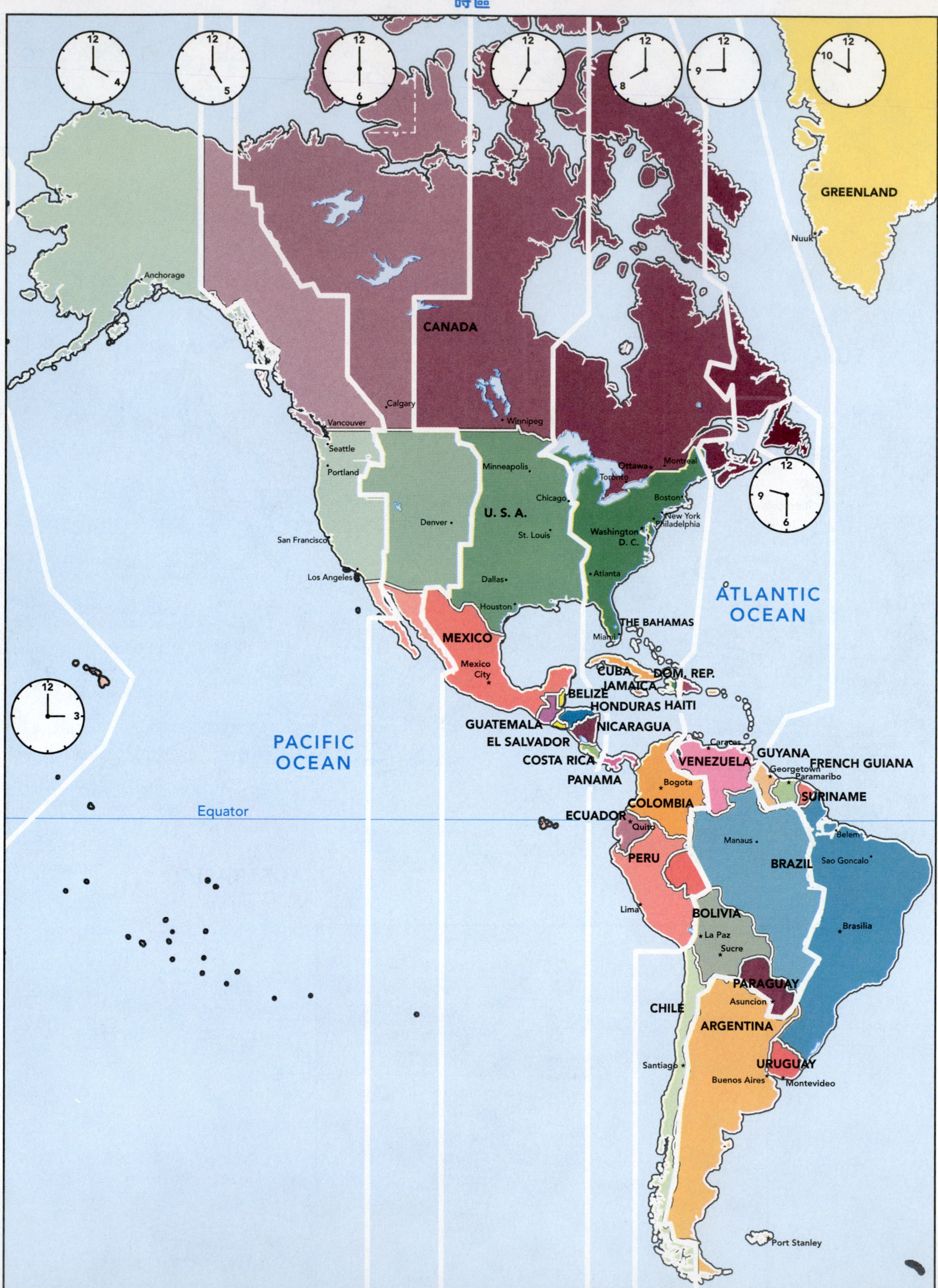
GREENLAND
Nuuk
Anchorage
CANADA
Calgary
Vancouver
Winnipeg
Seattle
Portland
Minneapolis
Ottawa
Montreal
Toronto
Chicago
Boston
U. S. A.
Denver
New York
Philadelphia
Washington D. C.
San Francisco
St. Louis
Atlanta
Los Angeles
Dallas
Houston
ATLANTIC OCEAN
THE BAHAMAS
Miami
MEXICO
Mexico City
CUBA
DOM. REP.
JAMAICA
BELIZE
HONDURAS
HAITI
GUATEMALA
NICARAGUA
EL SALVADOR
COSTA RICA
PACIFIC OCEAN
Caracas
GUYANA
VENEZUELA
FRENCH GUIANA
Georgetown
Paramaribo
PANAMA
Bogota
SURINAME
COLOMBIA
Equator
ECUADOR
Quito
Belem
Manaus
PERU
BRAZIL
Sao Goncalo
Lima
BOLIVIA
Brasilia
La Paz
Sucre
PARAGUAY
Asuncion
CHILE
ARGENTINA
URUGUAY
Santiago
Buenos Aires
Montevideo
Port Stanley

Country	Nationality	Language
Afghanistan	Afghan	Afghan
Argentina	Argentine	Spanish
Australia	Australian	English
Bolivia	Bolivian	Spanish
Brazil	Brazilian	Portuguese
Bulgaria	Bulgarian	Bulgarian
Cambodia	Cambodian	Cambodian
Canada	Canadian	English/French
Chile	Chilean	Spanish
China	Chinese	Chinese
Colombia	Colombian	Spanish
Costa Rica	Costa Rican	Spanish
Cuba	Cuban	Spanish
(The) Czech Republic	Czech	Czech
Denmark	Danish	Danish
(The) Dominican Republic	Dominican	Spanish
Ecuador	Ecuadorian	Spanish
Egypt	Egyptian	Arabic
El Salvador	Salvadorean	Spanish
England	English	English
Estonia	Estonian	Estonian
Ethiopia	Ethiopian	Amharic
Finland	Finnish	Finnish
France	French	French
Germany	German	German
Greece	Greek	Greek
Guatemala	Guatemalan	Spanish
Haiti	Haitian	Haitian Kreyol
Honduras	Honduran	Spanish
Hungary	Hungarian	Hungarian
India	Indian	Hindi
Indonesia	Indonesian	Indonesian
Israel	Israeli	Hebrew

Country	Nationality	Language
Italy	Italian	Italian
Japan	Japanese	Japanese
Jordan	Jordanian	Arabic
Korea	Korean	Korean
Laos	Laotian	Laotian
Latvia	Latvian	Latvian
Lebanon	Lebanese	Arabic
Lithuania	Lithuanian	Lithuanian
Malaysia	Malaysian	Malay
Mexico	Mexican	Spanish
New Zealand	New Zealander	English
Nicaragua	Nicaraguan	Spanish
Norway	Norwegian	Norwegian
Pakistan	Pakistani	Urdu
Panama	Panamanian	Spanish
Peru	Peruvian	Spanish
(The) Philippines	Filipino	Tagalog
Poland	Polish	Polish
Portugal	Portuguese	Portuguese
Puerto Rico	Puerto Rican	Spanish
Romania	Romanian	Romanian
Russia	Russian	Russian
Saudi Arabia	Saudi	Arabic
Slovakia	Slovak	Slovak
Spain	Spanish	Spanish
Sweden	Swedish	Swedish
Switzerland	Swiss	German/French/Italian
Taiwan	Taiwanese	Chinese
Thailand	Thai	Thai
Turkey	Turkish	Turkish
Ukraine	Ukrainian	Ukrainian
(The) United States	American	English
Venezuela	Venezuelan	Spanish
Vietnam	Vietnamese	Vietnamese

A. Where are you from?
B. I'm from **Mexico**.

A. What's your nationality?
B. I'm **Mexican**.

A. What language do you speak?
B. I speak **Spanish**.

Tell about yourself: Where are you from? What's your nationality? What languages do you speak?

Now interview and tell about a friend.

動詞列表

規則動詞

規則動詞的過去式及過去分詞有四種拼寫形式。

1 在動詞後加**–ed**。例如：

act → act**ed**

act	cook	grill	pass	simmer
add	correct	guard	peel	sort
answer	cough	hand (in)	plant	spell
appear	cover	help	play	sprain
ask	crash	insert	polish	steam
assist	cross (out)	invent	pour	stow
attack	deliver	iron	print	stretch
attend	deposit	kick	reach	surf
bank	design	land	record	swallow
board	discuss	leak	register	talk
boil	dress	learn	relax	turn
box	drill	lengthen	repair	twist
brainstorm	dust	lift	repeat	unload
broil	edit	listen	request	vacuum
brush	end	load	respond	vomit
burn	enter	look	rest	walk
burp	establish	lower	return	wash
carpool	explain	mark	roast	watch
cash	faint	match	rock	wax
check	fasten	mix	saute	weed
clean	fix	mow	scratch	whiten
clear	floss	obey	seat	work
collect	fold	open	select	
comb	follow	paint	shorten	
construct	form	park	sign	

2 在動詞最後字母的**e**後加**–d**。例如：

assemble → assemble**d**

assemble	declare	grate	pronounce	shave
bake	describe	hire	prune	slice
balance	dislocate	manage	raise	sneeze
barbecue	dive	measure	rake	state
bathe	dribble	microwave	recite	style
bounce	enforce	move	recycle	supervise
browse	erase	nurse	remove	translate
bruise	examine	operate	revise	type
bubble	exchange	organize	rinse	underline
change	exercise	overdose	save	unscramble
circle	experience	practice	scrape	use
close	file	prepare	serve	vote
combine	gargle	produce	share	wheeze

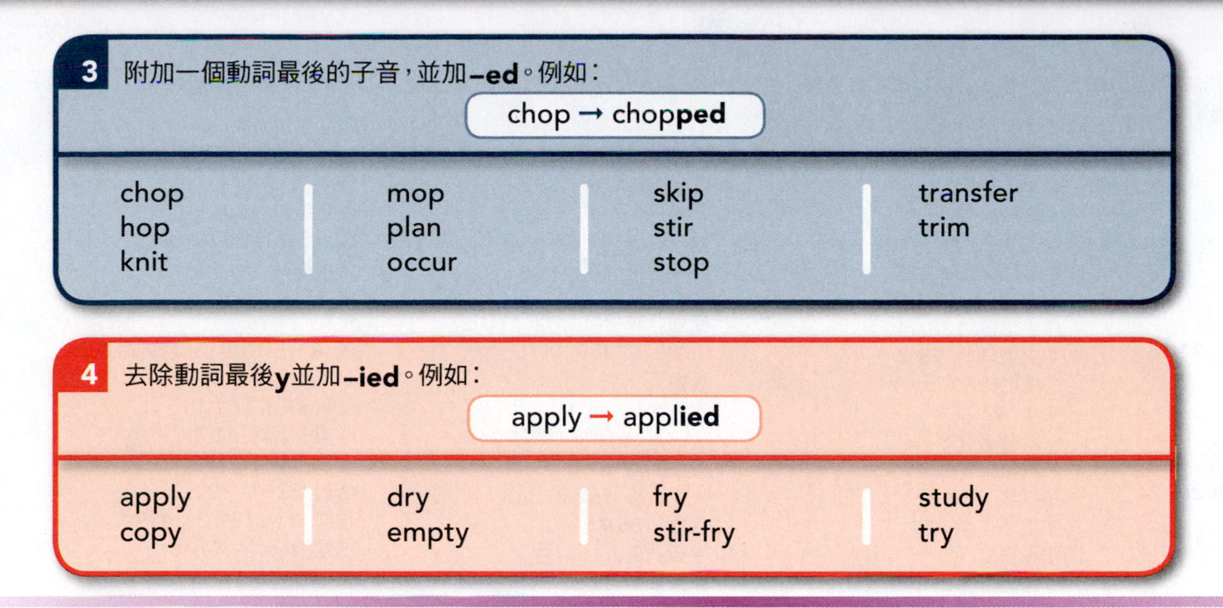

不規則動詞

下列動詞的過去式及過去分詞為不規則形式。

be	was/were	been	know	knew	known
beat	beat	beaten	leave	left	left
become	became	become	let	let	let
bend	bent	bent	make	made	made
begin	began	begun	meet	met	met
bleed	bled	bled	pay	paid	paid
break	broke	broken	put	put	put
bring	brought	brought	read	read	read
build	built	built	rewrite	rewrote	rewritten
buy	bought	bought	run	ran	run
catch	caught	caught	ring	rang	rung
choose	chose	chosen	say	said	said
come	came	come	see	saw	seen
cut	cut	cut	sell	sold	sold
do	did	done	set	set	set
draw	drew	drawn	shoot	shot	shot
drink	drank	drunk	sing	sang	sung
drive	drove	driven	sit	sat	sat
eat	ate	eaten	sleep	slept	slept
fall	fell	fallen	speak	spoke	spoken
feed	fed	fed	stand	stood	stood
fly	flew	flown	sweep	swept	swept
get	got	gotten	swim	swam	swum
give	gave	given	swing	swung	swung
go	went	gone	take	took	taken
grow	grew	grown	teach	taught	taught
hang	hung	hung	throw	threw	thrown
have	had	had	understand	understood	understood
hit	hit	hit	withdraw	withdrew	withdrawn
hold	held	held	write	wrote	written
hurt	hurt	hurt			

中文索引

以黑體呈現的數字表示該單字所在的頁數。該黑體數字後的數字表示該單字在該頁圖解及單字表中的位置。例如："地址 **1**-5"表示 *地址* 在第1頁單字表的第5項。

火部

英文索引

The bold number indicates the page(s) on which the word appears. The number that follows indicates the word's location in the illustration and in the word list on the page. For example, "address **1**-5" indicates that the word *address* is on page 1 and is item number 5.

主題索引